C000179849

DOUBLE TAKE
AND FADE AWAY

By the same author

Halliwell's Filmgoer's Companion
Halliwell's Film Guide
Halliwell's Television Companion (with Philip Purser)
The Filmgoer's Book of Quotes
Halliwell's Movie Quiz
Mountain of Dreams
The Clapperboard Book of the Cinema (with Graham Murray)
Halliwell's Hundred
Halliwell's Harvest
The Ghost of Sherlock Holmes (fiction)
Seats in All Parts: Half a Lifetime at the Movies
Return to Shangri-La (fiction)
The Dead That Walk

Halliwell on Comedians

DOUBLE TAKE AND FADE AWAY

LESLIE HALLIWELL

GRAFTON BOOKS

A Division of the Collins Publishing Group

LONDON GLASGOW
TORONTO SYDNEY AUCKLAND

Grafton Books
A Division of the Collins Publishing Group
8 Grafton Street, London W1X 3LA

Published by Grafton Books 1987

Copyright © Leslie Halliwell 1987

British Library Cataloguing in Publication Data
Halliwell, Leslie
Double take and fade away
1. Comedy films—History and criticism
2. Moving picture actors and actresses
—History
I. Title   II. Series
791.43'028'0922   PN1995.9.C55

ISBN 0-246-12835-6

Photoset in Linotron Bembo by
Rowland Phototypesetting Ltd
Bury St Edmunds, Suffolk

Printed in Great Britain by
Butler and Tanner Ltd, Frome and London

All rights reserved. No part of this publication may be
reproduced, stored in a retrieval system, or transmitted,
in any form or by any means, electronic, mechanical,
photocopying, recording or otherwise, without the prior
permission of the publisher.

JACK BENNY: 'You wouldn't say that if my writers were here!'

Usually, a comedian's scriptwriters go unsung, because the public is supposed to think that he makes up his material as he goes along. Tribute however must be paid to a few stalwart practitioners for contributions which have proved to be milestones in the history of comedy:

H. M. WALKER
for at least some of Laurel and Hardy's dialogue

FRANK MUIR and DENNIS NORDEN
for *Take It From Here*

MARRIOTT EDGAR, J. O. C. ORTON and VAL GUEST
for *Oh! Mr Porter*

JONATHAN LYNN and ANTONY JAY
for *Yes Minister*

EDWIN JUSTUS MAYER
for *To Be or Not to Be*

JIMMY PERRY and DAVID CROFT
for *Dad's Army*

JOHN GRANT
for Abbott and Costello's best routines

NORMAN PANAMA and MELVIN FRANK
for *The Court Jester*

and SYLVIA FINE
for Danny Kaye's songs

IAN LA FRENAIS and DICK CLEMENT
for *Porridge*

SID GREEN, DICK HILLS and EDDIE BRABEN
for the Morecambe and Wise shows

TED KAVANAGH
for *It's That Man Again*

RAY GALTON and ALAN SIMPSON
for *Hancock's Half Hour* and *Steptoe and Son*

AND TO ALL THE STARS WHO DID WRITE THEIR OWN

WAY OUT WEST. On the right, James Finlayson is about to go into his famous double take, and possibly his fade away also. Oliver Hardy seems aghast at the very thought, but Sharon Lynne has seen it all before.

GROUCHO MARX: You have the brain of a four-year-old boy, and I'll bet he was glad to get rid of it!

CONTENTS

ABBOTT: How much would you charge to haunt a house?
COSTELLO: How many rooms?

So the eldest son got married and he came into a fortune. A fortune. And he was a millionaire. And he came home one night to see his father, who'd fallen on bad times, and he said Dad, I'm sorry to hear about your bad luck, and you know I've come into all this money. And his dad said yes. So the son said, I don't want you to think I'm not grateful for all you've done for me, so now I want to do something for you and Mum. I'm going to write out a cheque for a hundred pounds, right now. No, go on, I'll make it two hundred. So there you are, dad. I see, said his father. Well, thank you, son. And since we're talking about family matters, here's one thing you should know. Your mother and I were never married. What, said the boy, do you mean to say I'm a bastard? Yes, said his father, and a right mean bastard at that!

– Max Miller, 1895–1963

Let us have wine and women, mirth and laughter,
Sermons and soda water the day after!

– George Gordon, Lord Byron, 1788–1824

GRATEFUL THANKS

are due not only to the writers listed in the tribute which follows the title page, but to all those briefly quoted; to Fred Turner of Rank for the long excerpt from *Oh! Mr Porter*; and to Don Gale of MCA for the dialogue of Mae West, W. C. Fields and Abbott and Costello.

OLIVER HARDY: Pardon me for a moment, my ear is full of milk!

PREFACE

We have all heard the definition of pessimism and optimism: the pessimist says his glass is half empty, the optimist calls his half full. So it is with tragedy and comedy. Tragedy is the human condition writ large, seen in sombre mood. Life is indeed a serious business: but very often we all feel the need, if madness is not to prevail, for a little alleviation. We are pleased then to see a man slip on a banana skin, or lose his trousers, because it comforts us to reflect that we are no more incompetent than the comedian we are watching. A major part of the appeal of the much-revered Tony Hancock was that the world always seemed to owe him a living; his grouches were ours, and by putting the weight of the world on his shoulders we could remove it from our own.

Put it another way: tragedy by its very nature invokes the grand manner, whereas comedy can be an occasional whisper in the ear, a spontaneous rumble in the belly, the regular chuckle in the throat which keeps us going through days of drudgery. It must always involve the loss of dignity, though sometimes through a facial reaction rather than a pratfall. Heaven knows that you can't take people seriously if they are undressed, so comedy exposes us as mercilessly as it can, points to our weaknesses and shortcomings, tells us what fools we are. In its very early days, as part of the Dionysiac rituals, it was relentlessly fundamental or phallic, more so than we can imagine today even in the night club performances of Lenny Bruce and Billy Connolly. The miracle and mystery plays of the Middle Ages were crammed with low comedians, and even Shakespeare's comic relief was more crude than clever, depicting the need for relief from sobriety and hardship. ('Dost thou think, because thou art virtuous, there shall be no more cakes and ale?') That age after all was one which found imbecility hilarious, and the groundlings had to be satisfied. Today, by one of those strange reversals to which society is apt, it is the sophisticates who clamour for the cruel satirical humour of late-night television programmes like *Not the Nine O'Clock News*, *Spitting Image* and *Who Dares Wins*, and the proletariat which is shocked by them (though the proletariat still revels in jokes about chamber pots and breaking wind).

If styles of humour have become a matter of taste (or tastelessness), the intent and effect have remained much the same through the centuries. Mel Brooks said that humour is just another defence against the universe; to Charles Chaplin, 'In the end, everything is a gag.' Thurber called his comedy 'emotional chaos recollected in tranquillity'. When life is bad, sometimes the only recourse people have is to laugh at it. They will laugh at anything, even at death. Well, almost anything: extreme political sensitivities during the latter half of the twentieth century have rendered it taboo even for the recognized bad taste comedians to laugh at another person's race, colour or religious beliefs, even though it is now accepted that members of the royal family are fair targets. (Some of the latter have responded by becoming occasional comedians in their own right.)

When the medieval kings, through the weight of their responsibilities, found it difficult to be optimistic or frivolous on their own account, they employed jesters to mock the weaknesses of themselves and their courtiers. Today we buy a theatre ticket or pay a TV licence in the hope of obtaining the same release, for if we laugh loud enough we can be certain of at least temporary respite from sadness at the follies of a world beyond our control (or anyone else's). Without our favourite laughtermakers our lives would be duller and the suicide rate higher; yet we should not be surprised to hear that most comedians are subject to depression off stage, for they bear our miseries and misfortunes as well as their own.

Cinema and television are the arts of the twentieth century, yet most practitioners of comedy had their apprenticeship on some sort of stage, facing a live audience. Not all of them in close-up were sufficiently photogenic or *simpatico* to make a full-time career on screens big or small, but in this superficial survey I have not let that deter me from including them for consideration, often as the setters of a style perfected by someone else. Those who did become screen stars, however, found themselves in the best of all possible worlds: their wisecracks still worked, but their sight gags could be made even funnier by sharp editing and the inclusion of reaction shots. Spectacle had been added to simple fun.

Introduction:

A LITTLE MONOLOGUE ENTITLED
'IT'S A POOR WORLD
IF YOU CAN'T LAUGH AT IT'

The world I first surveyed, when I was old enough to sit up and take notice, was the world of darkest Lancashire in the middle thirties; and if ever a world needed cheering up, that was it. Luckily the local brand of fun was plentiful, though on the black side: sickness and death were so commonplace that one made jokes about them as though to ward them off, or perhaps to make them so familiar that they should not come as a shock later on. I remember a story told by a semi-professional comic in a Saturday-night concert at the palatial local Co-op Hall. One dark night a capacious boozer had to go home from the pub by way of the cemetery, and he was known to be afraid of ghosts. A friend decided to play a trick on him, ran ahead by an alternative route, and as the drunk staggered past hid in an open grave, moaning: 'Oh, I am so cold!' Thunderstruck for a moment, the drunk did a double take, then looked left and right, and allowed his consideration for others to get the better of his fright. He began to shovel loose dirt on to his unseen friend, muttering: 'Of course tha's cold, tha's not gradely covered up!'

Sickness jokes were legion, starting with the one about the patient who said to his doctor: 'I'm afraid I'm at death's door this time.' 'Don't worry,' said the doctor absent-mindedly, 'we'll pull you through . . .' Funerals too were sufficiently commonplace to be funny: every family experienced them, and they were always followed by a slap-up ham tea at the Co-op Restaurant. (The Co-op was the centre of Lancashire life.) My first sight of Frank Randle on the stage of the Grand Theatre, Bolton's Palace of Varieties, had him dressed as an ancient hiker, all bony knees and no teeth, recounting as follows: 'Ah went to a funeral t'other day. A feller at graveside said to me, 'e said, How old art, gaffer?

Ah says, Ah'm ninety-three. Eeh, 'e says, it's 'ardly worth while tha goin' 'ome again, is it?'

Those comedians who about once a year, almost as regular as clockwork and much more welcome, stood before the Grand's new modernistic backdrop depicting chic cars and flat-roofed buildings in an empty street, telling stories hastily adapted to local geography ('I was standing waiting for a tram at Moses Gate – no, really!'), eventually put their acts on record. On gramophone record, mostly: my family chuckled time and again through Tommy Handley's rendition of 'Maggie's Cold' ('Was it by the fire with Jeremiah that Maggie caught a cold last night?'), while 'Sandy Powell at the Zoo' provided me with a catchphrase – 'See you in the monkey house' – which astonished a good many people when I tried it on them in later life. A few went through their familiar routines for the motion picture camera, either as a cameo in a feature film or – more probably – as the tailpiece of a weekly ten-minute 'magazine' called Pathé Pictorial. In the latter case the artists were expected to perform against the dimmest of studio sets, with flat lighting and no audience, so they were never at their best, and one had to add for oneself the inevitable extra tinge of blueness in the stage material as well as the enthusiastic audience reaction which was often the life and soul of the show. One accepted of course that the wireless, being in one's own home, was more decorous than the variety theatre or even the movies: BBC Radio in the thirties often seemed like one long party, with grown-ups in evening dress playing parlour games such as those which made up *Monday Night at Eight* with its insidious theme tune:

> It's Monday night at eight o'clock,
> Oh, can't you hear the chimes?
> They're telling you to take an easy chair.
> So settle by your fireside,
> Pick up your *Radio Times*,
> 'Cos Monday Night at Eight is on the air . . .

This curious hour consisted of a package of regular puzzles and sketches, often with audience participation. Listeners were expected to help Syd Walker with his human-interest problems, to spot Ronnie Waldman's deliberate mistake, to guess from a carefully dropped clue which of Inspector Hornleigh's suspects was the murderer. Then on Saturday night at eight there was *Music Hall*, with its theme tune 'The Spice of Life' performed in perfect rhythm by Charles Shadwell and the BBC Variety Orchestra. This was like being at the Grand without the acrobats or the jugglers, and with the comedians' patter bowdlerized.

(Max Miller more often than not was banned from the airwaves altogether.) But at least radio preserved the audience laughter, and the fireside ambience did suit the prevailing gentility. Besides, once you had actually *seen* Will Hay do his schoolmaster sketch, with fat Albert and ancient Harbottle for pupils, imagination easily sustained the mind's eye through Hay's many radio variants:

HAY: What's the matter with your grammar?

HARBOTTLE: She's ill.

HAY: Who is?

HARBOTTLE: Me grandma.

HAY: I didn't say your grandma, I said grammar. I am, thou art, he is, we ain't, and so on. What were you arguing about with Albert just now?

HARBOTTLE: About you. He said some nasty things about you.

HAY: What things?

HARBOTTLE: He said you hadn't the brains of a donkey.

HAY: And what did you say?

HARBOTTLE: I stuck up for you. I said you had.

HAY: Well, that's enough of that. Let's have general knowledge. What are the inhabitants of Malta?

ALBERT: Please sir, Maltesers.

HAY: How do you make a Maltese cross?

HARBOTTLE (*chuckling*): Stamp on his foot!

HAY: I'll do you in a minute. Now, Albert, what are semi-colons?

ALBERT: Commas with knobs on.

HAY: I'm wasting my time. Who was Noah's wife?

HARBOTTLE: Joan of Ark.

HAY: No wonder you know that, I'll bet you went out with her, you old fool. Now, on what mountain did the ark land?

ALBERT: Ararat. See?

HARBOTTLE: My mum gave me some of that when I had a bad tummy.

HAY: Gave you some what?

HARBOTTLE: Arrowroot.

ALBERT: What's arrowroot?

HAY: It's like celery.

ALBERT: What is?

HAY: Rhubarb. Oh, go and put some coal on.

Exeunt severally to music, as Shakespeare might have said. Or perhaps not.

Will Hay was a natural favourite at our house, especially in a film when he got confused by the question: How high is a Chinaman? (It turned out not to be a question at all, but a statement: How Hi is a

Chinaman.) There was a supplementary: What time do you make an appointment with a Chinese dentist? Answer: Two-thirty (tooth hurtee). But we had a lot of family favourites. And despite the sooty atmosphere and the unemployment and the later assorted hardships of the war years, we laughed a lot when I was growing up. Curiously enough, in that narrow, largely ignorant northern society, some of our laughs travelled six thousand miles to reach us, all the way from California. Stan Laurel was of course a Lancashire lad, and I have written elsewhere how he and Olly came to seem part of my family, their curious attempts at respectability amid life's pratfalls having an undeniable correspondence with the activities of my father and his relations, who when in their Sunday suits and away from their daily manual labour seemed lost and accident-prone. (The sniffy propriety of Laurel and Hardy's screen wives also had its mirror image, on my mother's side.) Certainly all my father's efforts at domestic improvement ended, like Stan and Olly's, in catastrophe, and it was through him that I began dimly to discern how all good comedy has its basis in truth. Perhaps for this reason I have tended for nearly sixty years to see life as a comedy, to echo the optimist who says his glass is half full rather than the pessimist who says his is half empty. It is not simply that one insists on a happy ending: I have taken great pleasure in hearing the likes of Laurence Olivier plumb the depths of 'To be or not to be'. On the whole, however, I would rather hear Danny Kaye singing 'Life Could not Better Be', even if it could. Putting it another way, when I first heard the couplet

> Two men looked through the prison bars,
> The one saw mud, the other stars

it was the second man with whom I identified. And yes, it was a comedy act from which I learned it, one of those in which a serious performer is constantly interrupted by an apparent idiot who manages to get all the laughs. The reciter had paused significantly at the end of the couplet, and his partner's response was:

> It must have been a gorgeous scrap!

This book is an attempt to bring together, briefly but in some sort of meaningful sequence, all the comedians who have given pleasure in my lifetime, on radio and television as well as the big screen. I have generally excluded such flexible comic *actors* as Roland Young and Roland

Culver and Edna May Oliver, concentrating rather on those players whose persona is at least partly that of the stand-up comic, the joke-teller, the waspish reactor against life's vicissitudes, the larger-than-life funny man in all of us. In medieval times, almost all my subjects would have been employed as jesters, and by dramatists they would have been classed as 'humorous'. They adopt variously the guise of coward or braggart or henpecked husband; they make play with their own eccentric physical attributes. Through these exaggerations, and at however great a distance, they tell us something about the human condition.

I did once try to repay my great debt to these people by writing a radio play about a cross-talking comedy team who passed the age of retirement and found themselves kicking against the traces in a home for the aged. And what happened? Neil Simon wrote *The Sunshine Boys*, that's what happened. So although this is a tribute of a more direct kind, I have retained my original title, which was *Double Take and Fade Away*; and that may take a little explaining. Almost everybody can tell you what a double take is: something odd happens, and the comedian fails to take it in at first glance. He nods pleasantly, turns away . . . and then realization dawns, and his head swings back, with some degree of eye-popping, to discover whether or not his eyes or ears deceived him. Cary Grant was among the subtler exponents of this art, but in a more extrovert way Oliver Hardy may be its most familiar performer, if only because his reaction is always to the camera. Among the entourage of Laurel and Hardy, however, was a comedian of Scottish origin who for a brief period was more popular than either of them. His name was James Finlayson, and Stan and Olly kept him in as many of their films as they could, for he was a splendid comedy villain and their most perfect foil: the house owner in *Big Business*, the sergeant in *Bonnie Scotland*, the conniving Mickey Finn in *Way Out West*. Every movement made by Finlayson was on the grand scale, his eyes a-pop, his limbs flailing: he never walked into a room if he could jump into it, and when he fumed in anger he used his whole body. His dialogue, in retrospect, seemed to consist largely of 'Aha!' and 'Oho!' and 'Hee hee!' It sounds horribly over the top, but such was Finn's enthusiasm that his luxuriant moustaches were always a welcome sight even though they hid one of the ugliest faces on screen: he looked, someone said, as though he had been weaned on a pickle. It was he who invented – and tried to copyright – the fade away, as a unique refinement of his double take. Finn would make the expected pop-eyed gesture, with so many accompanying grunts and little explosions that one felt it should be called a quadruple take at least. He would then, as a final and untoppable expression of fury, jerk his head backwards so sharply that it often seemed in danger of falling off his neck. That was the fade away, and once he did it so violently that he knocked himself out on a wall he hadn't noticed.

The title seemed to have a second aptness. Almost all the comedians of whom I write have indeed faded away, and replacements of equal worth are hard to find. Such training grounds as music halls and burlesque theatres are no more, and television has tended towards situation comedy rather than towards a new breed of funsters who can face the cameras alone. Only in occasional efforts of revival can we enjoy such shows as the BBC's *The Good Old Days*, or the unexpected success in America of *Sugar Babies*. Luckily there has grown up in both countries a very considerable nostalgia market, so that the skilled work of past comedy exponents can still be studied; video cassettes have helped, and in Britain Channel Four has lovingly unearthed many a hundred comedy extravaganzas of the thirties and forties which might otherwise have mouldered in archives, or been jettisoned as not worth keeping at all. In fact, though the performers themselves may have faded away, most of their work is enjoying a double take.

BOB HOPE: I was lucky, you know. I always had a beautiful girl, and the money was good. Although I would have done the whole thing over for, oh, perhaps half.

1
---

*A funny thing happened
on my way to the Colosseum:*

ROMANS, FRENCH
AND COUNTRYMEN

There is of course nothing new under the sun. British family audiences are well used to laughing at blue jokes which only the elders understand; but I doubt whether many of the elders, when they sat in the seventies through a long series of half-hour television comedies called *Up Pompeii*, realized that they were watching something basically designed from what Romans used to laugh at a couple of hundred years BC. Plautus was the gentleman credited with most of these low comedies, one at least of which had a long life indeed. *The Twin Menaechmi* was about identical brothers who are constantly mistaken for each other. Shakespeare nearly two thousand years later made it the basis of *A Comedy of Errors*, which is still a favourite for international revival, and on Broadway in 1940 it became a musical called *The Boys from Syracuse*, later filmed. Plautus' *The Haunted House* is about a clever slave who wants to use his master's house and forces the owner away by convincing him that it is full of dreadful apparitions; that situation was the basis of countless films of the thirties and forties, notably Abbott and Costello's *Hold That Ghost*. *The Pot of Gold* is about a miser whose hoard is stolen by a slave; Molière rewrote it as *L'Avare*, and versions of it under the title *The Miser* were offered by Fielding and Shadwell.

Most of the low comedies of Plautus centred on a cunning slave who outwitted his masters after confiding his schemes to his audience. In *Up Pompeii* Frankie Howerd, a tousle-haired camp comedian who always had an Ancient Mariner's way with his listeners, addressed the audience directly as the slave Lurcio, who alternately observes the intrigue going on in his master's house, and is responsible for it. There are many echoes of this in the French turn-of-the-century farces of Feydeau, and also in the British twenties ones of Ben Travers; but the most recent revival of the

A FUNNY THING HAPPENED ON THE WAY TO THE FORUM. Michael Hordern (second from left) seems quite at home in the film version with three seasoned Broadway funsters: Jack Gilford, Zero Mostel, Phil Silvers.

Roman setting and style was provided by the Broadway musical *A Funny Thing Happened on the Way to the Forum*, conceived in 1958 by its book author Burt Shevelove as an adaptation of Plautus into 'a scenario for vaudevillians'. The writers had no confidence that it would work commercially, but it ran and ran and is still running, having enjoyed more revivals than most Broadway musicals. This may be partly because it is funny and tuneful, partly because it is simple to stage, but principally because there is never a shortage of ageing comedians eager for one more chance to do their stuff. The original Pseudolus was Zero Mostel, followed in London by Frankie Howerd; the somewhat ill-conceived film version of 1967 chose Mostel and added Jack Gilford, Phil Silvers, Michael Hordern, Buster Keaton and Michael Crawford, scene-stealers all. (Milton Berle always regretted backing away from the original show when he couldn't get script approval.) It is a show which, professionally handled, gets an audience in the right mood almost from the opening strains of its theme tune:

> Something familiar, something peculiar,
> Something for everyone, a comedy tonight!
> Something appealing, something appalling,
> Something for everyone, a comedy tonight!
> Nothing with kings . . . nothing with crowns . . .
> Bring on the lions, lovers and clowns!
> Old situations, new complications,
> No recitations to recite . . .
> Open up the curtain, comedy tonight!

Soon everybody is running in and out of doors, and when the audience needs a breather the four leading comics come on and do 'Everybody Ought to Have a Maid' as a sort of soft shoe shuffle.

Almost everywhere you look in literature you will find characters who can be translated virtually as they stand on to the twentieth-century vaudeville stage, or into movies or television. In the medieval miracle plays a character of comic relief cries out for the thick Zummerset accents of Bernard Miles, who in the nineteen forties told rude stories while leaning on a cartwheel:

> Here come I, old Doctor Grub,
> In my hand I carry a club.
> Under my arm I carry a bottle
> And a great big volume of Harristotle.

Chaucer in the thirteenth century provided for his 'Miller's Tale' a yarn bawdier than the 'Carry On' team of more recent days ever knew how to be. Modern comedians with sufficient brio could be cast in most of Shakespeare's comic parts: indeed the aforesaid Frankie Howerd has successfully played Bottom in *A Midsummer Night's Dream*, while Roy Hudd in *The Blood Beast Terror* came on at half time, for comic relief amid the mayhem, as a garrulous servant clearly second cousin to the porter in *Macbeth*. Will Hay and Moore Marriott (in his Harbottle persona) would have made light work of Dogberry and Verges in *Much Ado About Nothing*:

> LEONATO: What is it, my good friends?
> DOGBERRY: Goodman Verges, sir, speaks a little off the matter. An old man, sir, and his wits are not so blunt as, God help, I would desire they were; but in faith, honest as the skin between his brows.
> VERGES: Yes, I thank God I am as honest as many living that is an old man and no honester than I.

DOGBERRY: Comparisons are odorous: *palabras,*★ neighbour Verges.

LEONATO: Neighbours, you are tedious.

DOGBERRY: It pleases your worship to say so, but we are the poor duke's officers; but truly, for mine own part, if I were as tedious as a king, I could find it in my heart to bestow it all on your worship.

LEONATO: I would fain know what you have to say.

VERGES: Marry, sir, our watch tonight, excepting your worship's presence, have ta'en a couple of as arrant knaves as any in Messina.

DOGBERRY: A good old man, sir; he will be talking: as they say, when the age is in, the wit is out. God help us! An two men ride on a horse, one must ride behind.

As for *Twelfth Night*'s willing but unable Sir Andrew Aguecheek, led along by the self-important hedonist Sir Toby Belch, they seem almost written to be played by Laurel and Hardy:

SIR ANDREW: Sir Toby Belch: how now, Sir Toby Belch!

SIR TOBY: Sweet Sir Andrew!

SIR ANDREW *(to Maria)*: Bless you, fair shrew.

MARIA: And you, sir.

SIR TOBY: Accost, Sir Andrew, accost.

SIR ANDREW: What's that?

SIR TOBY: My niece's chambermaid.

SIR ANDREW: Good Mistress Accost, I desire better acquaintance.

MARIA: My name is Mary, sir.

SIR ANDREW: Good Mistress Mary Accost . . .

SIR TOBY: You mistake, knight. *Accost* is front her, board her, woo her, assail her.

SIR ANDREW: By my troth, I would not undertake her in this company. Is that the meaning of accost? . . .

SIR TOBY: Oh knight, thou lackst a cup of canary. When did I see thee so put down?

SIR ANDREW: Never in your life, I think: unless you saw canary put me down. Methinks sometimes I have no more wit than a Christian or an ordinary man has: but I am a great eater of beef, and I believe that does harm to my wit.

SIR TOBY: No question.

You can almost see Olly's shake of the head and disgusted glance at the audience as he makes that last remark.

Osric in *Hamlet* is all the high camp comedians you can think of: Larry Grayson or John Inman would make a delicious meal of the part without

---

★ *Palabras* is a Spanish word, later corrupted to *palaver*: Dogberry is reproving Verges for idle chatter.

HENRY V. Shakespeare's low comedy does not come much lower than in this 'chronicle history'. Braggart Ancient Pistol (Robert Newton) is forced by Fluellen (Esmond Knight) to eat a leek.

damaging the surrounding suspense. And Ancient Pistol, the braggart in *Henry V*, may have waited four centuries for Robert Newton to play him, as he did in Olivier's 1944 film.

In the seventeenth and eighteenth centuries, high pomp of dress and manner set comic styles which were less easily copied by succeeding generations, but anyone who in 1985 witnessed Donald Sinden in full stage flight as *The Scarlet Pimpernel*, asking a passing hunchback whether he had rung any good bells lately, can have no doubt that the tradition of actors stepping out of role to make jokes with the audience is a long and fairly honourable one. It is an easy step from Christopher Sly, commenting on the main action from a primitive stage box in *The Taming of the Shrew*, to Olsen and Johnson telling the romantic lovers in *Hellzapoppin* to get on with it, or for that matter to the ancient hecklers Statler and Waldorf in *The Muppet Show*. Sinden in top comic form would be a natural for the periwigged Lord Foppington in Vanbrugh's *The Relapse*, with his strangulated cries of 'Stap me vitals!', just as John Inman was born to play the busily inventive actor-manager Mr Puff in

THE MUPPET SHOW. In the ancient tradition of hecklers, Statler and Waldorf tell the performers what they think of them.

Sheridan's *The Critic*. Even the somewhat effete skills of the *commedia del'arte*, with its classical mime figures of Harlequin and Pantaloon, find their twentieth-century equivalents not only in Marcel Marceau but in Charlie Chaplin and Harpo Marx.

But it was the more modern farces which really established the range of comic types on which television situation comedy is still trying out variations. Georges Feydeau in 1890s Paris produced one extravaganza after another filled not only with deceiving husbands, outraged wives and military lovers, but with oblivious priests, precocious children, benevolent uncles, maiden aunts, pregnant wives and nosy neighbours, as well as a few decorations in the form of choirboys, nuns, policemen and men who stammer, limp or suffer from a cleft palate. The genre was revived by the BBC in the seventies and proved to have lost none of its vivacity. In *Ooh La La*, Caryl Brahms's opening song told the audience what to expect:

> Lechery, treachery, swinging of hips,
> Dressing, undressing and longing for lips . . .
> Coryphées, negligées, passions that burn,
> Lovers discovered when husbands return . . .

A cinematic example of the farcical storms of Feydeau is *Occupe-toi d'Amélie* or *Keep an Eye on Amelia*, filmed by Claude Autant-Lara in 1949 and later reworked for the stage by Noël Coward as *Look After Lulu*. The film adds to the plot complications by presenting itself as a stage play within a movie, à la *Henry V*: one follows a motor car along a street and finds that it is being pushed by stage hands into the wings of a small theatre, to be applauded by the audience. This alienation effect intensifies the comic madness, and it is a pity that this fine film can be appreciated only by those competent to read subtitles at a rate of knots; for dubbing would entirely blunt its finesse. The plot builds up to a fine pitch of frenzy with hero and heroine going through a fake marriage of convenience at which the official in charge will supposedly be impersonated by an actor called Toto Béjard, who however fails to turn up and is replaced by someone with the real power to marry them. The way in which comic hysteria is generated by mere repetition of the actor's name is a supreme example of creative skill.

The end of the nineteenth century also marked in England the high point of popularity for the Gilbert and Sullivan operettas, all of which placed comedy above sentiment, and popularized the patter song for performers with well controlled larynxes. Take the 'Nightmare Song' in *Iolanthe*:

When you're lying awake with a dismal headache and repose is taboo'd by
    anxiety
I conceive you may use any language you choose to indulge in, without
    impropriety;
For your brain is on fire – the bedclothes conspire of usual slumber to plunder
    you:
First your counterpane goes, and uncovers your toes, and your sheet slips
    demurely from under you;
Then the blanketing tickles – you feel like mixed pickles, so terribly sharp is
    the pricking,
And you're hot and you're cross, and you tumble and toss till there's nothing
    twixt you and the ticking.
Then the bedclothes all creep to the floor in a heap and you pick 'em all up in a
    tangle;
Next your pillow resigns and politely declines to remain at its usual angle!
Well, you get some repose in the form of a doze, with hot eyeballs and head
    ever aching,

But your slumbering teems with such horrible dreams that you'd very much
    better be waking . . .

And after the dream:

You're a regular wreck, with a crick in your neck, and no wonder you snore,
    for your head's on the floor, and you've needles and pins from your soles
    to your shins, and your flesh is a-creep, for your left leg's asleep, and
    you've cramp in your toes, and a fly on your nose, and some fluff in your
    lung, and a feverish tongue, and a thirst that's intense and a general sense
    that you haven't been sleeping in clover;
But the darkness has passed, and it's daylight at last, and the night has been
    long – ditto ditto my song – and thank goodness they're both of them
    over!

Almost three-quarters of a century later one may be surprised to
learn that Sylvia Fine and not W. S. Gilbert is the author of 'The Maladjusted Jester', a song for Danny Kaye in his 1955 film *The Court
Jester*:

When I was a lad, I was gloomy and sad, as I was on the day I was born;
When other babes giggled and gurgled and wiggled, I proudly was loudly
    forlorn;
My friends and my family looked at me clammily, thought there was
    something amiss,
For when others found various antics hilarious the best I could manage was
    this:
        Boo hoo! Boo hoo! Boo hoo!
My father he shouted 'He needs to be clouted, his teeth on a wreath I will
    hand him';
My mother she cried as she rushed to my side 'You're a brute and you don't
    understand him';
So they sent for a witch with a terrible twitch to ask how my future impressed
    her:
She took one look at me and cried 'He he he he, what else could he be but a
    jester?'
        No butcher, no baker, no candlestick maker, and me, with the look
        of a fine undertaker impressed her – as a jester?

But where else could I learn any comical turn that is not in a book on the
    shelf?
No teacher to take me, to mould me or make me a merry mad fool or an elf?
But I'm proud to recall that in no time at all, with no other recourses than my
    own resources, with firm application and determination I impressed
    her . . .
                    . . . as a jester!

THE COURT JESTER. Danny Kaye, maladjusted or not, puts all he's got into his act.

Talking films changed a great many comedy styles, but if we look at the last decade of the silents we shall find that the most popular plays on the London stage were fast-talking farces, mostly identified with the company loosely in residence at the Aldwych Theatre. The leading actors were a splendid assortment of comic types. Tom Walls played young and old versions of the bibulous racing gent with an eye for a trim ankle. Ralph Lynn was the monocled silly ass who got into trouble only

from the highest motives. An imperishable trio was completed by
Robertson Hare, a small, meek and utterly conventional man who was
terrified of his large wife and relentlessly bullied by his co-conspirators:

> HARE: I am a man of peace!
> WALLS: You'll be a man of pieces if you don't do what you're told.

(Hare had a way of intoning his catchphrase, 'Oh, calamity!' which was
widely imitated throughout the land; and when in the thirties the team
split up he used it against an even more domineering bully, the bald-
headed Alfred Drayton.) Mary Brough impersonated the battleaxe of a
mother-in-law or landlady, ever suspicious of 'goings-on' beneath her
roof, as in *A Cuckoo in the Nest* when she makes the illicit lover even
more nervous by insisting that he sign the hotel register:

> BROUGH: You don't write very clear.
> LYNN: No, I've just had some very thick soup.

Although that particular exchange was said to have been inserted by
Lynn himself, it perfectly exemplifies the kind of googly dialogue at

ROOKERY NOOK. An essential ingredient of any Aldwych farce: Robertson
Hare (centre) finds himself at the mercy of monocled silly ass Ralph Lynn and
man-about-town Tom Walls.

which Ben Travers, who wrote all the genuine Aldwych farces, excelled (and continued to excel into his nineties). In *Plunder*, when the silly ass hero is grilled by the police, the worm finally turns:

LYNN: Rats!
INSPECTOR: I should advise you, sir, to moderate your language.
LYNN: Oh, very well. Mice!

The characters in these plays seldom commit any sin. Unlike their French precursors in Feydeau, their adultery is in the mind only, geared to contriving a totally innocent comic situation in which the heroine can explain that she said nuts to Putz, who made her eat wurts. Nor is the range of characters quite so extensive as Feydeau's, though it includes a stammerer or two: Travers adds inane constables, innocent vicars, flighty popsies in camiknickers, explosive Germans, peppery old admirals, *nouveaux riches* matrons and sonorous butlers. When the threat of naughtiness palls, this company of eccentrics can be just as funny in a haunted house:

WALLS: Somebody moaned.
LYNN: I think it was the wind.
WALLS: I don't know the cause of his affliction, but somebody moaned.

They live in a world so essentially proper that it can scarcely have existed outside the age of the comic postcard, when everyone knew about sin but not many had tried it.

The comic postcard must in fact be germane to our thesis. Almost unknown in America, it dared rather more than Britain's music hall comedians were allowed to, and virtually set the working-class style of public house humour. Popular for more than sixty years now, these cards are not merely 'blue' but ultramarine, yet most churchgoing mothers and spinster aunts north of Watford would have acknowledged them, even in the narrow-minded thirties, as the acceptable source of a good laugh. Donald McGill, who signed many of the cards, is often instanced as the prime begetter, though others certainly contributed. McGill's visual style is unmistakably right for the delineation of this vulgar world: clean colours, smooth firm lines, no shadows, and always in the caption the possibility of a double meaning, so that the beholder can be blamed for having a dirty mind when he sees a picture of a small child sitting between the legs of a fat man in a bathing suit, with the caption: 'I can't see my little Willy.' As Max Miller often complained, with tongue firmly in cheek: 'It's not what I say, lady, it's what you *think* I say!'

Here are some other postcard captions which have weathered the years, often with modernized drawings:

Flapper to her companion, as they escape the attentions of a camera fiend: 'Is he going to focus?'
Companion: 'Not if I can help it.'

Wife to friend, as husband makes heavy weather of repairing the garden gate: 'That's the trouble with George, can't screw without grunting.'

Doctor to girl: 'Have you had a check-up before?'
Girl: 'No, I think he was a Pole.'

Woman in department store: 'I want you to give this man in charge: he tried to tickle me in the bargain basement!'

Magistrate: 'What brought you here?'
Defendant: 'Two policemen, sir.'
Magistrate, to clerk: 'Drunk, I suppose.'
Defendant: 'Yes, sir, both of 'em.'

Doctor to girl: 'Have you been X-rayed?'
Girl: 'No, but I've been ultra violated.'

Delivery ward nurse: 'Your wife's had triplets.'
Father: 'Well, I never did.'
Delivery ward nurse: 'Go on, you must have.'

First mother: 'Did his father have hair like that?'
Second mother: 'I don't know, he kept his hat on.'

Complaining lady to waiter: 'There are two things I like firm, and one of them's jelly.'

First stork: 'Any business today?'
Second stork: 'No real business, but I put the wind up a couple of typists!'

'What are you doing with that cow, little girl?'
– 'Taking her to Farmer Smith's bull.'
'Good gracious, can't your father do that?'
– 'No, sir, it has to be the bull.'

Man trying to eat shellfish:
  'I can't get my winkle out, isn't that a sin?
  The more I try to get it out, the further it goes in!'

Peeping Tom looking at girl in bath: 'I wish I was a piece of soap!'

Doctor to wife: 'I suppose you're giving him anything he wants?'
Wife: 'Oh, doctor, he's been too ill to think of anything like that!'

'There's the vicar, sponging his aspidistra.'
'Horrid old man, he should do it in the bathroom.'

'I like taking experienced girls home.'
– 'But I'm not experienced.'
'You're not home yet!'

And so on, ad infinitum. This is a world of people on holiday, a world in which all the girls show a suspicion of frilly knickers and most of the men are inebriated. Both sexes have eyes that almost pop out of their heads at the thought of sex, but marriage makes an instant transformation: the men are all exhausted, the women grotesquely fat. Another curtain falls, and now the participants are even more grotesquely aged, cackling lasciviously at their remembrance of things past: as Jacques remarked in *As You Like It*, they are now sans eyes, sans teeth, sans taste, sans everything. But still good for a laugh!

Dost thou think that because thou art virtuous, we shall have no more cakes and ale?

SIR TOBY BELCH, *Twelfth Night*

2

Queueing on the right for the second house:
MASTERS OF THE MUSIC HALL

In the history of comedy entertainment the British experience has often diverged from the American, and after a superficial examination one might say never more surely than in the mid- to late nineteenth century and the early years of the twentieth; for music hall, even in its lowest form, was generally thought respectable, and burlesque was not. Yet in both cases it was the working man who called the shots, and Britain's now celebrated music hall tradition originated with the working man's need for a drink. The first music halls were glorified pubs, akin to the saloons in western movies, and what could possibly be more disreputable than those? The entertainment was added deliberately, so that men would not be ashamed to bring along their wives, and thus increase consumption. This touch of hypocrisy did not last long, for it turned out that British ladies were quite as fond as their menfolk of a good off-colour joke; while what might be going on in the upstairs rooms did not bother them so long as they knew where their husbands were.

Surprisingly few films have tried to reproduce the great vigorous age of the music hall, with famous names belting out songs loud enough without benefit of microphone to be heard in the bar behind the stalls. *Champagne Charlie*, made at Ealing in 1944, tells the fairly true story of a singing entertainer called George Leybourne and his rivalry with the Great Vance. Tommy Trinder and Stanley Holloway are well suited to the roles, and there is a strong impression of historical accuracy about the vast, echoing, bare-boarded halls in which we know that performers of the 1860s had to demonstrate their talents: but the production has a chill feel to it. *Those Were the Days*, made in 1934 by Thomas Bentley for Associated British, is based on a Pinero farce called *The Magistrate*, and tackles a later period, the nineties, when music halls had become cosier,

CHAMPAGNE CHARLIE. Tommy Trinder as George Leybourne takes the stage in a carefully recreated music hall of the 1840s.

smoke-filled places, with a table below the footlights from which the chairman of the evening robustly controlled the entertainment. By now it was deemed fashionable for officers and gentlemen to amuse themselves in such places, less perhaps in the main hall than in the private rooms upstairs. It was in this noisy and licentious atmosphere, beloved of the villain of *Gaslight* and the anonymous author of *My Secret Life*, that the really great names of music hall made themselves famous. If they had anything in common, it must have been the loudness of their voices, for there was a lot of hubbub to rise above, and audiences of the day were none too polite, if once allowed to become bored. The best-loved stars were not so much comedians as comic singers, some of whose most effective ditties were sold profitably, as sheet music or gramophone records, in remote parts of the kingdom to which the performer himself might never penetrate. I have never discovered who originated the song 'Hard Times', but it was handed down through the jovial uncles of my family, and its cheeky verse might raise an eyebrow or two even today:

> Long ago, years ago,
> Said Eve to Adam: 'I want a dress.'
> Said Adam: 'Look here, madam,
> As sure as my name's Adam,
> Times are bad, awful bad,
> In fact, they've never been worse before:
> Go round behind the barn –
> Your fig leaf you must darn!
>
> 'In these hard times,
> You've gotta put up with everything,
> In these hard times,
> You mustn't pick and choose.
> And things have come to such a pass
> To talk of fig leaves is a farce –
> You're lucky to get a blade o'grass
> In these hard times!'

A pause and a drum roll after the word 'farce' have been found effective. 'Dirty Work' is a splendid song for a sinister trio:

> Do you want any dirty work done, any dirty work today?
> Here we are, ready and willin'
> To murder your mother-in-law for a shillin';
> And if you've got a wife or two you want put out of the way . . .
> We're the boys to do the job.
> We do 'em in, a tanner a nob –
> 'Ere you are, then – three for a bob!
> Any dirty work today?

In more elegant vein, Charles Coborn, a gentleman entertainer since the 1870s, put on film in 1942, when he was ninety-four, his most celebrated ditty:

As I walked along the Bois Boolong with an independent air,
You could hear the girls declare, he must be a millionaire;
You could hear them sigh and wish to die, you could see them wink the other
    eye
At the man who broke the bank at Monte Carlo!

But there is nothing on film of Albert Chevalier delivering his equally famous piece of low life sentiment:

> We've been together now for forty year,
> And it don't seem a day too much;
> There ain't a lady livin' in this land
> As I'd swap for my dear old Dutch.

Nor, even more sadly, of the ebullient and wild-living Marie Lloyd, in social and sexual relations the equal of any man. Her most beloved piece of character comedy, as she totters along with her caged bird after a furniture van, is still in many repertoires sixty years after her death:

> My old man said follow the van
> And don't dilly dally on the way . . .
> Off went the van with me old man in it;
> I followed on with me old cock linnet.
> I dallied, and dillied, I dillied and I dallied,
> I lost me way and don't know where to roam,
> Cos you can't trust the specials like the old-time coppers
> And I can't find my way home.

The fastest music hall song was undoubtedly 'Any Old Iron', which, as performed by the increasingly short-winded Harry Champion, became a competition with the audience to see which could finish first:

> Just a week or two ago, me poor old Uncle Bill
> Went and kicked the bucket, and he left me in his will.
> The other day I went around to see poor Auntie Jane:
> She said, 'Your Uncle Bill has left to you his watch and chain.'
> I put 'em on – right across me vest –
> Thought I looked a dandy as they dangled from me chest –
> Then just to flash 'em off, I started walkin' round about,
> But all the kiddies followed me, and they began to shout
>
> 'Any old iron, any old iron, any any any old iron?
> You look sweet, talk about a treat,
> You look dapper from your napper to your feet!
> Dressed in style, brand new tile, and his father's old green tie on –
> But I wouldn't give you tuppence for your old watch chain,
> Old iron, old iron!'

The last verse was always treated by Champion, before the rousing finale, in solemn mock-operatic style:

> Shan't forget when I got married to Selina Brown,
> The way the people laughed at me, it made me feel a clown;
> I began to wonder when their dials began to crack
> If by mistake I'd got me Sunday trousers front to back!
> I wore me chain on me darby kell,
> The sun was shinin' on it and it made me feel a swell . . .
> The organ started playin' – the bells began to ring –
> Me chain began to rattle as the choir began to sing . . .

Et cetera, et cetera, et cetera.

The range of these songs will now have been perceived as sentimental, social-historical, vulgar, catchy and generally brisk. Some were also romantically melancholy, others military; most concerned affairs between the sexes ('Joshua', 'There was I Waiting at the Church', 'Tell Me Pretty Maiden'), and a few were determined to appear indelicate:

> Don't have any more, Mrs More;
> Mrs More, please don't have an encore.
> The more you have, the more you want, they say
> And enough is as good as a feast any day.

Whether the redoubtable Lily Morris was referring to babies, sex or just a glass of stout was not immediately clear, but the number was always climaxed by an amazing dance in which she clumped about with her skirts held high. There was also the occasional song based on a pun, in the manner of Benny Hill a hundred years later:

> I'm 'Enery the Eighth I am,
> 'Enery the Eighth I am, I am,
> I got married to the widder next door,
> She'd been married seven times before;
> Ev'ry one was an 'Enery,
> She wouldn't have a Willie nor a Sam;
> I'm her eighth old man called 'Enery –
> 'Enery the Eighth I am!

These songs made a great many popular reputations: Gus Elen, Dan Leno, Florrie Forde, Eugene Stratton, Gertie Gitana, Vesta Tilley, Nellie Wallace. A comedian called George Robey was even knighted, on little firmer basis than a pair of painted eyebrows and a song about a Peeping Tom called 'I Stopped, I Looked, I Listened'. (A public house called the Sir George Robey stands to this day in the Seven Sisters Road in London.) Such stars established with their audiences a total intimacy, being looked upon as members of the family. Their catch phrases were much imitated, especially that of the tubercular George Formby Senior, who died at forty-four and had often interrupted his rendition with a spasm followed by an explanation: 'Coughin' better toneet'. He also sometimes ate a flour cake during his act. It was all part of what a critic once called 'the gusty uplands of the British music hall tradition', and although not much of it got on to film, and what did is faded, scratched and badly recorded, it did set a few standards for the artists who, coming later, managed to get at least a semblance of their stage material on to celluloid which could be recalled and cherished.

SIR GEORGE ROBEY. No one was more surprised than him at the knighthood.

These later acts are the particular heritage of my father's generation, and to some extent of my own, though even when the stars were in their older heyday I was still too young to understand all their jokes. When they came to the Bolton Grand, however, I queued for them all on

almost a weekly basis, though I privately detested such ballad singers as
Cavan O'Connor, Talbot O'Farrell, Monte Rey and Josef Locke, and
grew bored with the repetition of novelty acts like the Ganjou Brothers
and Juanita, the Trio Mogador, Bob and Alf Pearson and even the much
lamented Wilson, Keppel and Betty, who had but one act and that a
comic sand dance called 'Cleopatra's Nightmare'. (Betty's part was to
sprinkle the sand.) My appreciation of singers at pianos depended on
what they sang: the jovial Flotsam and Jetsam were fine, but I was less
happy, on a descending scale, with the Western Brothers ('Jolly bad show,
chaps!), Norman Long and Hutch. Pianos without songs (Charlie
Kunz, Rawicz and Landauer) were generally more to my taste than
light singers without pianos (Terry Wilson, Albert Whelan); magicians
were better than either; acrobats, jugglers and trick cyclists were fine if
they didn't outstay their welcome.

 But it was the comedians I went to see. Almost any comedians:
Hatton and Manners, Murray and Mooney, Collinson and Dean. By the
time I was in short pants, Gracie Fields, George Formby (Junior), Will
Hay and the Crazy Gang were beyond the live reach of ordinary
mortals, having become film stars; but a few real luminaries still
consented to tour, and always drew full houses at the gilt-and-plush
paradise which was the Grand Palace of Varieties (unless you went in the
fivepenny gallery, which was bare and miserable and smelled of unmen-
tionable things). I remember one Saturday night feeling privileged to
get in, after queueing for more than two hours, to the final performance
of Lucan and MacShane in their famous sketch 'Bridget's Night Out'.
They too had become film stars by then, and there is one film in which
Arthur Lucan can be glimpsed as a man, but for 99 per cent of his
professional career he appeared in the guise of a sprightly, indignant,
unquenchable Irish washerwoman called Old Mother Riley. This was
essentially a dame figure from pantomime (of which more later), but
Lucan was seldom a pantomime star. Mother Riley worked best against
a semi-realistic background of drab poverty, the background which
Chaplin used for his little tramp. For most of the audience that was the
background against which they lived, and laughing at it helped them to
rise above it. Mother Riley did just that: she was constantly railing and
ranting about society's oppressors, and in her films always came up
trumps after a great deal of farce and knockabout. But 'Bridget's Night
Out' was the original concept, in which her trouble came entirely from
her errant daughter, played by a talentless Irish girl called Kitty Mac-
Shane, whose cries of 'Oh, mother, darlin'' were enough to make an
audience wince, especially as she was still uttering them forty years after

OLD MOTHER RILEY JOINS UP. Arthur Lucan, in standard drag, seems to be at the mercy of master spy Garry Marsh: but help is doubtless at hand.

her debut, with the same trill in her voice. MacShane had married Lucan, and promptly began to give him all kinds of hell, not only infidelity but the mistaken conviction that she could best manage his career. Their unhappy private life was already public gossip when I saw this live performance, and I could not understand in view of it how, having smashed enough crockery to fill a shop, they could end the sketch in each other's arms; but what possessed me for long afterwards was Lucan's perfect mimicry at the start of the performance of several old Lancashire women I knew (and he didn't) as he sat, slightly tipsy, by a dying fire and waited for his daughter to come home:

> I wonder where she is. I wonder who she's with. I wonder what she's doing. I hope she's all right.
>   I don't know how long she's been out. I've been asleep. And I can't read the clock till it strikes. That's where she has me, and she knows it. I don't know whether it's daytime, night time, half time, lilac time, early closing time or next Wednesday.
> *(The clock strikes three.)*
> One o'clock three times! I've been sitting here since yesterday, waiting for her to come home tonight, and now it's tomorrow. Something's happened to her. She's been abstracted. My only child, gone forever! If she doesn't come soon I shall have a nervous breakdown, a total eclipse. I shall

go right off the gold standard. I'm going to my bed. Half my life I waited
for her father to come home. I'm not spending the other three quarters
waiting for *her* to come home.

But when Bridget does arrive, the attack is immediate:

Where've you been, who've you been with, what've you been doing, and
why???

More than one play has been written about Lucan and MacShane, but
who can say whether the tragic or the comic mask is more fitting? The
brilliance of Arthur Lucan was never recognized in his lifetime, but now
it shines through his ramshackle films, of which several good prints
survive.

Frank Randle, also undervalued while he lived, was one of us, a
Lancashire lad from the laces of his pit boots. Born Arthur McEvoy in
Wigan in 1901, he seems to have led a somewhat mysterious youth
before emerging on the halls in the late thirties as a toothless, lurching,
spasmodically brilliant but totally unreliable vulgarian whose ability to
keep his audiences in stitches had more to do with rude noises than with
funny jokes. When you went to see Randle, you knew that whatever he
said would be aimed firmly below the belt and accompanied by a few
belches. (If he had lived a bit longer he would probably have farted too;
after all, Le Pétomane made a whole career of that accomplishment,
back in the 1890s in Paris.) Randle's act was a monologue on the simple
pleasures available to the working classes, principally beer and sex. He
could not pass a pretty girl without having his eyes almost pop out of his
head as he exclaimed, 'Bah gum, ah'll bet tha's a hot 'un'; and his usual
greeting to his audience was a prolonged bout of stomach gurgling
followed by the announcement: 'Ah've supped some ale toneet.' When
physically threatened, he usually escaped with a laugh: 'I've got only one
thing to say to thee.' – 'What's that?' 'Get off me foot.' He might then
proceed on the following lines (or might not, according to whether he
could remember them):

Ah'd just started me fifth pint, and Ah'd to go to the little lads' room, so
Ah left a notice propped up against the glass, 'Ah have spat in this beer.'
When Ah come back, somebody had written on't bottom, 'So 'ave I.'
(*A scoutmaster passes.*)
Ee, there's a young feller wi' 'is whistle danglin'. – Ah said to the
landlord, it's a bit thin, is this ale. He says, you'd be thin if you'd come up
t'same pipes as that ale 'as. Ah says it's all arms and legs, there's no body in
it. 'E says, a feller yesterday told me 'e'd never tasted owt like it. Ah says

FRANK RANDLE. As the ancient hiker, his favourite characterization, he seems about to expire from over-stimulation. A scene from *Somewhere in England*.

nor 'ave I, but Ah've paddled about in it. Ee, Ah'm not the man I was. Ah've just come back from t'chiropoddle. Ah says, look after that corn, it's killin' me. 'E says that's no corn, it's a collar stud stuck in thi stock. Aye. Ah don't like this ale, but Ah'll sup it if it keeps me up all neet. There's about thirty-six burps to the bottle. Last week Ah sent a bottle up to be analysed. The card came back, dear sir, your 'orse is in perfect condition . . .

Hardly prime material, but with Randle as with so many others it wasn't the jokes so much as the way he told them. He and his stooges often got the biggest laughs by abandoning the script altogether and coming on in funny clothes to stare at each other. I remember sitting in the front stalls of Bolton's Theatre Royal, waiting in eager anticipation for Randle to play Buttons in *Cinderella*. (Randle in a family pantomime? That had to be worth a visit.) The performance began very late because Randle at the appointed time was nowhere to be found. He turned up eventually, and drunk or not he steered the performance to a fine climax when he was being dressed for the ball and had trouble with the cut of his silken drawers. 'Come on, stand up straight,' urged an Ugly Sister, 'I want to see your dignity come out!' Randle milked that one for five minutes, establishing instant rapport with his audience and in particular with a woman in the third row who did not so much laugh as cackle. Randle had only to bare his toothless gums at her for the cacophony to be resumed, leaving the rest of the audience – and the cast – in stitches.

Randle's speciality, in his touring show *Randle's Scandals*, was to appear just before the final curtain as an ancient hiker, leaning on a shepherd's crook, a man clearly kept alive and vigorous by ogling the passing damsels and fantasizing about doing more, especially to those in shorts:

> There were one of them girls wi' so many veins in 'er legs she looked like a route map. Ah were busy lookin' for the Great North Road . . . There were a kid outside 'ere, 'e took one look at me and ran off, shoutin' 'Mother, Ah've just seen a monkey up a stick . . . Anyroad, Ah found a girl to goo out wi' me, and we went for a walk in t'country. Ah said, a penny for thi thoughts, and she clapped mi right across mi lughole. I said what's up wi' thee, I only said a penny for thi thoughts. She said oh, I thought you said a penny for me shorts . . .

Needless to say, Randle's film appearances were muted. To begin with, he seemed bewildered by entrances and exits, he had no concept of filmcraft, and all concerned found it easier, in *Somewhere in England* and *Somewhere in Camp* and *Somewhere on Leave*, to let him do his old acts before the camera, or as much of his old acts as the censor would allow. The films came to seem like protracted displays of Randle getting drunk, being unsteady on his pins, failing to get up stairs, taking a bath with his clothes on, losing his place in the script, and belching. Always, belching: he could without too much effort have composed a belching symphony. As a bonus, he garbled what dialogue there was, and played about with a few rude words. 'Do you jitterbug?' asked a girl at an army dance. 'Oh, aye,' he replied, 'Ah'm a reet jitterbugger!' Then there was the film which discovered him on parade, astride a donkey. 'What the hell do you think you're doing?' bellowed the colonel. 'Ah'm sittin' on me ass,' replied the imperturbable Randle.

When the star gained control of production, and often kept the crew waiting until he turned up drunk in mid-afternoon, the films got even sloppier. They were weird entertainments at best, with their cheap sets, their total lack of direction, their abysmal dialogue and their impossibly upper-class lovers. Only Randle instinctively turned the dross into fool's gold, and he was enough of an alchemist to do that whenever he came on screen, even when, as sometimes happened, he bewilderingly popped in his false teeth for the musical finale and looked totally out of character, with marcelled hair and a beaming, avuncular smile. Alas, the puzzle of Randle will never be solved. He drank himself to death at fifty-six (the certificate said gastro-enteritis) and the films, three at least, are all that remain; only accident has preserved even them. But his personality struck more than a spark in all who saw him on stage. There still exists in Britain a Frank Randle Appreciation Society, and in 1978 there appeared a would-be biographical work called *King Twist*, on the lines of *The Quest for Corvo*: the real Frank Randle was sought through the recollections of those who had known him. At the end of the book he remained a mystery.

Another performer emasculated by the requirements of cinema codes was Max Miller, the fabled 'cheeky chappie'. Max was not essentially photogenic, and on screen a little of him was sometimes too much. But to be in the same theatre with him was an electric experience, even before he uttered a word: he seemed to fill all the available space, leaving one breathless. To the strains of 'Mary from the Dairy', his signature tune, he would stride through the inner curtains in his silk floral suit, and stand back for a full minute of audience titters at his playful effeminacy as he displayed the garments, in profile and full frontal. He would then demand: 'Well, what if I am?' His ensuing monologue could last anything from fifteen to fifty minutes, depending on whether Max was on form and in a good mood. He usually was. Basically his character was that of the fast-talking market spieler, the Cockney with the ready smile who dazzles you by his verbosity and ingratiates himself in order to sell you something you don't want. The difference was that the audience always wanted what Max had to sell, which was a few saucy jokes, or maybe a poem:

> A boy and a girl went out hiking.
> Of course they were both wearing shorts.
> They stopped at the old Pig and Whistle
> And there had a couple of snorts.
> When they got back home the same evening,
> The neighbours all started to quiz.
> For *he* came back home wearing *her* shorts,
> And she came back home wearing – 'ere!

As a rule Max allowed the audience to supply the last word, so that he could tell them they were a dirty lot, and he was ashamed of them. While they rocked with laughter at their own daring – not his – he would flash a cheeky grin and remind them:

MAX MILLER, ready as ever to chat up anything that looks female.

Miller's the name, lady. There'll never be another. They don't make 'em today. When they made me, they broke the mould. When I'm dead and gone, that's it.

Max's act was so fast that the joke was over while you were still following it, and to save time, while he was waiting for the laughter to subside, he would oblige with a few dance steps. ('Here's a clever one. Scissors. Now, applause.') The ruderies followed each other in some sort of order, but the order could change according to his whim:

> There was a little girl
> And she had a little curl
> Right in the middle of her forehead.
> When she was good
> She was very very good,
> And when she was bad she was very very popular.

It's right, isn't it, lady? I have a terrible time with women. I was trying to get on this bus, see, and the clippie says can't you see we're full, do you want to get me into trouble? I said all right, what time do you finish? So I met her. I met her. She says what do you want to do? I said well, I thought we might go for a walk in the woods, and then we could pause and look at the moon. She said we'll go in the woods, and we'll look at the moon, but you keep your pause to yourself. Here, did you hear the one about the donkey? This feller had a donkey, and it was going to be twenty-one, and he didn't know what to get it for its birthday. Straight up. No, listen. So he asked the donkey, and the donkey said there's a fine thing. It was a talking donkey, you see. It said haven't you any feelings? It said here am I, slaving away for you for twenty-one years, and never a spot of female companionship. So that's what I want for my birthday. So this feller felt bad – well, you would, wouldn't you? – and he looked everywhere for a female donkey he could hire for the night. But he couldn't get one. No, he couldn't, really. The best he could do was a lady zebra, so that was all fixed up, and when the birthday came he put the zebra in with his donkey. And next morning the zebra was taken away, and the feller hurried in to ask his donkey did everything go all right. 'No, it bloody well didn't,' said the donkey, 'I spent all night trying to get her pyjamas off!'

That didn't get into the films, of course. And nor did this:

This girl had a little dog, and it was very hairy. So she went to the chemist and said, do you have anything for removing superfluous hair? And he said yes, I've got my own prescription, you just rub it on your legs and ten minutes later the hair will be gone. Oh, she said, but it isn't for my legs, it's for my little chihuahua. He said, in that case don't ride your bike for a fortnight . . .

And nor did this:

I came here by tube, lady. Can't afford a taxi, not at these prices. And I had to straphang, it was so full. Just in front of me there was this little old lady, sitting sound asleep, and suddenly the train gave a lurch and threw me forward, right across her lap. And she woke up with a start, and said: 'Is this Cockfosters?' I said: 'No, lady, Miller's the name!'

And nor did the one about the honeymoon picture which the bridegroom proudly showed to his friend. But why, asked the friend, are you sitting in the chair with Gertie standing up behind you? Because, the bridegroom replied, I was too tired to stand up and she was too sore to sit down. But the one that supposedly got Max banned from some halls concerned his dream of walking along a narrow ledge on a mountainside when he met, coming from the other direction, a luscious blonde with no clothes on. 'You see my problem,' he said. 'I didn't know whether to toss myself off or block her passage.' He was in trouble too after a Royal Variety Performance: his material was judged too near the knuckle for royalty. His tongue-in-cheek excuse to the press was that he'd brought along the wrong joke book. He had a blue one and a white one, you see. And after that, most of Max's stage appearances would begin with his producing two little books, one blue and one white, and asking the audience which they wanted. It was always the white one he threw away . . .★

The films in all honesty were not very good, because by the time the scripts had passed the censors there were no jokes left. *Hoots Mon* even presents Max more or less as himself, a cheeky comedian, floral suit and all, but the act we see contains an impenetrable last-minute censorial bloop and is otherwise all style and no substance:

> Aye aye, I'm 'ere. Thank you. I expected more, but I'm satisfied. It's raining outside, ducky: you all right in 'ere? I know what you're saying to yourself. You're saying, why is he dressed like that? I'll tell you why I'm dressed like that: I'm a commercial traveller and I'm ready for bed. Now listen, the last time I played this theatre I cracked a joke and someone told the manager, and they're not entitled to do that. It's jealousy. Now how do I know that? Because as a rule he sits in that box, and tonight he's not there. Now, I'm going to tell the same joke, but don't you laugh. If you laugh, he'll know it's rude. I think he's round the back.
> *(For the rest of his act Max keeps going to the back of the stage and glancing left and right.)*

★ A measure of Max's ingratiating skill was that fifty years after his heyday, in 1986, a television comic called Jim Davidson ran into trouble when he used on the box some fragments of Max's material, plus some naughties of his own. ('These Chinese girls, I had two in one night. Well, it's like Chinese meals, isn't it? No sooner you've had one, you want another.') Davidson was denounced on Channel Four's *Right to Reply* as sexist, racist and generally offensive, but one can't help imagining that the beaming Max would in 1986 have got away with it, even on prime time television.

Now, don't move. And don't go out. Don't you go out till I get back. He's at the side. Sitting in a bath chair with a silk hat and a whip. Haven't I got a nice figure, lady? No, I have. But don't they ride up in this weather? I've got a new one, all rubber next the skin, with little holes in it. You know. When I take it off, I look like a golf ball. I always have a row with the wife when I go on holiday. Course, I haven't got one of those wives that say where did you go, and who did you go with? She doesn't say that. She comes with me. She didn't come with me this time, though. I went to Blackpool. I found some digs and knocked at the door. A nice lady came – a nice lady – you know, a little bit up here, and then some more, not quite so much and then perhaps. And that's all I want, just a little encouragement. So I said surely you could squeeze me in a little back room? She said I could, but I haven't got time now.

Max knew his limitations. He didn't think much of his movies, and he didn't do pantomime. It wasn't that his act would have been unadaptable to family audiences – after all, Frank Randle got away with it – but Max was already a fantasticated version of a chap you might meet in any market town, and half the fun of pantomime lies in having a bit of fun with performers who are normally dignified or gawpish. Unless, of course, they can play the dame; and Max was all man. Besides, he was only credible against a modern urban setting: in ancient China or the Sleeping Beauty's castle he would have been so out of place as to seem irrelevant rather than funny. Pantomime is a curious off-shoot of music hall, a tradition known only to the British and mystifying to foreigners. Though it developed from such high-class period entertainments as the masque and the harlequinade, by the mid-nineteenth century it had become distinctly lower class, a mid-winter romp when children were allowed into the music hall and a pretence was made of telling a fairy tale for their benefit. Since the show had to appeal to adults also, the story stopped quite frequently to allow the insertion of the stars' standard acts, and just for fun, the leading heroic part was played by a girl (probably because she looked ravishing in tights). Even more oddly, the female comic character, usually the hero's mother, was played by a man, a popular comedian who took full advantage of the opportunity to dress in grotesque garments and make-up. Part of the fun was for the audience to join in with the singers, sometimes divided into left and right in order to see who could sing the loudest; and it was essential to hiss the villain at each entrance, and to help the hero with cries of 'He's behind you'. Farcical highlights might include wallpapering, baking a cake, or spending the night in a haunted house; while for a finale, the cast would troop on wearing fresh sets of clothes, and there would be another spot of community singing, with the words lowered from the flies, before the curtains finally closed.

Even today it is a poor comedian who is not engaged in pantomime, somewhere in the country, every Christmas; and although pop stars and television personalities may sometimes get top billing, it is the comedian whom the majority of the audience goes to see, for he is the one who

PANTOMIME. Stanley Holloway plays the Demon King in *Meet Mr Lucifer*.

makes them feel most at home, engaging in repartee across the footlights and indulging in all the traditional hilarities, including local jokes,
political jokes and television jokes. Above all, he must indulge with his
second banana in the time-hallowed cross-talk routines. The division of
spoils is one, with the smart ass doing the counting and getting the best
of it:

> There's one for you, and one for me. There's two for you, and one, two
> for me. There's three for you, and one, two, three for me. There's
> four . . .

This is usually followed by the 'you're not here' routine:

> I'll bet you a fiver I can prove to you that you're not here.
> – You can't.
> I can.
> – Well, there's my five pounds.
> And there's mine. Right. Now tell me: you're not in Manchester, are
>   you?
> – No.
> And you're not in Birmingham, are you?
> – I don't think so.
> Well, if you're not in Manchester and you're not in Birmingham,
>   you must be somewhere else. And if you're somewhere else, you
>   can't be here.
> – I see.
> Hey, where are you going?
> – Eh?
> You're taking the money . . .
> – Don't be silly, how can I be taking the money when you've just
>   proved I'm not here?

Some of these routines originated in American vaudeville (for which
see the next chapter), and many of Abbott and Costello's sketches were
on similar lines, but English comics made a score of them their own. The
closest an American movie ever came to English pantomime was Danny
Kaye's rather surprising 1955 piece *The Court Jester*, with its script so
well researched, or so well remembered, by Norman Panama and
Melvin Frank. The 'pellet with the poison' routine, reproduced on page
174, must be the supreme flower of its kind, but its roots are all English,
not only in pantomime but in revue sketches such as Dion Boucicault's
'A Double Dozen Double Damask Dinner Napkins', also quoted later.
    It was important for any music hall artiste to have some short piece
which would be remembered, to instant applause, whenever he strolled

on to the stage. Thus Will Fyffe would be unable to count the number of times he sang the song by which he is still kept vivid in our memories:

> I belang to Glesga,
> Guid auld Glesga toon,
> An' there's naethin' the matter wi' Glesga
> But it's goin' roond and roond;
> I'm nobbut a common auld working chap
> As anyone here can see . . .
> But when I get a couple o' drinks on a Saturday
> Glesga belangs tae me.

Nor could Albert Whelan have counted the number of times he whistled 'The Jolly Brothers' while pulling off (or putting on) his white gloves. Equally familiar mementoes of different kinds were Little Tich's big boots, Cicely Coutneidge's full-bottomed military walk, Sandy Powell's ventriloquist bit, Vic Oliver's violin, and the diminutive Arthur Askey's bee song:

> Oh what a glorious thing to be
> A healthy, grown up, busy busy bee:
> Whiling away all the passing hours,
> Pinching all the pollen from the cauliflowers.
> I'd like a be a busy little bee,
> Being just as busy as a bee can be.
> Flying round the garden, brightest ever seen,
> Taking back the honey to the dear old queen.

Why this mild little verse, an admitted favourite on the ends of seaside piers, should have made Askey a national star is not at all clear, but it may have had to do with the fascination of his short stature and almost perpetual motion.

Not all comedians sang or told jokes. There were also monologuists, beginning with serious (or sentimental) ones like Bransby Williams, with his Dickensian delivery, and proceeding through the skits of Billy Bennett, who in 'The Green Tie on the Little Yellow Dog' was the first to mock the most imitated and parodied monologue of all, Milton Hayes's 'The Green Eye of the Little Yellow God':

> There's a one-eyed yellow idol to the north of Khatmandu,
> There's a little marble cross below the town.
> There's a broken-hearted woman tends the grave of mad Carew,
> While the yellow god forever gazes down.
> He was known as Mad Carew by the subs at Khatmandu,

ARTHUR ASKEY. The 'silly little man' in his silly little hat, with equally silly glasses.

He was hotter than they felt inclined to tell.
But for all his foolish pranks, he was worshipped in the ranks,
And the colonel's daughter smiled on him as well . . .

Bennett's version ran a little differently:

There's a little sallow idle man lives north of Waterloo,
And he owns the toughest music hall in town.
There are broken hearted comics, it's a graveyard for them too;
And the gallery gods are ever gazing down.
He was known as Fat Caroo in the pubs round Waterloo,
And he wore a green tie with a diamond pin;
He was worshipped in the ranks by the captain of the swanks,
And the coal man's daughter loved his double chin.

Stanley Holloway was a man with a long and extensive film career, famous the world over after playing Alfred Dolittle in *My Fair Lady*. Yet he never filmed the recitations which first made him a household name, though they are still available on audio cassette. He didn't write them either – Marriott Edgar, who also wrote for Will Hay and the Crazy Gang, is the rhymster mainly responsible – but the doings of Albert and the Lion, Sam Small and the lady who 'with 'er 'ead tucked underneath 'er arm, walks the Bloody Tower' were party pieces always associated with Holloway. A Londoner by birth, he had a dark and resonant voice which made him a perfect recounter of north-country doings, and I am especially partial to a story called 'Three Ha'pence a Foot' which uses dry Lancashire wit to tell a little known anecdote about Noah:

I'll tell thee an old-fashioned story
That Grandfather used to relate,
Of a joiner and building contractor:
His name, it were Sam Oglethwaite.

One day Sam were filling a knot hole
Wi' putty, when in through the door
Came an old feller, fair wreathed i'whiskers.
T'ould chap said: 'Good morning, I'm Noah.'

Sam asked Noah what was 'is business,
And t'ould chap went on to remark
That not liking the look of the weather
He were thinking of building an ark.

What Noah wants of Sam is some birdseye maple to line his bunk, but they can't agree on the price: Sam says three ha'pence a foot, Noah stands fast at a penny ('and I'll give you a ride in me ark'). They part in high dudgeon, and then the flood begins.

The 'ouses was soon under water,
And folks to the roof 'ad to climb.
They said, 'twas the rottenest summer
That Bury 'ad 'ad for some time.

Soon Blackpool Tower is the only building sticking out of the water. Sam swims there and defiantly takes up his position. Noah passes by in his ark, but they still can't agree, so Sam still doesn't get his ride. Forty days later Noah returns, to find Sam's head just above the water level:

> Said Noah: 'Ye'd best take my offer;
> It's last time I'll be hereabout.
> And if water gets half an inch higher
> I'll happen get t'maple for nowt.'
>
> 'Three ha'pence a foot it'll cost yer,
> And as fer me,' Sam said, 'don't fret.
> The sky's took a turn since this morning:
> I think it'll brighten up yet.'

Holloway, by courtesy of writers R. P. Weston and Bert Lee, also thrived on funeral jokes:

> I've been very poorly, but now I feel prime.
> I've been out today for the very first time.
> I felt like a lad as I walked down the road;
> Then I met old Jones, and he said: 'Well, I'm blowed!
> My word, you do look queer! My word, you do look queer!
> Oh dear, you look dreadful. You've had a near shave;
> You look like a man with one foot in the grave!'
> I said: 'Bosh! I'm better. It's true I've been ill . . .'
> He said: 'I'm delighted you're better, but still,
> I wish you'd a thousand for me in your will!
> My word, you do look queer!'

And the one about the relation who came to a funeral in unsuitable footwear:

> Brahn boots. I ask yer, brahn boots.
> Fancy comin' to a funeral in brahn boots!
> I will admit 'e 'ad a nice black tie,
> Black fingernails and a nice black eye;
> But you *can't* see people off when they die,
> Not in brahn boots!

Holloway will inevitably be associated with the unfortunate Albert as long as either is remembered, but the less-known sequels are at least as funny as the original. In 'The Return of Albert', for instance, the lad's timing is so bad that, having been disgorged by the lion in Blackpool Tower, he gets back home just as Dad is collecting the insurance money due on his death – nine pounds four and two.

Young Albert came in all excited,
And started his story to give.
And Pa said: 'I'll never trust lions
Again, not as long as I live.'

Then giving young Albert a shilling,
He said: 'Pop off back to the zoo.
'Ere's your stick with the 'orse's 'ead 'andle:
Go and see what the tigers can do!'

Muddleheaded Robb Wilton, his stubby fingers always in his mouth
as he wrestled with the burning problems of the day, was another who
seldom told formal jokes: the humour came from his character. In his
earlier days he did have a formidable range of monologues, including
the inimitable 'Back Answers':

I pal on to people while standing in bars, and tell them my private affairs.
Once in a saloon a chap offered cigars; I responded with scotches in pairs.
As we drank, we got bragging of girls we had had. I described a sweet thing
    dressed in red.
I described her all right, 'cos my pal went half mad – 'twas the one he
    intended to wed.

He said: 'I'll punch your nose.' I said: 'Whose?' He said: 'Yours.' I said:
    'Mine?' He said: 'Yes.' I said: 'Oh.'
Then he said: 'Want to fight?' I said: 'Who?' He said: 'You.' I said: 'Me?' He
    said: 'Yes.' I said: 'No.'
At last words got to words, and he called me a cad. I said: 'Cad?' He said:
    'Yes.' I said: 'Who?'
He said: 'Who?' I said: 'Yes.' He said: 'You.' I said: 'Me?' He said: 'Yes,
    you're a cad'; I said: 'Boo.'

Robb Wilton did get himself on to the cinema screen, but only as a
cameo performer in generally inferior comedies, playing the fire chief
who could never actually bring himself to go to a fire, or the JP who
couldn't make up his mind in favour of a by-pass or against it. But his
real moment of glory came during World War II, when he stood alone
centre stage, or by a microphone, and mumbled his way through
accounts of his bumbling war effort. They always began with the same
ten words:

The day war broke out . . . my missus said to me . . . she said, what are
you going to *do*? I said, do? I've done it! Oh, she's a hard woman, the wife.
She said, done what? I said, I've joined the Home Guard. She said, the
Home Guard, what good is that, what do you actually *do*? I said, defend
this country against Hitler's invasion. She said, what, you? I said no, not

ROBB WILTON. The darling of the northern circuits, and a much bulkier performer than his henpecked image would suggest.

just me: there's Wilf Smith and Charlie Parker and Ted Robinson, there's quite a few of us . . .

Alternatively:

She said, you'll have to go back to work. She's got a cruel tongue, the wife. She said, our Harry's bound to be called up, and when he's gone there'll only be his army allowance, so what are you going to do about that? I said, I'll just have to try and manage on it. But she wouldn't give in. She said, what kind of work is there? I said, well, there'll be munitions. She said, now, how can *you* go on munitions? I said, I never said anything about going on them, I said there'll *be* some.

There is only a BBC tape record of Jimmy James's still celebrated drunk act, though it has been re-created for television by his son and two of his father's stooges. The bulky James, a teetotaller off-stage, was the professional epitome of the middle-aged, top-hatted wanderer, poleaxed by alcohol, a walking compendium of grimaces, shudders and double takes and the perfect foil for two apparent idiots, one of whom, in a high spot of surrealism, announces that, having recently returned from Africa, he has a lion in the shoebox under his arm. In due course it turns out that the box also contains a giraffe, and an elephant:

> JAMES: Is it male or female?
> STOOGE: No, it's an elephant.
> JAMES: I don't suppose it makes any difference to you whether it's male or female.
> STOOGE: It wouldn't matter to anybody. Except another elephant.
> JAMES: I shall have to stop you going to those youth clubs.

There were transvestite comedians too: G. S. Melvin and Douglas Byng and Clarkson Rose and the superb Norman Evans who played his act 'over the garden wall' and rested his huge false bosoms on that edifice. ('Ee, there was something wrong with me rice puddin' at dinner time. I swear I could taste that tom cat in it.') But of the pre-war crop of character comedians, the most successful in transferring his stage act to the screen, and in achieving star status for himself, was the aforementioned schoolmaster comic Will Hay. True, he wasn't always a schoolmaster, and after a few years he mistakenly decided to dispense with his stooges, but he was always the same shifty, sniffing old windbag with an eye to the main chance, and the public quite improperly took him to its heart. Graham Moffatt and Moore Marriott were much smarter than him, but they required his bluster and bravado to get them going. Between them, and with the help of scriptwriters Marriott Edgar, J. O. C. Orton and Val Guest, they produced in *Oh Mr Porter* (1937) at least one genuine classic of English music hall comedy on film. Hay, an incompetent stationmaster, has been banished to the run-down halt of Buggleskelly, in Ulster near the Irish border. From the moment of his soaking wet arrival he is besieged by ghosts and gun-runners, but above all by his own amiably corrupt staff of two, who have become used to a regime of few trains and no work. The following dialogue covers his arrival by night in the vicinity, shabby-suited and carrying his presentation clock and the minimum of luggage, in an ancient bus full of stage Irish characters and a squealing pig:

POSTMAN: That's a grand clock you've got there!

WILL: Eh? Oh, this? It's a little present from my staff when they heard I was leaving London.

POSTMAN: And what might the inscription say?

WILL: 'To William Porter' – that's me – 'from his fellow workers on the occasion of his promotion to stationmaster at Buggleskelly.'

(General consternation.)

FARMER: What was that he said?

WOMAN: This gentleman's the new stationmaster for Buggleskelly.

POSTMAN: Poor man – and him a stranger!

WILL *(uneasily)*: Why, what's wrong with it? Is it damp or something?

POSTMAN: Did you never hear tell of One-Eyed Joe, the Phantom Miller?

WILL: No, I never follow greyhounds. ★

POSTMAN: Follow, is it? You'll be a lucky man if One-Eyed Joe never follows you. He was murdered by the railway, so he was. He owned the Pookha Hill and the mill that stands atop of it – and what did the railway do but run a tunnel right through the heart of it, without saying by your leave or nothing.

WILL: That's hardly sic transit gloria. He should have sued them.

POSTMAN: He did better. He put a curse on the line, and swore that any train that entered the tunnel should never come out again.

WILL: That would mess up the timetable, wouldn't it?

POSTMAN: The first train came along. There in the mouth of the tunnel stood One-Eyed Joe, his arms upraised. 'Go back, go back,' he cried – but the engine driver went straight ahead.

WILL: What? Over Cockeyed Joe?

POSTMAN: Next morning his body was found on the line . . .
    And every night when the moon gives light
    The miller's ghost is seen
    As he walks the track
    With a sack on his back
    Down to the black borheen;
    And the mill wheels turn though the night is still,
    And the elf lights flash from the ruined mill,
    For he haunts the station, he haunts the hill,

★ A reference to Mick the Miller, greyhound champion of the day.

And the land that lies between . . .
(The bus pulls up with a jerk.)
DRIVER: Buggleskelly!

It's actually the *signpost* to Buggleskelly, which is two miles away, 'past the Witch's Oak and down into Hell Hollow'. By the time the gets through the driving rain to the dark and dilapidated station, Will is soaked to the skin. A feeble gaslight flickers over the ticket office, illuminating a sign: Leave Half a Pint. He knocks hesitantly; abruptly the hatch flies open and ancient Harbottle's face briefly appears:

HARBOTTLE: Next train's gone!
WILL: Here, come back! . . . What's the idea, keeping me out of my
    own station? What are you doing here anyway?
HARBOTTLE: Me? I'm porter and shunter and signalman and deputy
    stationmaster – when there isn't a stationmaster, which is more
    often than not.
WILL: Well, there's one now, see?
HARBOTTLE: Where?
WILL: Here. Me. I'm the stationmaster.
HARBOTTLE *(narrowly)*: Where's your clock?
WILL: What clock?
HARBOTTLE: Your presentation clock.
WILL: How'd you know I'd got one?
HARBOTTLE: They all bring one. Bung it with the others.
(We see a long mantelpiece laden with clocks.)
    Look nice when they're new. William Porter – another William.
    That was William O'Shea. Poor Bill.
WILL: Why, what happened to him?
HARBOTTLE: They put him away. *(Taps his forehead.)* Had to.
WILL *(reading)*: Mick McGuire. What was his trouble?
HARBOTTLE: Nobody knows. He went out after dark.
WILL: Where to?
HARBOTTLE: Don't know. Never saw him again. But we heard him.
    At least, Albert did.
WILL: Albert? Who's Albert?
HARBOTTLE: He functions for me when I'm not here.

Albert, the fat boy, arrives and proves to be even more disrespectful than Harbottle. Will coughs to attract his attention.

ALBERT *(to Harbottle)*: What's he want?
HARBOTTLE: New stationmaster.
ALBERT: Got a nasty cough, ain't he?

OH MR PORTER. Whatever Will Hay does, he does wrong in the eyes of Moore Marriott and Graham Moffatt, who greatly enjoy his discomfiture.

WILL: Never mind my cough. Show more respect to your superiors. And take your hat off. Both of you! What have you got there?

ALBERT: Supper beer. Want some?

WILL: Certainly not. This place is too free and easy altogether. I don't hold with a man in my position hobnobbing with his staff. You keep your place and I'll keep mine. What is it? Bitter?

They settle down to supper, but Will soon finds that the cheese has a delivery label on it.

WILL: What's the idea of this? You're eating stuff that doesn't belong to you.

HARBOTTLE: We haven't had any pay since we came to Ireland. We can't starve . . . so we borrow things.

WILL: You mean you steal things from the railway?

ALBERT: I wouldn't call it stealing: call it living off the country.

WILL: And I suppose you got this beer straight from the wood?

HARBOTTLE: Oh no, we paid for that.

WILL: What with?

HARBOTTLE: Ticket to Belfast.

WILL: Do you mean to say you're giving away the company's tickets
 for . . . well, I never heard of such a thing. It isn't right. In future
 you're going to make sure the tickets come back.
ALBERT: How?
WILL: Give 'em return tickets.

With this high level of easy dialogue, which in the cinema delivers a
laugh on every line, we have left idle backchat behind and arrived at
character comedy. Music hall has become humanized and respectable,
for Albert and Harbottle and even Hay himself are images recognized as
lifelike by a wide audience, loved as much because of their defects as in
spite of them. Albert is the smart young whippersnapper with a ready
lip; Harbottle the indefatigable old codger who gives us all hope for our
senior years, and Hay the conniver in all of us who conceals his
ignorance and inefficiency by the skin of his teeth. They have come a
long way from the fourth form of St Michaels, where there was always a
row of footlights between them and the audience. They are stars.

The trio made six films together, and could have gone on indefinitely
had not Hay decided in 1940 that he must be the only king in his castle.
Graham Moffatt and Moore Marriott did stalwart duty for other
comedians, and Hay's star slowly (and predictably) sank, as would
Tony Hancock's, in similar circumstances, two decades later. Without
partners as crooked as he was, his character defects began to seem more
reprehensible than funny, and although he was never less than skilful in
the management of spectacles and other props, his wartime adventures,
The Goose Steps Out and *The Black Sheep of Whitehall*, revealed him as a
somewhat lonely figure. He took to a dual role in one, to female
impersonation in the other, but neither trick seemed to work. Two other
wartime films, *The Ghost of St Michael's* and *My Learned Friend*, marked a
distinct improvement, not only because the first brought him back to his
schoolroom setting and the other was a fast-moving black comedy, but
because in Claude Hulbert he had found a partner whose silly-ass
dithering perfectly matched Hay's proletarian bravado. Alas, Hay's
health now failed, and he spent his last five years away from the cameras,
after an impressive though brief screen career of which *Oh Mr Porter* is
the undoubted high spot.

WILL HAY: 'The character I play is really a very pathetic fellow.'

3

Split week in Pocatello, Idaho:

AMERICAN VAUDEVILLE
AND BURLESQUE BEFORE 1930

What the British called family variety, the Americans called vaudeville. The word derived rather obscurely, perhaps from comic songs which originated in France's Vire valley (Val de Vire), and why Americans should have preferred it to the more straightforward 'variety', which after all they took as the name of their entertainment trade paper, will now never be known. But vaudeville, or 'vodvil', it was, from the 1880s to the 1920s, and what it came to mean was a nation full of travelling acts: jugglers, singers, dancers, monologuists, magicians, acrobats, trick cyclists and comedians, all on the move each week from one corner of the forty-eight states to the other, all aspiring (after 1908 when it was built) to play the Palace on New York's Broadway, generally accepted as the number one vaudeville theatre in the land. The mood of those days can still be gleaned from films of the thirties and forties. *Mammy* and *Swanee River* take us right back to the blackface minstrel shows which first set the pattern, but for vaudeville at its height you can take your pick from *The Merry Monahans, Bowery to Broadway, Funny Girl, The Jolson Story, Show Business, Two Tickets to Broadway, Gypsy, The Great Ziegfeld, April Showers, Bright Lights, Babes in Arms, Yankee Doodle Dandy, Shine on Harvest Moon* and *There's No Business Like Show Business* – and that's just scratching the surface. Most of them have one thing in common: that only slightly varying montage of train wheels and town signs which so vividly evokes the life of the performing nomads. Many of the great names of vaudeville were never recorded on film except as imitations, and we have to interpret the films for an impression of what it was really like to sit in the front stalls and watch Nora Bayes or Frank Fay or Annette Kellerman or Harry Lauder (even more popular in America than on his native heath) or Lou Holtz or Weber and Fields or

Anna Held or the Dolly Sisters or Bert Williams. Other talents, however, hit the big time to the extent that they are to be remembered more as film stars than as vaudeville performers. They are covered in our later chapter on the golden age of talkies, and to that list one might almost add half a dozen others who never became so popular in Hollywood as to renounce their 'live' heritage, but who made enough films to be known by history for what they really were.

Such a comedy team is Clark and McCullough, Bobby and Paul of that ilk. McCullough was the straight man, and in real life a tragic figure: after several nervous breakdowns he committed suicide in 1936. They made a number of short comedies which survive, and Clark later appeared in *The Goldwyn Follies*, but it is typical of Hollywood that in return for this elevation he was made to abandon the painted spectacles which had been as much a trademark for him as a painted moustache was for Groucho Marx. His preferred act combined nonsense, puns and a lot of slapstick, much in the manner of Olsen and Johnson; Clark might even abandon dialogue altogether and start hitting everyone in sight with a bladder.

El Brendel made a great many films in the thirties, but apart from *Just Imagine*, a futuristic fantasy in which he comes out of deep freeze fifty years after 'dying', none of his performances is in the least memorable. This may be because his characterization was shy and self-effacing, apart from being limited by his Swedish dialect. (He was in fact born in Philadelphia, but could think of no other way to get laughs.) Fanny Brice made a few film appearances, coyly emphasizing her reputation as 'the ugliest girl in town', but in close-up this persona seemed no funnier than her Baby Snooks impersonation and she was not invited back to Hollywood after 1944; though radio continued to employ her, and thirty years later Barbra Streisand impersonated her in two major musical dramas, *Funny Girl* and *Funny Lady*. Similarly afflicted was Sophie Tucker, a heavyweight Russian *emigrée*, the original red hot momma: her personality was simply too big for the screen, as Florrie Forde's would have been in England. When she sings her famous 'Some of these Days' in *Broadway Melody of 1938*, the effect recorded by the camera is muted and disappointing: she needed to sing to the gallery.

George M. Cohan was a multi-talent – actor, producer, composer, dancer, playwright – who electrified Broadway for nearly forty years, and it is ironic that he will be best remembered for the impersonation of him by James Cagney in the historically not-too-accurate *Yankee Doodle Dandy*; but his one star talkie, *The Phantom President*, shows that despite his precise skill in everything he tried, his own personality, as revealed

"Vote every schnozzle!"

"When me and Cohan bust into the White House, it'll be a capital offense to eat apple pie for breakfast — New England States excepted!

"We'll write a new chapter in American hysterics and declare 365 national holidays a year!"

II THE

PHANTOM PRESIDENT II

with GEORGE M. COHAN CLAUDETTE COLBERT JIMMY DURANTE

A Paramount Picture

SCHNOZZLE FOR LAUGHS COHAN FOR SONGS—and COLBERT FOR ROMANCE

What this Country Needs is a Good Five-Cent Date!

The Only Babies I Kiss Are Grown-Up Babies!

GEORGE M. COHAN. A legend in his own lifetime, but only in the tight circle of Broadway. His only talking film, *The Phantom President*, was not a runaway success, and Jimmy Durante was the name that saved it.

by the camera, is hard and unsympathetic. Marie Dressler had been in vaudeville as a blackface singer before the turn of the century, and her star had waned by the mid-twenties when she appeared on a bill of 'old-timers'; ironically, sound brought her fresh luck in the movies, and when she died in 1934 she had become one of Hollywood's biggest stars, on the brink of a mammoth popularity which would have lasted well into her seventies. Perhaps luckily, she never had a chance on film to do her vaudeville act, which included such songs as 'Heaven will Protect the Working Girl' and 'I Never Liked a Nigger with a Beard'.

Jimmy Durante, of the hoarse voice and the Brooklyn accent, also had a lucrative Hollywood career, but it was intermittent at best, and most of the time he was performing versions of his stage acts, wrecking pianos and singing raucous staccato songs like 'Umbriago', 'Inka a Dink a Dink' and 'I'm the Guy that Found the Lost Chord'. He thrived on interruptions: 'Everybody wants to get into de act!' he would complain. 'Am I mortified!' And he had an infallible prop in his long luscious nose, which gained him the nickname of Schnozzle. In fact, another favourite song of his was 'It's My Nose's Birthday, Not Mine': according to this, the nose was born first, and Jimmy came along a fortnight later. On another occasion, when someone told him that what he was looking for was 'right under his nose', Jimmy retorted: 'Don't be so indefinite!' And his favourite exclamation was: 'Dere's millions of good-looking guys in the woild – but I'm a novelty!' His homely appearance prevented him from ever playing the hero, even in fun, but through the forties and fifties he became an essential part of MGM's musical comedy roster, just as Marie Dressler had been given special treatment in the early thirties. Only when given the whole burden of a film, as in *You're In The Army Now*, did he quickly wear out his welcome: it is significant that the climax of this film is old-fashioned slapstick about a house teetering on the edge of a cliff, with the star required only for reaction shots.

A vaudeville comedian who never quite achieved star status in Hollywood was Bert Lahr. His failure may have stemmed from the fact that much of his humour depended not on characterization but on exaggerations of speech and indeed of speech defects. Yet for one film role at least he has already joined the immortals. His thick-tongued Brooklyn delivery will delight generations of fans to come in *The Wizard of Oz*, in which by now he is the only Cowardly Lion one can possibly conceive:

> Oh, it's sad to be admittin'
> I'm as vicious as a kitten
>   Widout de vim and voive;
> I could show off ma prowess –
> Be a lion, *not* a mowess –
>   If I only had de noive!

He also had a number called 'King of the Forest' which seemed at the time an unnecessary *longeur* but well represented the kind of sentimental fooling which had made Lahr a Broadway hit. The trouble was that with his moon face and crescent grin he was not easy to cast in naturalistic roles, though in *Always Leave Them Laughing* he was effectively if somewhat ungraciously cast as the elder comic into whose shoes the brash hero quickly steps when a heart attack turns the funny man into an invalid. Lahr had a few apposite words of advice for his too-aggressive pupil: 'They don't feel *sorry* for you. It's the *nice* things a comic does that make people remember him.'

There were also a couple of fragments from a famous Lahr act about a zany cop arresting a stripteaser:

> COP: That'll be a fine of one year, or imprisonment for two dollars, or *e pluribus aluminum* . . .
> GIRL: I think you're intoxicated.
> COP: Well, if I'm not, I'm out four ninety. As soon as I saw you, I said that's got to stop. So I watched you for twenty minutes . . .

No, it wouldn't bring the house down these days, but Lahr in his prime was greatly loved, and it seems a shame that he died so soon after filming began on *The Night They Raided Minsky's*, which was partly designed as a tribute to him. He didn't even get the chance of his contemporary Ed Wynn, similarly handicapped in his youth by an exaggerated burlesque image and Jewish dialect, to grow old gracefully in Disney movies, for whom Wynn perfectly voiced the Mad Hatter and portrayed a variety of elderly eccentrics.

The aforementioned brash hero of *Always Leave Them Laughing* was played by Milton Berle, who also failed to be much of a Hollywood name, though in the late forties and early fifties his blend of slapstick and one-liners gave him the nickname of Mr Television. A memorable line from the later comedy series *Happy Days*, set in that period, has Mum knocking on the bathroom door to announce to Dad: 'Hurry up, Uncle Milty's on TV and he's wearing a *dress!*' Berle was known, with partial justice, as a man existing on jokes borrowed from other and better comedians, and also as a man who would do anything to get a laugh: off-colour jokes, impersonations, funny faces, custard pies. The fact was that within himself lurked no tangible comic personality, only an urge to succeed. It was odd and ironic that his biggest screen opportunity was to play this version of himself, a guy with no heart and no singular talent. It's just possible that he didn't notice the resemblance; or perhaps he thought he could bring out the pathos in such a character. The film now is tolerable only for its barrage of corn, and for whole stretches of it Berle is performing, whether supposedly on stage or off. Coming into a crowded dressing room, he quips: 'Will everybody exhale? I gotta find my pants.' He knocks at a chorus girl's door:

> BERLE: Hurry up, you're on.
> GIRL: Hey, wait a minute, I'm not even dressed.
> BERLE *(coming in)*: That's all I wanted to know. Don't worry, I spent two years in medical school.
> GIRL: How'd you get out of the bottle?

He calls on his agent:

> BERLE: Have you got a woman in your room?
> AGENT: Of course not.
> BERLE: Well, open the door and I'll throw one in.

Escorting a girl to a train, he is asked by a porter: 'Can I carry your bag, sir?' 'That's all right,' says Berle, 'she'll walk.'

The act which in the film propels him to stardom (as it did in real life) is a veritable barrage of one-liners, starting with a few gunshots:

> Nobody sleeps during my act. Ladies and gentlemen – I apologise for calling you ladies and gentlemen, you know what you are . . . Please don't applaud my act, if you like it just throw money. I've had a hard life, you know. At school I was teacher's pet: she couldn't afford a dog. My mother said for goodness' sake learn a business, so we'll know what work you're out of . . . But times are hard for everybody. A man came up to me and said he hadn't had a bite for three days. So I bit him. Ladies and gentlemen, I want you to note during my next trick that at no time do my fingers leave my hands. Meanwhile, there will now be a two-minute silence for the three jokes that just died.

Even if the stuff works, it somehow isn't personalized, and nor was Berle. He wasn't even particularly Jewish, just a smart-alec New Yorker whom nobody really wanted to like – except that early television audience. *Always Leave Them Laughing* was shot during the first flush of that immense small-screen success, and in it Berle can't resist an ironic joke when a knock is heard at the door: 'If that's someone with a TV contract tell him I'm not interested. Television will never catch on.'

Julian Eltinge was a unique vaudeville performer in that, as a female impersonator, his act was sufficiently subtle to be accepted by all classes. He starred in some silent films, mostly lost, but had no better luck in talkies than Britain's Danny La Rue. Frank Fay was an Irish monologist whose talent should have fitted well into films; one suspects that the causes of its failure to do so were his Irish temper and his caustic ad libs at the expense of other performers. (When Milton Berle challenged him to a duel of wits, he said: 'I never fight with an unarmed man.') Eddie Foy Senior, father of the seven little Foys, died before talkies could gain a foothold, but Eddie Foy Junior hung around the studios for decades without ever getting a role worthy of his talents other than Hines in *The Pajama Game*, which remains his best epitaph. Trixie Friganza was a fat lady who described herself as 'a perfect forty-six'; movie roles for her were hard to find. A famous double act was Gallagher and Shean, but Gallagher died during the twenties, and in the two film presentations of their famous 'travel' act, Al Shean (uncle of the Marx Brothers) uses other partners:

> Oh Mr Gallagher!
> – Yes, Mr Shean?
> In Egypt life is clearly European.
> – One can ride on camels' backs,
>   And one pays no income tax!
> Positively, Mr Gallagher?
> _ Absolutely, Mr Shean!

Umpa, umpa, umpa, umpa, umpa, umpa, um, vamps the band, and the audience, for no perceptible reason, becomes ecstatic.

Charlotte Greenwood is remembered as an immensely tall, graceless girl who could do astonishingly high kicks: she too made films, notably *Oklahoma!*, but never became a Hollywood fixture. Texas Guinan, a pallid version of whose life was filmed with Betty Hutton as *Incendiary Blonde*, was a hot potato, a consort of gangsters who burnt herself out and died young, younger even than Britain's Marie Lloyd about whom similar remarks might be made. Tex became a nightclub proprietress, but still performed regularly. Jack Haley had Hollywood success to approximately the same level as Bert Lahr, to whose Cowardly Lion he played the Tin Man in *The Wizard of Oz*; but his precise impersonation of a meek and mild young man prevented him from achieving top star status, and he seemed to have no other cards up his sleeve. Completing that famous Oz trio was Ray Bolger as the amiably vacuous Scarecrow:

> I could while away the hours
> Conversin' with the flowers,
> Consultin' with the rain;

THE WIZARD OF OZ. Judy Garland, a great performer in her own right, is supported by three giants from vaudeville: Bert Lahr as the Cowardly Lion, Jack Haley as the Tin Man, and Ray Bolger as the Scarecrow.

> With the thoughts I'd be thinkin'
> I could be another Lincoln
> If I only had a brain . . .
> And perhaps I'd deserve you,
> Or be even worthy erv you
> If I only had a brain . . .

Bolger made several tries at film stardom, partnering June Haver and Doris Day as well as Judy Garland, but despite his brilliant acrobatic dancing the producers never came clamouring a second time: he was simply not a hero type.

George Jessel, allegedly, spent the rest of his life regretting that he turned down the leading role in *The Jazz Singer*, a chance smartly snapped up by Al Jolson. Jessel never quite had Jolson's personality, but in later life he became a competent producer of Fox musicals, and a nationally known toastmaster and payer of tributes. (Stars complained that whenever Jessel glanced in their direction they felt he was preparing notes for their funeral eulogy.) Ted Lewis, another Jewish entertainer with great personal style, made a few pictures too, but his range, singing 'Is Ev'rybody Happy?' with his invariable props of cane and battered top hat, was limited. Ken Murray, known in later years for his home movies of the stars, never became much of a Hollywood actor himself, but had been known in vaudeville as a risqué comedian, and took this reputation later into the field of revue with *Ken Murray's Blackouts*:

> Do you have a fairy godmother?
> – No, but there's an uncle we're not too sure about.

Harry Richman had a similar fund of jokes, which meant similar difficulty in getting into movies, despite his immaculate song and dance act. He also had a reputation for consorting with gangsters, and another as a determined ladies' man: Mae West once said he had a great touch – 'even with a piano'.

Weber and Fields, top of the bill at the turn of the century, did a Dutch Jewish act, as Mack and Myer, which would probably not have endeared them to movie audiences in their day, and in any case they could make only silent films. Smith and Dale, correspondingly popular a quarter of a century later, appeared in several talkies, none of which is remembered; but they will go down in history as the cross-talking originals of Neil Simon's *The Sunshine Boys*; the 'Dr Kronkhite' sketch which is parodied in that play and film is theirs. Urban types from Hester Street, they gave the impression of never having seen a cow, nor wanting to. Their act was a relentless barrage of verbal gags with a heavy Jewish flavour, and their greatest merit was that they spoke the lines clearly, with a masterful command of timing:

> You should go to the mountains for your rheumatism.
> – Is mountains good for rheumatism?
> Sure, that's where I got mine. Hey, I gotta go back to the office. I forgot to lock the safe.
> – Why worry? We're both here.
> What we eating tonight?
> – Sardines. I gotta nice four-dollar can.
> Four dollars for sardines?
> – But they're imported.
> Why should I pay their fare over? I gotta lot of expenses, these days, with moving house.
> – Where do you live now?
> Rusty Cove, LH.
> – What state is LH?

Long Highland. And I just paid out a fortune for life insurance.
– You shoulda gone with my company. When you die they give you
    a beautiful cemetery plot by a lake.
What, with my rheumatism?

Audiences could not think of Dale without Smith, or vice versa, and
never had to. They were lifelong inseparables. When a pretty girl ogled
one and asked 'Have you got the time?', his reply was: 'Sure, but what'll
I do with my partner?' Hollywood or not, Smith and Dale went on
performing on stages across the country, and latterly finished their act
with a little verse:

> Over seventy years together,
> With a bond that never tore,
> And if somebody up there likes us
> We'll make it more and more.

One performer was as well known for his vaudeville appearances as
for the movies which he crowded into the last few years of his life. Will
Rogers, in some senses, didn't have much of an act. He had been a
cowboy, and started off doing roping tricks, but he had to say something in between them, and gradually he found that audiences responded better to his impromptu remarks than to the ropes. His
humour all passed for common sense, or crackerbarrel philosophy: later
in Britain, Bernard Miles would do something similar while leaning
over a cartwheel, and later still Buddy Ebsen as Jed Clampett stretched it
to nine television seasons of *Beverly Hillbillies*. 'A rope ain't bad to get
tangled up in,' Rogers would drawl, 'if it ain't round your neck.'
Whatever the real Rogers may have been, he came over to the public as
what Gary Cooper would have called 'the average Honest Joe American', and since the country felt that it needed such a thing, he quickly
rose to become star of the Ziegfeld Follies, still roping, but now making
homely remarks about the president, whom he treated as an equal.
When talkies came, he was an obvious candidate for Hollywood, and his
ranch on Sunset Boulevard is still preserved as a national monument.
    If vaudeville as a whole was dominated by Jewish performers, which
is only fair in view of that race's splendid confidence in self-expression, it
was also well supported by Irish, who are not far behind in bravado, and
by blacks. Bert Williams, Ethel Waters, Bill Robinson, Adelaide Hall
and Florence Mills were all bill-toppers, and following them was a
legion of blackface comedians and singers in imitation of Jolson and
Cantor. Though it causes squirms of embarrassment and protest today,

WILL ROGERS. A rope twirler who became America's favourite crackerbarrel philosopher.

blackface performing was originally intended as a tribute to the melodies and rhythms of the old spirituals sung by Southern slaves. These had been adapted into the format of the minstrel show by men like E. P. Christy and Lew Dockstader, and Jolson added a depth of feeling derived from Jewish religious singing. Between them these traditions produced the now honoured and purely American musical form of jazz, which can require no defence whatsoever.

Vaudeville was intended for the whole family, but there was a more adult form which came to be known as burlesque, or by trade distortion burlicue. The only movie which has gone some way towards recording the heyday of burlesque is *The Night They Raided Minsky's*, but even that was produced at a time (1967) when there were still restrictions on what could be shown. The entertainment undoubtedly centred on a line of girls wearing as little as possible, but in the twenties titillation was so rare that a little went a long way, and the bulk of the responsibility for a show's success lay with the comedians, who were provided with saucy routines and sketches which still stopped well short of being explicit. The flavour was well conveyed to American theatregoers in the early 1980s by a nostalgic revue called *Sugar Babies*, which had immense success around America and ran for more than three years on Broadway, revivifying the star appeal of faded luminaries Ann Miller and Mickey Rooney. Rooney had tried everything, from Andy Hardy to tragic drama, and now America was telling him that the way he was liked best was as a dirty old man in burlesque. His material certainly was

VAUDEVILLE, as represented by Hollywood in *Bowery to Broadway*. Rosemary de Camp and Frank McHugh lead a somewhat unlikely musical troupe.

VAUDEVILLE IN LATER DAYS, recreated for television by three star graduates: Bing Crosby, Jack Benny, George Burns.

raunchy: in one scene he was taken into a brothel and a companion described him as 'so short that he'll have to be put up to it'. But the chief interest of the show lay in its exhumation of blackout sketches from long ago, sketches which got big laughs without ever stating what was clearly in the audience's mind.

A man sits peacefully on the river bank, holding a fishing rod with nothing on the end of it. Enter to him a stranger on his way home, with two fish on the end of his line.
> FISHERMAN: Excuse me, sir, I'm not having much luck here. Would you mind telling me what you've been using for bait?
> STRANGER: Not at all. I'm a doctor at the hospital up the river, and I performed an operation this morning. So I just kept the bit of liver I cut away, and used that.
> FISHERMAN: I see. Thank you.

First stranger goes; second stranger appears with half a dozen fish at the end of his line.
> FISHERMAN: Excuse me, sir, would you mind telling me what you're using for bait?
> 2ND STR.: Why, certainly. I'm a doctor at the hospital just along the river bank, and I'm using a little spleen from an operation I performed this morning. It seems to have worked fine.
> FISHERMAN: Yes, it does. Thank you.

Exit second stranger. Enter third stranger, positively laden with fish.
> FISHERMAN: Excuse me, doctor . . .
> 3RD STR.: Vot doctor? I'm a rabbi!

Such blackout sketches often seem to work in three jabs, of which the third is the googly. Take for another instance:

> VOICE: Ladies and gentlemen, we take you now into the home of one of our foremost national poets. It is Saturday night, and his three nubile daughters are going out on dates for the very first time.
> POET: Tell me, daughter, tell me true,
> Who're you going out with, and what're you going to do?
> 1ST DAUGHTER: I'm going out with a guy named Bill,
> We're going for a walk, up over the hill.
> POET: Okay, be back by midnight.
> Tell me, daughter, tell me true,
> Who're you going out with, and what're you going to do?
> 2ND DAUGHTER: I'm going out with a guy named Pete,
> We're going downtown for something to eat.
> POET: Okay, be back by midnight.
> Tell me, daughter, tell me true,
> Who're you going out with, and what're you going to do?
> 3RD DAUGHTER: I'm going out with a guy named Chuck –
> POET: Get back to your room!

MAURICE CHEVALIER (left) in attention-getting form, seen here with Jack Buchanan: they played a couple of down-and-out vaudevillians in *Break the News*.

British music hall, perhaps, was vaudeville and burlesque rolled together. It was almost entirely urban, whereas amid the vastnesses of America there were rural audiences which demanded not to be sullied by the sins of the big city. French variety too must have appealed largely in the cities, for in the late twenties its most powerful star was the ebullient, effervescent and all-male Maurice Chevalier, who like many performers around the world had his eyes on a Hollywood career. He got two, widely separated; but the first one ended prematurely when the Hays Office found his stuff a bit too saucy for pure American ears. The five formative years of the talkies, however, were all his, after the talkies had displaced a very different comic art which created, developed and glorified the sight gag into one of the richest sources of laughter in all history. The silent cinema had also permitted a mood in which comedy was tinged with poetry and melancholy, and that was something which would not return, not even in disguise.

And now, a moment while the
operator changes reels:

THE GLORY DAYS OF SILENCE

The first kind of American comedy to become international knew no language barriers, and any ethnic origins it may have had were obscured by purely visual gags which any race, colour or creed could understand. The wonders of silent farce were devised and developed in Hollywood between 1912 and the coming of sound in 1927, after which almost all its most brilliant exponents suddenly discovered their talents to be unusable. Since those talents included such comedy geniuses as Buster Keaton and Harold Lloyd, and the supremely inventive entrepreneur Mack Sennett, one may well wonder why on earth this was so. The only good reason, if it can be thought sufficient, is fashion. Talkies had been invented and commercially adopted, and the new medium had to be used. Talkies were what the fans read about, and therefore what they thought they wanted to see. Silent gags were suddenly old-fashioned, the wonder of yesterday, and no producer of power thought it worth his while to 'present' the old talent in the new medium. It could easily have been done, with talking introductions and an apt musical background for the main part of the entertainment, but it *wasn't* done. Everybody on the new screen had to talk all the time, and because sound recording was in a primitive state, that meant that they had to stand still while they did so. Gone was the possibility of those symphonies of movement which so delighted the eye during the early twenties, as the Keystone Kops wove their dizzy patterns of madness, dutifully followed by an enquiring if bewildered camera.

Only Chaplin among the comedians was strong enough and rich enough to weather this storm out of sheer defiance, and he through the thirties made no more than two widely spaced feature films, in the second of which he hesitantly sang a couple of verses of gibberish, just to show that he did have a voice. Laurel and Hardy, who had established themselves only during the last year of silence, found that although basically visual performers they could adapt very well to the new medium, varying periods of high silent action with equally amusing stretches of conversation, and thus becoming the most richly inventive comedians of them all. (Even so, the trade paper *Variety* complained every time a new Laurel and Hardy film came out that the slowness of the gags harked back to silent days, failing to realize that it was the deliberate pace, stressing the inevitability of comic disaster, which kept audiences in stitches.) But Keaton turned to drink after seeing his first truly awful sound comedies (for anyone who needs to be convinced, *Free and Easy* is the nadir); Lloyd made occasional attempts, but gradually became disheartened and reclusive; the rest went to the bad in their various ways, accepting that for them the time was out of joint.

Thus one of the subtlest art forms of the twentieth century was allowed to wither and decompose in favour of wisecracks (which are fine in their way, but it is not the only way). Silent comedy might never have been rediscovered before the negatives fell to pieces had it not been for an article by the perceptive critic James Agee, who in 1949 wrote for *Life* an essay called 'Comedy's Greatest Era'. Oddly enough it caused its deepest ripple among younger readers, and when a few years later an obsessive, overweight film producer called Robert Youngson made a feature-length compilation of silent extracts under the title *The Golden Age of Comedy*, it was a box-office sensation. There followed several others: *When Comedy was King, Days of Thrills and Laughter, Laurel and Hardy's Laughing Twenties, The Further Perils of Laurel and Hardy, Four Clowns, Thirty Years of Fun*. They were all cursed with obnoxious commentaries and music tracks, but the excerpts were well chosen, and the very act of making the compilations underlined the commercial value of the old negatives and ensured that they would henceforth be properly looked after. Meanwhile Keaton's privately owned films had been rediscovered by Raymond Rohauer, a lawyer and theatre owner with an eye to the main chance and a liking for seeing his own name on the screen as custodian of the giants of the past; Harold Lloyd had sold his own backlog to Time Inc. for several million dollars; musical sound tracks were put to the Laurel and Hardy silents; and soon there was scarcely a piece of twenties comedy not available for re-examination and sale, even quite a lot which would have been better left in the vaults. Sadly, Robert Youngson died prematurely in 1974, and no other editor so far has assembled the material with equal skill; but at least the material

MACK SENNETT COMEDIES. A banisterful of Sennett bathing beauties and comedians. Billy Bevan, with moustache, centre.

remains, a treasure trove indeed, to be sifted by future scholars, among whom Kevin Brownlow has made an excellent start.

In Hollywood in the silent heyday there were two great impresarios of gag comedy, each with his studio factory full of stars under contract, running and jumping but seldom standing still. According to Agee, Mack Sennett divided his work into parodies (which have survived least well because the originals are no longer familiar) and plain unmotivated slapstick. The latter Agee describes as:

> a profusion of hearty young women in disconcerting bathing suits, frisking around with a gaggle of insanely incompetent policemen and of equally certifiable male civilians sporting museum piece moustaches. All these people zipped and caromed around the pristine world of the screen as jazzily as a convention of water bugs. Words can hardly suggest how energetically they collided and bounced apart, meeting in full gallop around the corner of a house; how hard and often they fell on their backsides; or with what fantastically adroit clumsiness they got themselves fouled up in folding ladders, garden hoses, tethered animals and each other's headlong cross purposes. According to legend (and according to Sennett) he discovered the speed tempo proper to screen comedy when a green cameraman, trying to save money, cranked too slow. Realizing the tremendous drumlike power of mere motion to accelerate, he gave inanimate objects a mischievous life of their own, broke every law of nature the tricked camera would serve him for, and made the screen dance like a witches' sabbath.

There can be no better description than that of a Keystone Kops comedy, with its absurd gesticulating figures subjected frequently and often to the kind of Tom and Jerry violence which never seems to hurt. Even when tossed from a high building on to the sidewalk below, men rise and walk away unconcernedly, and although they seldom manage to board the police car before it sets off, these determined custodians of the law happily cling to one another behind it, a giant snake of skittering humanity, whirling from side to side of the street as the vehicle zooms away into the distance. As Agee goes on to remember:

> toward the end of every Sennett comedy a chase built up such a majestic trajectory of pure anarchic motion that bathing girls, cops, comics, dogs, cats, babies, automobiles, locomotives, innocent bystanders, sometimes what seemed like a whole city, were hauled along head over heels in the wake of that energy like dry leaves following an express train.

Sennett himself was a quiet man who seems to have known his limitations, except that he always, curiously, fancied himself as a performer although the evidence shows him to have been uneasy in front of the camera. Hal Roach, with a more flexible approach, refused to give up at the advent of sound, and although after 1940 he made little of note he was still playing around with new ideas in his nineties. Lloyd had started with him, and in the twenties his big hits before Laurel and

THE KEYSTONE KOPS. Ford Sterling is at the wheel (or what's left of it) after
an unfortunate encounter with two streetcars.

Hardy were *Our Gang*, a motley collection of kids who regularly got
into spectacular mischief, and Charley Chase, a dapper go-getter who
usually got into trouble through misunderstandings with his wife or his
boss. The two-reeler was Roach's forte: at various times he had under
contract Snub Pollard, Mabel Normand, James Finlayson, Will Rogers,
Max Davidson and Edgar Kennedy, among others, and when sound
came, in addition to steering Laurel and Hardy safely through its
troubled waters, he tried other combinations: Thelma Todd and Patsy
Kelly, The Boy Friends, Thelma Todd and ZaSu Pitts, Franklin Pangborn and Bud Jamison, even the British Duggie Wakefield. When
two-reelers proved uneconomic he tried forty-minute featurettes
('screenliners'), but by then inspiration was wearing thin, and he seems
to have decided to leave the running of the studio to his son, who
botched the job to the extent that Roach had to sell up and never again
became a power in the business. This seemed doubly strange because in
the late thirties he made (and occasionally directed) a string of popular
features. One, *Of Mice and Men*, was a gloomy classic, and there was an

CHARLEY CHASE, the man-about-town of the twenties.

old-fashioned spectacular, *One Million BC*, as well as a couple of action epics, but most were comedies streaked with madness, and these have lasted particularly well: the *Topper* trio, *Turnabout*, *The Housekeeper's Daughter*, *Merrily We Live*. Posterity may applaud Roach most loudly for having allowed Laurel and Hardy to develop their own brand of comedy and come up with such brilliant pieces as *Sons of the Desert* and *Way Out West*; but as a comedy maker in his own right he was not to be despised.

Hollywood comedy in the zany, raucous twenties was aptly celebrated through re-creation in Twentieth Century-Fox's otherwise disappointing 1939 extravaganza *Hollywood Cavalcade*, and in the same year Sennett bade custard pies a fond farewell in a short called *Keystone Hotel*. More recently there have been tributes in *Abbott and Costello meet the Keystone Kops*, in *The Great Race*, and in Carl Reiner's *The Comic*, in which the character played by Dick Van Dyke is intended as an amalgam of Buster Keaton and Stan Laurel.

Who were these great American comics? Well, one of them was French, and might have proved a giant among them had not a morbid streak caused him to commit suicide at the age of forty-two. Max Linder played a dapper man-about-town, and his precise characterization and movements must clearly have influenced Chaplin, since he had been making films since 1907. In 1917 he moved to Hollywood and did some of his best work: it is collected in a 1963 compilation called *Laugh with Max Linder*, which contains the funniest known version of the mirror gag also attempted by Groucho Marx, Bob Hope and countless others. Roscoe 'Fatty' Arbuckle also pre-dates Chaplin: not especially appealing now, the roly-poly comic was a surefire crowd-pleaser in his day, until his career was ruined by a sensational murder trial in 1921. Though he was judged innocent of any complicity in the death of Virginia Rappe, Hollywood at that time was so careful of its image that it washed its hands of one of its most effective clowns, and Arbuckle stepped on to the road to ruin, as did his 'second bananas' Minta Durfee and Al St John. Not so however for a young tumbler who had been allotted increasingly sizeable parts in Arbuckle comedies, to the extent that when the trial took place he was his own uncontaminated man. His name was Buster Keaton, and his chief prop apart from a slight but agile body was his unsmiling poker face, which was imitated the world over. Keaton's forte was creating complex visual set-ups of breathtaking virtuosity, and his good luck lay in being allowed to stage them with painstaking preparation and at considerable expense. Think of the multi-Keatons in *The Playhouse*; of the location tricks in *Balloonatic*; of the house assembled then wrecked by a train in *One Week*; of one escape gag piling on another in *Cops*; of the house wall which falls on Keaton in *Steamboat Bill Jnr*, an open window neatly framing him as he stands among the debris; of his efforts in *The Navigator* to boil an egg on an empty ship with equipment which will boil only three hundred; above all of the

MAX LINDER, a dapper international comedian whose career was cut short by personal tragedy.

huge steam locomotive which he bent to his will for an endless variety of tricks in *The General*.

Our Hospitality has a different kind of genius. It begins as gentle parody of old-time melodrama; then there is a hilarious train journey with that unbelievable rescue swing across the waterfall which still dazzles all who view it; and the last section is situation comedy, the meek and mild Keaton as the house guest of people who he slowly realizes are out to kill him. When it was new, *Our Hospitality* must have provided the most satisfying sort of evening for civilized audiences, and it is doubly sad that only a few years later Keaton's career was wrecked by the talkies, and especially by his forced alliance with a big studio which would not allow him to direct his own films. At least he lived to see the revival of interest in his best work, which came with the seventies retrospectives in New York and around the world. As he said at the time, 'Who would not wish to live a hundred years in a world where there are so many people who remember with gratitude and affection a little man with a frozen face who made them laugh a bit, years ago when they and I were both young?' Agee had noted even earlier the basis of Keaton's lasting virtues:

> Beneath his lack of emotion he was also uninsistently sardonic; deep below that, giving a disturbing tension and grandeur to the foolishness, for those who sensed it, there was in his comedy a freezing whisper not of pathos but of melancholia. With the humour, the craftsmanship and the action there was often, besides, a fine, still and sometimes dreamlike beauty.

Harold Lloyd was a master of thrill comedy. He would climb, for purposes of plot, up the outside of a skyscraper building, braving on the way loose ropes, falling paint cans and collapsing clocks; and when he got to the top he would fall again, only a rope holding his ankle as he swung from side to side, upside down, among the burgeoning high rise buildings of Los Angeles. (Thank heaven for the brick construction which at least offered a few footholds!) *Safety Last* was the title of his best film, and it might well have been his motto: his daring astonished especially those who knew that half his right hand had been blown away by a trick bomb which had exploded prematurely. Like Keaton, he had but one characterization, though Lloyd's was less subtle, less susceptible to shades of meaning: he was a shy, pale-faced, bespectacled young man in a straw boater, always at the mercy of bad luck in whatever enterprise he attempted, be it taking a live turkey on a tramcar, trying out a new automobile, or reluctantly accompanying a giant prisoner in an escape from a banana republic's jail. The inventiveness of Lloyd's gags was endlessly delightful, but one suspected that beneath the white make-up was a basically dull fellow, one who would make an irritating husband

BUSTER KEATON in *The General*. Even in the trickiest of situations (i.e. behind enemy lines and under the general's dinner table) his face shows no emotion.

for the girl he invariably won in the last reel. Lloyd the man was certainly canny: his silent features made him a millionaire, and he lived in splendour; his Beverly Hills mansion was so famous that there was an attempt after his death to turn it into a state monument. (The attempt failed, though part of it was used for the Roman villa in *Westworld*.) Sadly, he never quite got the hang of talking pictures, and his best attempts, *Feet First* and *Movie Crazy*, are flawed by leaden pace; but in 1962 he issued two compilations of his silent climaxes which made the whole world laugh again.

Harry Langdon and Larry Semon, like Lloyd, used a whiteface make-up which detracted from any claim they might make to be human beings. In fact they made none. Semon, to judge from his few surviving films, was an acrobatic clown, a gagman *par excellence*; while Langdon got his laughs by looking perpetually close to tears, like an aged baby. Being so limited, he managed only three popular features before ennui set in; but modern critics look back on him longingly, as though wishing that some secret cache of unreleased films will some day be found to illustrate his true genius.

These were some of the comedy stars of the silent twenties, but in their day they were backed by a whole gallery of familiar faces who only in the judgement of posterity are held to be more lightly talented. Cross-eyed Ben Turpin in his parodies of better-looking heroes was an immense popular success, to such a mind-blowing extent that he used to introduce himself to strangers in the street as: 'Ben Turpin! Three thousand a week!' Louise Fazenda, who later married producer Hal Wallis, was the perennial prim spinster or farmer's daughter. Mack Swain, a great lump of a man, was a perfect dumb-bell or massive villain: remember him as Chaplin's hungry cabin-mate in *The Gold Rush*?

Billy Bevan, a dumpy English working type with a turned down moustache, later appeared in hundreds of talking films, usually as a comic policeman. His moment of glory came in a short called *Super-Hooper-Dyne Lizzies* (1924). Pushing his stalled car from behind, he unwittingly picked up several other cars which had been stationary.

HAROLD LLOYD in a typically dangerous stunt from his silent period. No faking here: it's a real bus and a real road.

SNUB POLLARD and BEN TURPIN, knockabout comedians who delighted millions in the twenties.

Up hill and down dale the little figure pushed this incredible snake of automobiles, until one by one they tumbled over a cliff!

Chester Conklin had an even bigger moustache and bleary features: he was the foreman who got mixed up in the machinery in *Modern Times*. Wallace Beery was around in silent comedies, incredibly doing female impersonations; so was Carole Lombard as a teenage flapper; and so of course was the most popular of them all, for a time, Douglas Fairbanks Senior, who might not have regarded himself as primarily a comedian, but whose adventurous leaps across rooftops and off moving trains and down ropes must have engendered many a satisfied smile.★

If I seem almost to have forgotten Charlie Chaplin, it is primarily because so much has been written about him that it seems presumptuous and even foolhardy to offer more. Yet since his death at a venerable age

★ Researchers of discrimination and devotion may yet uncover more gems from this fertile period. Youngson brought to light a brilliant 1928 short called *A Pair of Tights*. Apparently intended for Laurel and Hardy, and forgotten because they were replaced by Edgar Kennedy and Stuart Erwin as the tightwads who try to get away with buying their girl friends ice cream, instead of dinner, it packs into ten minutes more disasters devolving on four ice cream cones than anyone would think possible; and it boasts sterling work from two lady comics of the period, Marion Bryan and Anita Garvin. You can see most of it in *When Comedy was King*.

in 1977 his star had waned to such an extent that a whole generation of youngsters must be totally ignorant of the man who once cheered up the whole world and united highbrows with low in unqualified admiration of his comic art. Young people who do know something of him are these days plagued by his less than admirable private qualities. He was a

CHARLIE CHAPLIN. In this still from *A Dog's Life*, the dog seems to be getting all the laughs. Mr Chaplin probably had him fired next day.

comic who wanted to play Hamlet; a Jew who pretended to be Gentile; an incorrigible luster after young girls; a self-styled genius who thought that everything he touched must turn to gold; and a poor boy from the London streets who became an extremely mean millionaire. (The free list was always suspended for Mr Chaplin's pictures.) The abysmal misjudgements of his later years, especially *A Countess from Hong Kong*, are notorious, and the rot set in quite early. He was only fifty-eight when he released *Monsieur Verdoux*, a stiff and bewildering social comedy, admired at the time by a few but now a puzzle for historians; and *A King in New York*, the product of his seventies, is no more than a spewing up of gall at the United States for expelling him as a suspected communist.

Nevertheless, as a composer of sentimental songs he would have been hailed as the king of his kind; and the short comedies he made between 1915 and 1917, after emigrating from London with Fred Karno's comic army, still provide some of the funniest times anyone can spend in front of a moving picture screen, and must have been much more so in the days when prints could still be made from pristine negatives. The balletic comedy of the little man in the tramp outfit is seen at its best in *Easy Street*, where it is combined with sentiment and with the satisfaction of the worm turning as he outwits the slum street bully and wins the love of a Salvation Army girl. In *The Cure* he is a dude alcoholic, disrupting the sedate existence of health spa residents when his smuggled-in liquor is dumped in the public drinking fountain. *The Adventurer* presents him as an escaped convict, taking refuge in a country house and evading capture through a variety of disguises. But the majority of these early films had him as an urban down-and-out, never so disheartened that he can't help those less well placed than himself, be they ladies, infants or dogs. Between 1914 and 1922 Chaplin's art was at its summit. After that, the longer he laboured – and for some scenes he did hundreds of 'takes' – the limper his results tended to be. *The Gold Rush* in 1924 had wonderful moments but was patchy overall; *The Circus* in 1928 began well but then fell away. He persevered without speech for *City Lights* in 1931, but despite its enormous success at the time – due partly, one suspects, to nostalgia – it now evokes comparatively few laughs, and is cherished chiefly for the tramp's superbly lit final expression in the last shot, when the blind girl recognizes him as her benefactor. *Modern Times* also started brilliantly, and has marvellous moments throughout, but one is uncomfortably aware of pathos and political stridency struggling to take over. *The Great Dictator*, Chaplin's contribution to the raising of wartime morale, contains a sharp impersonation of Hitler but isn't otherwise very funny, while its final anti-fascist speech to camera was a sad mistake in a world already convinced.

Like Jacques Tati, Chaplin would never take advice, and in later years he paid for this failing. As Lord Acton said, all power tends to corrupt, and absolute power corrupts absolutely; and perhaps Chaplin gained too much power too soon. More seriously, he never felt the need to be liked, only to have people in their millions flock to see his brilliance; and without affection on both sides there can be no true greatness in the cinema.

CHAPLIN: All I need to make a comedy is a
park, a policeman and a pretty girl!

5

Silly little men:
THE THIRTIES HEYDAY
OF BRITISH COMEDY

The astonishing thing is that there was so much of it, but then you need to laugh in a depression. Even back in 1926, the year of the General Strike, British film comedies had abounded: Walter Forde in half a dozen two-reelers, Will Rogers in *Tiptoes*, Guy Newall in *The Ghost Train*, Peter Haddon in *Oxford Bags*, Sydney Fairbrother in *Mrs May*, Guy Newall in *What the Butler Saw*, George Robey in *The Prehistoric Man*. But as with most British silent films, it was hard to sit through them at the time; almost impossible now. Not until Hitchcock and the talkies supplied a fresh impetus did British film-making demonstrate any ability to emulate the finesse of Hollywood. Even then British films were usually slow and unsure of themselves: 1932's *Rome Express* and 1933's *Friday the Thirteenth* are rare exceptions for their years, smart and well-judged compendiums of drama and comedy. The flat, uncertainly paced failures are more typical, and they seem all the more effete now because most of the comedy was archly based on West End musical or farcical models, fantasies for the underprivileged in which nobody behind the camera took any real creative interest.

The early thirties, however, were fruitful apprentice years during which a new group of talking comedy stars, among others, learned their trade. Most of them succeeded, and it is largely the same names which were popular at the end of the decade as at its beginning: Jack Buchanan, Jack Hulbert, Leslie Fuller, Bobby Howes, Stanley Lupino, Gene Gerrard, Jessie Matthews, Seymour Hicks, Gordon Harker. Here and there in the early thirties a decent, well-formed comedy surfaced: a not bad version of *Three Men in a Boat*; a lively Hulbert–Courtneidge vehicle, *Jack's the Boy*; George Robey in a dressy version of *Chu Chin Chow*; a stylish Jessie Matthews musical, *Evergreen*, from Victor Saville;

Sydney Howard in *Tilly of Bloomsbury*. The Aldwych farces had their own kind of vigour: Tom Walls's idea of direction was to have everybody stand in a line and speak clearly, but the wit of Ben Travers and the theatrical skill of the performers usually showed through. Almost all these stars, however, repeated themselves in later vehicles, and we shall do ourselves no injustice if we mark down the first half of the thirties to experience.

By the beginning of 1935 the style and status to which British film comedies aspired was well established, but still the gap between aspiration and achievement was often incapable of being bridged. When World War II started nearly five years later, the men had been sorted out from the boys. Some comedians had gone back to variety, others had found themselves best suited to the fireside medium of radio, and just a few, aided by smart writers and producers, had seen their fairly frequent appearances round the cinema circuits turn into queue-forming events to be appreciated by all classes. The best overall view of this decisive period in British comedy may be gained by setting out the productions in order of release, with time to pause at the most notable names emerging. The sheer volume of output may cause surprise:

1935

Things Are Looking Up. A somewhat unhappy vehicle for the indefatigable Cicely Courtneidge, strident both as a stuffy teacher who goes over the wall and as her circus-owning sister who also plays tennis against Suzanne Lenglen. Max Miller for once is almost speechless in support.

Brewster's Millions. Jack Buchanan, the elegant, top-hatted, long-legged darling of West End cabaret and musical comedy, would possibly never have become a star post-war, despite his undoubted stage-filling qualities and his uniquely nasal, plaintive way with a romantic song. But in the thirties, when everybody loved a lord, he was liked by most people and adored by many, as much because of his somewhat neutral sexual quality as despite it. He was a charming, clean-living, debonair boy, the son every grandmother wanted, and he danced divinely, with or without his longtime partner Elsie Randolph. His films were variable, but do not deserve the neglect which has befallen them, despite the fact that they were seldom as well produced as they might have been; for it is still quite an experience to hear him sing a romantic melody like

JACK BUCHANAN (right). For the picture on page 63, Mr Buchanan descended to Mr Chevalier's level. Now Mr Chevalier mirrors his partner's usual debonair elegance.

'Goodnight Vienna', or even a simple comic ditty like this one, which he could turn (almost) into poetry:

> I like a nice cup of tea in the morning,
> Just to start the day, you see;
> And at half past eleven,
> Well, my idea of heaven
> Is a nice cup of tea.
> I like a nice cup of tea to my dinner
> And a nice cup of tea to my tea;
> And when it's time for bed
> There's a lot to be said
> For a nice cup of tea.

The Lad. Gordon Harker, he of the cockney accent and the jutting lower lip, had started his screen career as a character actor in Hitchcock's 1928 silent *The Ring*. By the mid-thirties, though his best days were still to come, he was well established in a variety of roles; he sometimes played straight, but it was a surprise if one did not hear that fruity voice say 'Yerss'. He had been excellent as a club car bore in the 1932 *Rome Express*, and later would make three amusing if basically unsuitable appearances as Inspector Hornleigh. He did in fact play a lot of policemen, but also had a partiality for jailbirds (to whom one instantly warmed), especially in adaptations from Edgar Wallace, of which this was one.

Strictly Illegal. Leslie Fuller was a burly, beefy, cheerful working-class comic, more credible doing something with his hands than with his brain. His low-budget vehicles, almost never revived, were not marked by production skill, but they entertained a wide audience. In this one he was a bookie posing as a clergyman: at other times he would be a stoker, a bargee, a soldier or a train driver, among other callings. For a while, with wee Georgie Harris as his side-kick, he was popular enough to produce his own movies, and take the profit.

Oh! Daddy! Leslie Henson, with his pop eyes, was a fine comedian in stage musical comedy, where every gesture reached the back of the gallery, but on screen he seemed overpowering, and with those grotesque features he was an unlikely candidate to get the girl, which made it difficult to build a script around him. *Oh! Daddy!* had been a stage farce, and for the screen version he recreated his role as a Purity League peer, but the movie passed without much remark despite a cast which included the delectable Frances Day (then highly popular on radio with a song about being lost in a London fog with her dog).

Dandy Dick. A fairly straight version of Pinero's play about a vicar accused of doping racehorses. Will Hay starred, but it seemed curious casting in view of the fact that his legions of music hall fans knew and loved him for broader stuff (which he was allowed to play for the first time later in the year).

It's a Bet. A forgotten comedian is Gene Gerrard, of Irish descent but born in Clapham, and most easily described as a British Danny Kaye without much of the talent. Or, if you like, Harold Lloyd. He was good-looking enough, but played nervous types. Alas, the further his films strayed from London, the less certain was their appeal.

Who's Your Father? An acrobatic comedian who had made some mark in Hollywood in silent days, Lupino Lane was now somewhat desperate for material, as may be guessed from his choice of this somewhat tasteless comedy about the hero's embarrassment when his parents divorce, his mother to marry an undertaker and his father a black woman. Lane still had glory to come, as the dapper, strutting cockney hero of the stage hit *The Lambeth Walk*, which he would film in 1939. (Thirty-five years later London's West End and New York's Broadway would hail it as a long-running smash hit under the title *Me and My Girl*.)

Fighting Stock. The Aldwych farceurs had now passed their peak, but fans still flocked to this contrivance for the sake of the amiable familiarity with which they skated on thin ice.

Off the Dole. An unkempt northern comic, son of another, starred in this low-budget extravaganza which was lucky to get bookings south of Manchester. The fact that it did, and that the essential talent of its star was recognized by entrepreneurs, enabled George Formby within three years to become Britain's number one box office attraction; but we will try to explain this when he has gained a little more stature.

Bulldog Jack. Jack Hulbert, essentially a revue comedian whose career had begun in the Cambridge Footlights, might have been a singing and dancing rival for Jack Buchanan had not his long chin turned his thoughts more to comedy than to romance. His forte was

JACK HULBERT. Britain's long-chinned, long-legged Mr Entertainment of the thirties steps out with Gina Malo in this scene from *Jack of All Trades*.

light-hearted nonsense, and his typical casting in the early thirties
would have been a cheerful playboy locked out of his Mayfair house
at two o'clock in the morning. For a time it seemed that every home
in the country had his gramophone recording of a silly song called
'The Flies Crawled Up the Window':

> The flies crawled up the window:
> They'd nothing else to do.
> They went up in their thousands
> And they came down two by two.
>
> The flies crawled up the window:
> They said, we love to roam,
> So once more up the window
> And then we'll all go home.
>
> And if those flies annoy you
> Then here's what I advise:
> You don't have any windows
> And you won't have any flies.

The popularity of the record – from *Jack's the Boy* – is made even
more mysterious by the fact that Hulbert's introduction is in French
and he spends part of the time arguing with the orchestra. His
marriage to the ebullient Cicely Courtneidge seemed somewhat
unlikely, but they remained in double harness for more than forty
years, though usually 'in character', since Cicely simply could not be
a romantic lead. Her forte was funny voices and faces, especially a
strutting walk when she stuck out her backside and marched around
the stage. She could be a tipsy spinster, a male impersonator, or
most memorably a memsahib, as in 'Under Your Hat', when she
gave frank advice to a group of questioning schoolgirls:

> When I was in Delhi,
> I lay on my – hm, hm,
> In a flat-bottomed canoe.
> They all thought me barmy –
> But I know the army.
> The nation depends on you!

Age may have diminished Jack's appeal – he became notably
arthritic – but Cicely remained a stage star into her eighties,
appearing gratefully in anything that came along, from revue to
Agatha Christie. She is best remembered for a song which was never
filmed. She sang it in 1953, in Ivor Novello's *Gay's the Word*, and it

was intended as a tribute to all the female stars of revue and music hall who over several decades had retained their vitality and star appeal:

Vitality!
It matters more than personality, originality, or topicality;
For it's vitality
That made all those top-liners tops.
Vitality!
They all had individuality, but in reality their speciality
Was a vitality
Enough to make hits out of flops.
They could knock you for six
They had vigour and drive
They'd no microphone tricks,
They were live, live, live!
Vitality!
The stars who gained their immortality
Knew with finality
The practicality
Of something that's lacking in us . . .
They all had vitality plus!

They had vigour, they were bigger, they had wonderful attack,
They were workers, never shirkers, never blasé, never slack,
They could thrill you, they could fill you with their energy and verve,
They were servants of the public, and by golly, did they serve!
They were singers who *were* singers, nothing canned and nothing tinned;
They were artists to their fingertips – I'm getting short of wind!
They were zealous, they were jealous of the fame that they had won;
They were vital, and entitled to that stardom. They were fun!
And if you think that that vitality has vanished, well, that's rot,
There's a certain Mr Churchill who has still got quite a lot,
And if we're getting very personal, I think that you'll agree
As a sample and example of vitality – there's me.★

Going back to Jack, you never knew whether he would turn up next in farce, comedy thriller, adventure or satire. *Bulldog Jack* is thought by many to be his best vehicle, and in it he is amiably supported by his 'silly ass' brother Claude, but in truth his jaunty assumption of the mantle of Drummond wears a little thin, and the

★ Two lines for the chorus boys would now need to be rewritten:

> Oh, the stars of the past, they are still stars today,
> And the reason they last, they were gay, gay, gay!

film is chiefly tolerable for Ralph Richardson's criminal mastermind
and for Walter Forde's snappy direction of the chase sequences
through the Underground.★

Vintage Wine. Seymour Hicks, who received a knighthood for services
to the theatre, never seemed quite on top form before the camera,
but this January–May caper was doubtless a fair rendering of one of
his more popular stage plays.

Look Up and Laugh. I met Gracie Fields in a lift in Los Angeles, just a
few months before she died in 1979. She was staying in the
Guadalahara suite of the Beverly Wilshire Hotel, and I was down the
hall. I could not help saying, as she stepped ahead of me into the
empty cubicle, 'I was born twelve miles from where you were born.'

'Where were that, love?'

'Bolton.'

'Ee, they say it were a gradely place, that. I only went there once or
twice. They used to say they were a snotty lot that came from
Bolton.'

A descent of five floors does not allow much time for conversation.
'Do you still sing "Sally"?'

'Aye, they won't let me stop. Isn't that daft? All me life I've been
singing a song written for a chap.' She murmured a few bars to
prove her point, and of course she was right: it is the song of a swain
swearing allegiance to his loved one. Suddenly the doors opened into
the lobby, and with a cheerful wave she was gone. I wanted to tell
her that a few months earlier I had tracked down the mill gates
through which in 1934 she had led back the striking workers to the
sound of 'Sing as we Go'; but I never saw her again.

> Sing as we go, and let the world go by . . .
> Sing me a song to chase away the grey skies.
>   Say goodbye to sorrow:
>   There's always tomorrow
> To follow today . . .

It was an exhilarating song for conquering the depression of the
thirties, and Gracie's unique north-country voice and timbre made it
more so. That voice had made her Britain's most unlikely musical
star of the twenties, for people said she was insufficiently photogenic
for the movies. They were wrong. The angular looks didn't matter,

★ Forde had himself been a silent comic, and performed a precursor of this chase in
the 1928 *Wait and See.*

GRACIE FIELDS in *Sing As We Go* sells Crunchy Wunchy to the crowds on Blackpool promenade.

because Gracie's sunny temperament and pawky good humour showed through. Her half a dozen key films are probably the closest the movies came to recording British working-class life of the time: certainly Blackpool's lodging-house system was unerringly depicted in *Sing as we Go*. But by the end of the thirties Gracie had been forced into sentimental drama (*The Show Goes On*) and flabby, unfocused comedy (*Shipyard Sally*). Despite a brief stop in Hollywood as a character actress, she never regained the nation's affection after hotfooting it to America when war broke out, even though she had the very good reason of protecting her technically alien husband, Monty Banks. *Look Up and Laugh* is on the farcical side for her, but J. B. Priestley wrote the story and the market backgrounds have the ring of truth. It's well worth comparing with later little-man-against-authority comedies from Ealing; and sharp eyes will spot Vivien Leigh in a small part, not to mention Robb Wilton as the mayor.

The Stoker. Leslie Fuller in fair form.

Me and Marlborough. Cicely Courtneidge and Tom Walls both sought fresh pastures in this curiosity, quite a well produced 'serious comedy' in which he plays the duke and she a woman who poses as a soldier in order to prove that her husband is not a spy. The public was decidedly puzzled.

Boys will be Boys. The 'real' Will Hay made his first screen appearance in this one, though he was slightly constricted by J. B. Morton's conception of Narkover, a school for the sons of criminals, and by the need to cram in comedy scenes for Gordon Harker and Claude Dampier.

Stormy Weather. Walls, Lynn and Hare in one of the thinner Ben Travers farces, with a Chinatown setting.

Jimmy Boy. An early appearance by the Irish comic Jimmy O'Dea, as a bootboy who unmasks a spy.

Where's George? Herbert Wilcox made several comedies starring the untypeable Yorkshire comedian Sydney Howard, whose humour lay less in dialect or characterization than in a curiously mannered walk and speech. George was a henpecked blacksmith.

The Deputy Drummer. Lupino Lane as a poor composer catching jewel thieves in a stately home.

The Private Secretary. A classic farce made famous by Charles Hawtrey (the elder). In this version Edward Everett Horton came across from Hollywood to play the mild-mannered cleric of the title, with Alastair Sim notable in a small part.

Honeymoon for Three. Stanley Lupino was another performer strayed from musical comedy. Rather curiously shaped, but game for anything, he tended to cast himself in effete high society musicals with good comedy numbers. The prime example of this came in 1937's *Over She Goes*, in which he, Laddie Cliff and a pleasant young man called John Wood line themselves up in evening dress, after dinner in a stately home, and launch into one of the smartest, snappiest and most physically dextrous three-for-one routines I have ever clapped eyes on:

> Side by side we'll pull together
> True and tried – we'll face the weather
> Face to face, back to back, achieving our ambitions,
> Cheek to cheek, beak to beak and other strange positions,
> Side by side, we'll march to glory
> Far and wide they'll hear our story,
> East to west, north to south,
> Chest to chest and hand to mouth,
> Our fame will ride side by side.

STANLEY LUPINO (centre) in *Over She Goes* shares Laddie Cliff's puzzlement at Syd Walker's merriment.

Stanley Lupino comedy-musicals came along pretty regularly during the thirties, and demand investigation in case they contain any other such plums.

A Fire has been Arranged. Flanagan and Allen were already well known in the music halls, but this curious comedy-musical, packed with plot and revue sidelights, was their first venture before the camera. They play ex-convicts who try to burn down a store under which their loot is buried, but this reprehensible behaviour passes for fun in the film's atmosphere of extravaganza. Robb Wilton and Alastair Sim are lost in the shuffle.

No Limit. George Formby's first properly produced picture was an instant success, and not only in Lancashire. Apart from the gormless charm of the ukulele-playing north-country idiot he plays, *No Limit* is valuable as an indication of what life was like on the Isle of Man during the holiday season. George goes there to take part in the T.T. motorcycle races, and of course he wins not only the trophy but the girl, both of which seem unlikely in view of his unco-ordinated body and regressive personality. But he had a star quality which was

recognized, and even fifty years later impressionists are still making
hay with his shy, toothy grin as he innocently strums a ukulele and
sings his surprisingly vulgar ditties:

> Now I've a job, it just suits me,
> A window cleaner you would be
> If you could see what I can see
> When I'm cleaning windows.
>
> Pyjamas lying side by side,
> Ladies' nighties I have spied,
> I've often seen what goes inside
> When I'm cleaning windows.
>
> In my profession I work hard
> But I'll never stop.
> I'll climb this blinking ladder
> Till I get right to the top.
>
> The blushing bride, she looks divine,
> The bridegroom, he is doing fine,
> I'd rather have his job than mine,
> When I'm cleaning windows.

The very first song George recorded was an instant nationwide
hit. Oddly enough it was intended as the flip side to one which didn't
get anywhere: 'Do De O Do' isn't even remembered as a Formby
song, but he could never get off a stage without singing 'Chinese
Laundry Blues':

Now Mr Wu is a laundryman in a shop with an old green door;
He'll iron all day my linen away, it really makes me sore;
He's lost his heart to a Chinese girl, and his laundry's all gone wrong:
All day he'll flirt, and scorch my shirt, that's why I'm singing this song:

Oh Mr Wu, what can I do? I've got these kinda Limehouse Chinese Laundry
     Blues.
This funny feeling keeps round me stealing:

Why don't you throw your sweetheart over? Do . . .
My vest's so short that it won't fit my little brother,
And my new Sunday shirt has got a perforated rudder,
Mr Wu, what can I do? I've got these kinda Limehouse Chinese Laundry
     Blues.

It's not a very clever song, and the lyrics are clumsy to say the least,
but George's style was infectious and the public loved to imagine his
mischievous grin as he put in the variations:

> Now Mr Wu at washing shirts is very handy
> But he'd go broke if all the men wore shirts like Mr Gandhi

or:

> Now Mr Wu, he's got a naughty eye that flickers:
> You ought to see it wobble when he's ironing ladies' blouses . . .

Oddly enough, George never sang this song in a film. It was used in the primitive *Boots Boots*, but only as background music for Beryl Formby's clog dance. Beryl was George's wife and manager, and though she propelled him unerringly to the top she became the bane of his existence, just as Kitty MacShane turned Arthur Lucan's life into a misery. Every movement George made was supervised, even to the extent that when (miraculously) getting the girl in a film he was never allowed to kiss her. Without Beryl, George might never have been a star, but he would almost certainly have been happier. Still, for twenty years he accepted unquestioningly her view of life. I met him once at a civic function in Bolton, when he was gracing our local theatre with his presence. 'Eeh, George,' said our blunt-speaking Labour mayor, 'it mun be a great thrill to see your name up in lights outside yon theatre. Good luck to you, son. But tell me this: how is it that when *you* come to see us, the prices go up?' George was nonplussed for a moment, then produced his shy grin. 'Well,' he offered, 'Beryl says, if they want to see me, they mun *pay*!' The song that got George into trouble with the BBC – who banned it – was 'With My Little Stick of Blackpool Rock':

> One afternoon the band conductor up on his stand
> Somehow lost his baton, it flew out of his hand,
> So I jumped in his place and then conducted the band
> With my little stick of Blackpool rock.
>
> A fellow took my photograph, it cost one and three,
> I said when it was done, is that supposed to be me?
> You've prop'ly mucked it up, the only thing I can see
> Is my little stick of Blackpool rock.

Whole books have been written about Formby, for there is something in him of the tragic hero as well as the clown. When Beryl died in 1960 he was free at last to marry the schoolteacher he had loved secretly for some time. But George had been a sick man for years, and a heart attack carried him off before they could make it

GEORGE FORMBY. What more need be said? It makes you laugh to look at
him.

to the church. Still, he had been one of Britain's greatest stars, and
internationally popular too, even in Russia, where they gave him the
Order of Lenin in 1943. And his films, from *No Limit* on, survive
remarkably well, much better than the Norman Wisdom comedies

of the fifties which tried to copy them. Every now and then George tried to vary his image, but the way the public wanted him was the way he had been when they first took him to their hearts: the cheerful idiot who wins through against all odds. They made one exception, for the pleasant little love song George crooned in *Feather Your Nest*:

I'm leaning on a lamp,
And if you think I'm just a tramp
I'll tell you why I'm here and what my motives are.

I'm leaning on a lamppost at the corner of the street in case a certain little lady
    comes by.
Oh, me. Oh, my. I hope the little lady comes by.
I don't know if she'll get away, she doesn't always get away, but anyway I
    know that she'll try.
Oh, me. Oh, my. I hope the little lady comes by . . .

It became one of the standards which he had to sing before any audience would let him go home.

Get off my Foot. A lost Max Miller film in which he played a butler who became heir to a fortune, so that the master of the house wanted him for a son-in-law. The title seems odd: as a catchphrase it belonged to Frank Randle, not Miller.

No Monkey Business. Gene Gerrard again, pretending to be the missing link. Renee Houston, Peter Haddon, Claude Dampier and Richard Hearne are other comedians in attendance.

Captain Bill. Leslie Fuller as a bargee.

Come Out of the Pantry. A nobleman on his uppers pretends to be a butler. A decade on, this served as plot for *Spring in Park Lane*; here it was a Jack Buchanan vehicle.

Can You Hear Me, Mother? A low-budget independent vehicle for roly-poly music hall comedian Sandy Powell, another north-countryman. The title was his catchphrase, deriving from his first nervous radio appearance; the plot concerned a lost baby. In his old age Powell became a television institution with his comedy ventriloquist act, but as a film comedian he never rose above witless cheapjack productions far below the standard of his excellent gramophone recordings.

1936

Don't Rush Me. Robb Wilton's only starring vehicle, a lost film derived from a Fred Karno sketch about an anti-gambling propagandist forced to become a racetrack bookie.

Cheer Up! Stanley Lupino as a poor author mistaken for a millionaire.

Queen of Hearts. Gracie Fields as a seamstress pretending to be rich in order to marry her heart's desire. A rather odd mixture of sentiment and farce.

When Knights were Bold. A nobleman wins his girl by dreaming of medieval days. Based on a once popular play, this oddity seemed rather amateur even at the time for a Jack Buchanan vehicle, especially so since Fay Wray had come from Hollywood to play the lead.

Jack of All Trades. Something really worthy of revaluation, based on a play called *Youth at the Helm* by Paul Vulpius, which was a BBC radio standard for many years. Jack Hulbert appears as an unemployed man who talks his way into high finance, and admiration is due not only for his star performance but for the slick writing and direction and some musical numbers which remind one of Astaire and Rogers. Only a farcical fire sequence at the end tends to let the style down.

King of Hearts. Will Fyffe as a docker bribed by a rich woman to break his daughter's romance with her son. A probably boring exposition of the class theme: Fyffe, a pillar of the Scottish music hall stage, was better at being pawky than being sentimental.

Public Nuisance Number One. Inane Riviera-set comedy about a waiter who saves the hotel belonging to his girlfriend's uncle. Arthur Riscoe only once found his feet in the cinema, as Chitterlow in Carol Reed's 1941 *Kipps.*

The Big Noise. A lost quota quickie with Alastair Sim as a timid clerk made the scapegoat of his bosses.

Fame. Sydney Howard as a shopwalker who becomes a film star. One of his better vehicles, it offers plenty of scope for his funny walk, with arms akimbo, like a sea lion walking upright on its flippers.

Hot News. Lupino Lane as a reporter chasing crooks.

In the Soup. A solicitor pretends to be a butler in order to persuade his rich uncle of his worthiness. A curious independent venture for Ralph Lynn in an unseaworthy craft, yet again depending on the division between master and man.

Pot Luck. The routing of a crime gang specializing in oriental antiques.

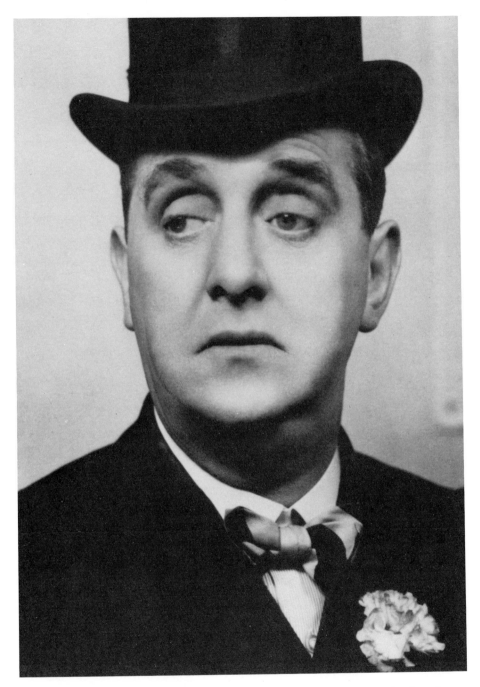

SYDNEY HOWARD, the lugubrious Yorkshireman. Forgotten is the fact that he even made a film in Hollywood with Jack Benny. *Transatlantic Merry-Go-Round* was the name, but it didn't cause much of a tinkle at the box office.

A Ben Travers original and the last of the Aldwych farces with the original team of Walls, Lynn and Hare. Entertaining stuff, but with more action than comedy.

Where's Sally? Gene Gerrard has trouble finding his wife when on their honeymoon she learns of his naughty past and runs away.

Someone at the Door. That lightest of light comedians Billy Milton gets a rare starring role as a man who fakes a murder to interest house buyers, then finds that the murder comes true.

One Good Turn. Leslie Fuller as a coffee-stall keeper.

Where There's a Will. Will Hay as a shyster lawyer: a fairly good vehicle, but the best was yet to come.

Keep your Seats Please. George Formby in the film which established him as a number one box-office star, an adaptation of the Russian story about a fortune hidden in one of six chairs. The cast includes Alastair Sim, Florence Desmond (a skilful impressionist), and music hall star Harry Tate as an engineer. Note also one Hal Gordon as a sailor: he was the burly grinning man who always responded so infectiously to Formby's songs that he became a kind of mascot.

Educated Evans. Max Miller as a racetrack bookie.

It's in the Bag. Nervo and Knox, not yet part of the Crazy Gang, as market porters who come into money.

Two's Company. Gordon Harker is teamed with the American Ned Sparks as a visiting millionaire whose daughter wants to marry an earl's son.

Wolf's Clothing. Claude Hulbert is a timid Foreign Office official mistaken for a Paris assassin.

Love up the Pole. Ernie Lotinga was a comedian and pantomime dame from the north-east, locally famous for his characterization of the much put-upon Jimmy Josser. His ventures into films never rose above the lowest level, and in any case he was 60 when he appeared in this extravaganza about a waiter who catches jewel thieves.

Millions. A Gordon Harker comedy which also starred Frank Pettingell and Richard Hearne, and revived quite well into the fifties. Harker was a rich man trying to separate his daughter from his rival's wastrel son.

Land Without Music. This Ruritanian musical vehicle for Richard Tauber would scarcely qualify as a comedy had not someone had the odd idea of importing Jimmy Durante to provide a few laughs.

Everybody Dance. Cicely Courtneidge gets herself into complex impersonations when her American relations come to stay.

The Man in the Mirror. Another American import, Edward Everett

Horton, scores in this pleasant and quite skilful fantasy about a timid man's success after his mirror image takes over his life.

Skylarks. Nervo and Knox as reckless airmen. Eddie Gray, a Crazy Gang colleague-to-be, was also in the cast.

This'll make you Whistle. One of Jack Buchanan's best remembered vehicles, about a Riviera playboy pretending to be a crook in order to scare off the girl he doesn't want to marry.

Sporting Love. Stanley Lupino in a version of his own successful play: an impecunious racehorse owner pretends to be married in order to please his rich Aunt Fanny.

Windbag the Sailor. A patchy Will Hay comedy climaxing on a cannibal isle: chiefly notable as his first teaming with Moore Marriott and Graham Moffatt as Harbottle and Albert.

For the two years so far surveyed we have seen a new film comedy rather more than once a fortnight; but now, perhaps because Hitler is looming ever larger on the horizon, the frequency begins to diminish.

1937

Well Done, Henry. Forgettable and forgotten, this Will Fyffe vehicle had him as a henpecked husband helping his daughter to elope.

Aren't Men Beasts? An adaptation from a stage play provides the first screen teaming for Robertson Hare and Alfred Drayton. A few years later came a semi-sequel called *Women Aren't Angels*.

Take a Chance. Claude Hulbert and Binnie Hale in yet another racetrack comedy. Cabaret-oriented support included Henry Kendall, Enid Stamp Taylor and Guy Middleton, but Harry Tate was there to wave the flag for the music hall.

Good Morning, Boys. At last, the real Will Hay, though sadly lacking Moore Marriott on this occasion. As a schoolmaster in charge of a Paris trip, Mr Hay prevented the Mona Lisa from being stolen by the father of one of his pupils; but what people went for were the schoolroom scenes, which included 'How Hi is a Chinaman' and 'What is a watt?'; while one of the boys, asked to name six animals found in India, replied 'A tiger and five elephants'. The boys included Will Hay Jnr and Charles Hawtrey, who made several appearances with Hay before going on to be a regular member of the 'Carry On' team.

Splinters in the Air. The perennially occupied Sydney Howard starred in this slack RAF comedy derived from the original 1929 *Splinters*, an army concert party on film, and the 1931 *Splinters in the Navy*.

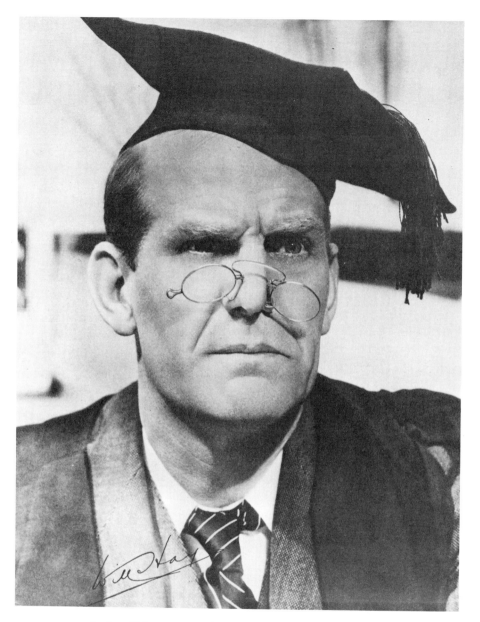

WILL HAY as he is still best remembered: the schoolmaster in *Good Morning Boys* who is well aware that his pupils know more than he does.

It's a Grand Old World. Sandy Powell wins a football pool and helps a
  down-and-out actress.
Please Teacher. Bobby Howes, diminutive graduate from the musical
  comedy stage (he was the original Mister Cinders), made a few quite

respectable star comedies in the thirties. Here he poses as an explorer to find a will hidden in a girls' school, and has redoubtable support from the weighty ladies Vera Pearce and Bertha Belmore, who often appeared with him on stage, and played Margaret Dumont to his elfin Groucho Marx.

Feather Your Nest. A George Formby film which contrived to please while avoiding most of his usual knockabout. The plot found him in the record business, becoming an accidental star when one of his amateur recordings is substituted for a broken one.

It's Not Cricket. Claude Hulbert in a comedy of adultery written by co-star Henry Kendall.

Don't Get me Wrong. Max Miller well in character as a fairground spieler promoting a petrol substitute which works – for a while.

The Vulture. Claude Hulbert as an inept detective.

For Valour. Tom Walls and Ralph Lynn trying something different: three generations in a family of soldiers.

Okay for Sound. The Crazy Gang had been a great hit at the Palladium in George Black's *Crazy Weeks* and *Crazy Months*, and something

PLEASE TEACHER. Madness prevails in this sleepwalking scene with Wylie Watson (left) and Bobby Howes. The bewildered ladies, left to right, are Rene Ray, Vera Pearce and Bertha Belmore.

THE CRAZY GANG. Teddy Knox (centre), gripping Charlie Naughton's neck; then (clockwise) Bud Flanagan, Chesney Allen, Jimmy Gold, Jimmy Nervo.

similar would shortly happen in New York with *Hellzapoppin* 'where anything can happen and it probably will'. In essence what the Gang presented was a ragbag of old music hall jokes and sight gags, interspersed with knowing winks to the audience, but together their impact was overwhelming, and as they grew older they became a national institution, capable even of kidding royalty: when the Queen made her first appearance in the Royal Box after the birth of Prince Charles, Jimmy Nervo came on with a rocking horse and said: 'Here you are, missus, here's something for the nipper.' Nervo and Knox had in fact been among the first to exploit crazy comedy on the stage. Teddy Knox was dapper, but had a spluttering lisp ('Don't be thilly, Thethil'). Jimmy Nervo excelled in grotesque female impersonations. Together they did a side-splitting act of slow-motion wrestling. Naughton and Gold were more routine practitioners, and the fragments which survive of their original material are fairly pitiful, but Jimmy Gold was a good stooge or straight man, and Charlie Naughton developed into a pathetic butt for the team, an elderly baby always blamed for the communal misfortunes. Flanagan and Allen had been the most prominent on their own account, partly because Chesney Allen was such a gentleman and Bud Flanagan could alternate pratfalls with Jewish schmaltz. Their vocalizing of a score of lilting melodies produced enduring classics, and the one especially associated with them, in their characters as optimistic underdogs, is 'Underneath the Arches':*

> Underneath the arches
> We dream our dreams away;
> Underneath the arches
> On cobblestones we lay.
> Ev'ry night you'll find us
> Tired out and worn;
> Happy when the daylight comes creeping,
> Heralding the morn.
> Sleeping when it's raining,
> Sleeping when it's fine,
> Trains rattling by above;
> Pavement is our pillow,
> No matter where we stray;
> Underneath the arches
> We dream our dreams away.

Bud and Ches also developed a species of verbal cross-talk later taken up by Abbott and Costello. Here is Bud as a jockey being given his instructions:

CHES: It's a 2.30 race. You start off at 10 to 1.
BUD: What about the other horses?
CHES: They start off at 5 to 4.
BUD: I'll have won it before they get there.

Then there were atrocious puns, reminiscent of the Chico/Harpo routines in the Marx Brothers films:

BUD: I went to the opera. It was Friendly Joe.
CHES: Friendly Joe?
BUD: Chummy Dick?
BOTH: Pagliacci . . . oi! ('Pally Archie')

* The arches referred to were the railway arches at Charing Cross, where tramps foregathered.

From time to time other members were admitted to the gang. Caryll and Mundy were a man-and-wife act: he had started as an upside down dancer, and specialized in 'romantic' rhymes such as:

> I wish I was a little egg, as bad as bad can be.
> I'd nestle in my little nest, away up in the tree.
> And when a little girl like you came jumping round with glee,
> I'd burst my little naughty self and sprinkle you with me!

Eddie Gray was another favourite, originally a juggler who found fractured French an aid to laughs:

In *un minute, moi* will juggle with two clubs: not *un*, but *deux*.

Like the rest of them when they got together, Eddie was as uncontrollable off-stage as on. A story is told of him sitting in his dressing room stark naked with the door open, and using bad language. Well, not quite naked: he wore his luxuriant black moustache, his collar with dicky attached, and shoes and socks with suspenders. When he observed a woman pass his door with a shocked expression, he leapt to his feet and insisted on accompanying her to the stage entrance, apologizing for anything he had said . . . He was also fond of practical jokes, like talking to a pillar box which he swore had a man inside, and asking a crowd to stand by and keep the poor fellow cheerful while Eddie went for the police (and never came back).

Here is a selection of Gang material:

Bud enters as a Roman emperor, with a slave girl chained to his chariot: 'Every time I pull the chain, she flushes!'

'If a bomb fell in a field and a bull ate it, what would it be?' – 'Abomin-able!'

'Would you like a little son, darling?'
'Yes, we've been having some shocking weather lately!'

'Why is a picture house like a fat lady?'
'I don't know.'
'One draws the crowds and the other crowds the . . . oi!'

'I've just come back from Scotland. All the Scotsmen were wearing kilts.'
'Did you see the Trossachs?'
'No, it wasn't windy!'

'Ladies and gentlemen, here is a special announcement. If Mr Jones, who met Miss Smith last year at Brighton, will kindly contact Miss Smith's solicitors, he will learn something which will wipe that silly grin off his face!'

'Have you heard? They don't want London Bridge any longer.'
'Why not?'
'It's long enough!'

Okay for Sound had virtually no plot: the Gang was simply set loose within a film studio, and their material was separated by other specialities. Their best ensemble number is the high-speed one in which they act out film titles. Charlie enters eating a flower: *Tudor Rose* (chewed a rose). Jimmy Nervo has two paving stones on his head: *Under Two Flags*. Bud knocks the upper limbs off a statue: *A Farewell to Arms*. Jimmy Gold sells a musical instrument: *Trader Horn*. Charlie goes out with spade and bucket: *The Camels are Coming*. Nervo and Knox enter sans trousers: *We're not Dressing*. Yes, it does become infectious, even if not all the jokes work these days. Some of them didn't even work at the time. As Eddie Gray used to warn his audience, 'You can't have all big stuff, you know. You've got to have little stuff in between.'

Take my Tip. Hulbert and Courtneidge as yet more noble people pretending to be their own servants, with Robb Wilton popping up as a jury foreman.

Spring Handicap. Will Fyffe as a miner who comes into money.

Cotton Queen. Will Fyffe again, in a rather dim Lancashire comedy about a mill owner whose daughter goes to work for his rival. With Stanley Holloway and, in a tiny part, Gibson Gowland, the hero of Stroheim's *Greed*.

Boys will be Girls. Leslie Fuller can inherit a fortune if he stops smoking.

Keep Fit. One of George Formby's best, parodying a current government campaign to improve the health of the nation. George is a department store barber who becomes a multi-talented sportsman and exposes his rival for Kay Walsh as a thief. (Miss Walsh then sported the most excruciating upper-class accent to be heard in British films.) A smartly made comedy by any standards, with a catchy title tune:

> Keep fit – don't bend the knees –
> Don't sit – be careful please,
> You'll split your do-re-me's,
> Whatever you do, keep fit.

KEEP FIT. George Formby finds himself in a rather embarrassing situation with Kay Walsh.

The Penny Pool. Another gormless hero wins a fortune on the pools. Duggie Wakefield was Gracie Fields's cousin.

Wise Guys. Naughton and Gold alone again, having to borrow a modest fortune in order to prove themselves capable of taking over a loan company.

Old Mother Riley. Something of a milestone in British comedy, though it didn't seem so at the time. Unfortunately this first film is lost, but many others followed, in descending order of merit. See under Arthur Lucan.

Over She Goes. The Stanley Lupino vehicle with 'Side by Side', previously quoted. Also notable for a policeman's ballet featuring Syd Walker and Richard Murdoch, and for a few musical numbers that look as though they might have been frightened by the ghost of Busby Berkeley.

You Live and Learn. Glenda Farrell, imported from Hollywood, made a curious partner for Claude Hulbert in this modest hands-across-the-sea comedy in which both are miscast.

Smash and Grab. Jack Buchanan in a detective comedy-thriller on the lines of *The Thin Man.*

Leave It to Me. Sandy Powell in more trouble, as a policeman after a Chinese gang.

Transatlantic Trouble. Max Miller as a boxer mistaken for a millionaire.

Oh Mr Porter. Perhaps the true classic of British comedy, dealt with in detail on page 44. Apart from the central trio, it's a pity we never saw more of Dave O'Toole, who played the postman. ('You're wasting your time!')

Paradise for Two. Jack Hulbert and Arthur Riscoe as Frenchmen. The audience didn't believe it either.

Sam Small Leaves Town. Stanley Holloway as an actor seeking anonymity in a holiday camp.

The Sky's the Limit. Jack Buchanan as an aircraft designer.

What a Man. Sydney Howard as a photographer looking for missing club funds.

1938

Sweet Devil. Bobby Howes as a rich playboy who falls for a typist.

Second Best Bed. Tom Walls as a magistrate suspected of adultery.

I See Ice. George Formby as a photographer on the ice hockey rink, with Cyril Ritchard as the heavy.

Glamour Girl. Gene Gerrard as a smart photographer brought down to earth by his secretary.

Blondes for Danger. Gordon Harker as a taxi driver who picks up a dangerous fare. Good comedy-thriller material.

Oh Boy! A chemist invents a rejuvenating potion. Albert Burdon played the gump from the north, and was never a national success.

Almost a Honeymoon. A playboy is suspected of adultery. Tommy Trinder makes an inauspicious debut.

Convict 99. A solid but somehow unsatisfying Will Hay vehicle, with Hay mistaken for a prison governor and Moore Marriott taking the honours as Jerry the Mole.

Almost a Gentleman. Cheapjack vehicle for Billy Bennett, as a nightwatchman mistaken for a millionaire.

Thank Evans. Max Miller back on the racetrack.

Break the News. Buchanan and Maurice Chevalier teamed up for this lightweight René Clair confection about a dancer who 'kills off' his partner for publicity and is then arrested for murder. The theme turned up again more than thirty years later in Universal's curious *The Art of Love.*

Alf's Button Afloat. The supreme achievement of the Crazy Gang,
perhaps an extravaganza rather than a comedy but still perfectly
controlled by director Marcel Varnel. The Gang accidentally become
marines, and Bud has a button on his tunic which when rubbed
summons a lugubrious genie in the person of Alastair Sim (his most

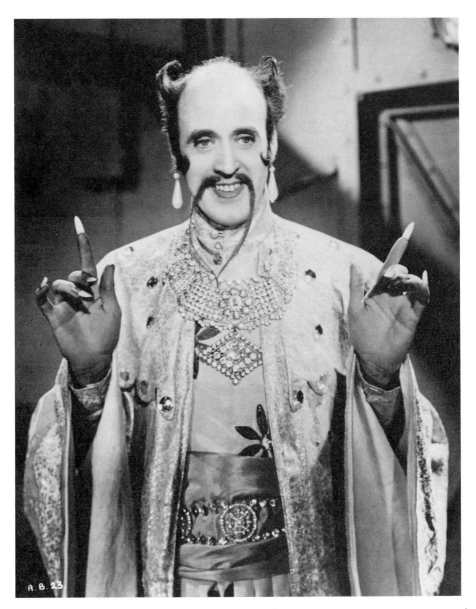

ALASTAIR SIM. Even in the mid-thirties a budding star, he made a delightful
genie, and managed to upstage the Crazy Gang, in *Alf's Button Afloat.*

effective role to date). When Bud exclaims 'Strike me pink!' the genie mishears and *stripes* him pink instead, but this is only the first of many complications, the last being that the film's nominal hero and heroine are eaten (offscreen) by a bear, in Kent.

No Parking. Gordon Harker as a car park attendant mistaken for an American assassin.

Hold my Hand. Stanley Lupino in another film version of one of his own plays, this time set in the newspaper world and co-starring Fred Emney.

A Spot of Bother. Hare and Drayton in a farce about the misuse of cathedral funds.

I've got a Horse. Sandy Powell at the racetrack.

Penny Paradise. Jimmy O'Dea's contribution to the list of football pool comedies.

Hey! Hey! USA! A misguided attempt to make Will Hay popular in the States by casting Edgar Kennedy as co-stair in a kidnapping comedy.

Yes, Madam. Bobby Howes's best remembered comedy of misadventure: heirs to a fortune must act as servants for a month.

It's in the Air. George Formby in top form, joining the RAF. The title tells almost all, and the catchiest song was 'Our Sergeant Major'.

Keep Smiling. Gracie Fields's last really cheerful film, about a touring revue. Eddie Gray can be spotted in support.

Many Tanks Mr Atkins. The prolific Claude Hulbert in an army spy comedy.

Everything Happens to Me. Max Miller as a salesman involved in local politics.

1939

So This is London. A British bakery resists an American takeover. Hare and Drayton join forces for once; Revnell and West can be glimpsed in support.

Let's be Famous. Jimmy O'Dea becomes a radio singer.

Inspector Hornleigh. The radio series featuring smoothly anonymous S. J. Warmington was retailored for Gordon Harker, with Alastair Sim stealing some of the show as his mournful sergeant. Two sequels followed.

Trouble Brewing. George Formby uncovers counterfeiters using a brewery as cover.

The Lambeth Walk. Lupino Lane in the film version of his stage smash, with Seymour Hicks representing the nobility. As noted on p. 82, it was to have a longer life than either of them could have imagined.

Home from Home. Sandy Powell becomes involved with escaped
  convicts.
A Gentleman's Gentleman. Eric Blore, back from Hollywood, does his
  valet act.
The Gang's All Here. Jack Buchanan unmasks jewel thieves. The cast
  included Edward Everett Horton, Ronald Shiner and Robb Wilton.
The Good Old Days. An odd period piece for Max Miller: travelling
  players save a noble child from kidnapping.
Shipyard Sally. The daughter of a Clydeside publican persuades a
  magnate to reopen a shipyard. Pre-echoes of Ealing exist in this
  rather slim vehicle for Gracie Fields, with Sydney Howard in
  attendance.
Ask a Policeman. Essentially a reworking of *Oh Mr Porter*, with the
  incompetent trio now policemen at Turnbottom Round, trying to
  work up a few arrests in a crimeless village. The first film had
  borrowed its 'ghost', covering up for gun runners, from *The Ghost*

ASK A POLICEMAN. The incompetent trio of Marriott, Hay and Moffatt have
been warned that they must make more arrests. Unfortunately the motorist
they try to frame for speeding is the Chief Constable (Peter Gawthorne).

Train; now it became a headless horseman covering up for
smugglers. Ancient Harbottle was given a father who remembered
the rhyme which was the key to the mystery:

> When the tide runs low in the smugglers' cove,
> And the headless horseman rides above,
> He rides along with a wild hallo,
> And that's the time the smugglers go in their little boats to the schooner
>   and bring back the kegs of brandy and rum and put them in the Devil's
>   Cave below.

(This was the equivalent of *Oh Mr Porter*'s

> Every night when the moon is bright
> The miller's ghost is seen . . .
> He haunts the station, he haunts the mill,
> And the land that lies between . . .)

Ask a Policeman has a few splendid moments of its own, as when
Albert's girlfriend, having seen the horseman, staggers into the
police station and faints from fright. 'Feel her heart, feel her heart,'
cries Harbottle. 'Nark it,' says Albert, 'she's my bird.'

Cheer Boys Cheer. The Romeo and Juliet story worked out against rival
breweries. Jimmy O'Dea leads the plot, with Marriott and Moffatt
in support.

Old Mother Riley M.P. The title tells all.

The Frozen Limits. The Crazy Gang in the Yukon, assisted by ancient
prospector Moore Marriott (whose big year this clearly was). Not
their best, but full of fun, with such skilful touches as the Gang
undressing to music associated with the seven dwarfs.

Where's that Fire? Hay, Moffatt and Marriott meet for the last time in a
script which, though written by the same team (Orton, Edgar,
Guest) as devised *Oh Mr Porter*, seems too similar and too thin. This
time they are village firemen foiling an attempt to steal the Crown
Jewels, but the best scene involves a pole holding up traffic outside
the fire station.

Inspector Hornleigh on Holiday. Generally accepted as the best of the
three Hornleighs, with a most ingenious plot.

Come On, George. Formby in top form as a jockey. Immaculately
produced, the film is a little reminiscent of the Marx Brothers' *A
Day at the Races*, released a year previously.

All at Sea. Sandy Powell joins the navy.

Old Mother Riley Joins Up. A presage of the future: soon all the comedy stars would be doing the same.

Hoots Mon! Max Miller in a valuable if cleaned-up record of his stage performance. The plot proves him, as a big-headed comedian, wise to refuse to play Scotland. (In reality Max seldom ventured north of Watford.) Florence Desmond gave as good as she got.

Lucky to Me. Stanley Lupino in a slight effort about a clerk who gets involved in a rich client's romantic affairs.

She Couldn't Say No. Tommy Trinder and Fred Emney impersonate doctors and catch jewel thieves.

The Middle Watch. Jack Buchanan at sea in a much filmed romantic manoeuvre; Leslie Fuller has now dwindled to a supporting role.

Jailbirds. Albert Burdon and Shaun Glenville (the famous pantomime dame) in a prison break comedy based on a Fred Karno sketch.

And so to war. What have we learned from this extensive inventory of British film vehicles for comedians during the five years leading up to the outbreak of hostilities? Principally that only a few of the great stars of music hall made the transition with absolute certainty. Will Hay,

HOOTS, MON! Hal Walters, the perennial stooge, helps Max Miller to dress in his floral suit. Max clearly approves of the result.

SHE COULDN'T SAY NO. An astonishingly young Tommy Trinder tangles with Fred Emney, who looked the same for forty years.

George Formby and Gracie Fields were the undoubted successes, to some extent because they landed the best scripts and production. At a lower level, Arthur Lucan as Old Mother Riley maintained a following, by sheer force of personality, in inferior vehicles; but other stalwarts such as Robb Wilton and Harry Tate had to be content with cameo roles. One suspects that Max Miller's devoted music hall fans never thought much of his movies, and if so they would have been right. On the musical comedy plane (which meant that the stars' previous reputations began and sometimes ended in the West End of London), there was usually a welcome for Jack Buchanan and to a lesser extent for Stanley Lupino and Bobby Howes, despite material which many hard-headed northerners would consider 'soft'; and although Hulbert and Court-neidge tried many different styles, their public never ignored them. The Crazy Gang lit up the scene with one film a year for three years: greater frequency would have been unwise. And in the really cheapjack movies, designed for an uncritical following, Sandy Powell and Will Fyffe and Claude Hulbert and Leslie Fuller kept slogging along.

The plot is not the reason why one goes to see a comedian, yet many of these films were plotbound because plots are easier to write than original comedy material, and it is interesting to see what popular themes emerged. One notes first of all that, apart from one or two Aldwych-type farces, the middle classes are conspicuous by their absence; broadly speaking, the heroes of British comedies in the thirties were either playboys or proles, silk scarves at midnight or mufflers on the morning shift. A very frequent theme is the master pretending to be his own servant, and although the dialogue always stresses the great dignity and pleasure of working for one's living, the sigh of relief as the nobleman abandons his impersonation is almost audible. Sometimes connected with this is the Romeo and Juliet plot: two powerful magnates who hate each other have sons and daughters who love each other. (By the final reel, reconciliation is naturally the order of the day.) Mistaken identity is also good for a sustained laugh, especially if the gormless hero is mistaken for someone very rich, very brainy, or very villainous. (The last alternative later served both Bob Hope and Danny Kaye very well, and Hitchcock was still having fun with it in *North by Northwest*. Deliberate impersonation is equally popular.

The threat of unemployment sometimes appears, but the factory owner always turns out to be basically benevolent, misled by his underlings, and work starts again over the end title (though it remains clear that such benevolence can be withdrawn at the magnate's whim). Henpecked or drunken husbands are common, but they always turn or reform. Sudden wealth is a good bet, acquired by winning the pools or a lottery: the moral is that it brings responsibilities with it. The most popular crime is jewel theft: it does no harm to anyone the audience cares about, and it has about it a romantic air. The same thing goes for valuable art. Female impersonation gets a terrific laugh. But without doubt the overall winner is the theme of the gormless incompetent who wins through more by good luck than good management, for this covers all the greatest movie comedy stars of the period: Hay, Formby, Fields, the Aldwych farceurs and Jack Hulbert. (It would give equal cover later on to Norman Wisdom and the 'Carry On' team.)

The most amazing thing of all is that so many comedy vehicles were required in such a short space of time. But in the later thirties Great Britain had five thousand cinemas to fill, and the economics were such that one week in each town was enough to recoup. Very few of these films could be exported, but that didn't matter. Less than half of them ever played the 'number one' spots. Less than a third of them were professionally made. Less than a third of that third have really stood the test of time, so far as entertainment is concerned. But for the social historian they are all valuable, and at least half a dozen stand up as masterworks in their own right, fit to be set beside anything of the type that Hollywood could produce.

Ooh, mother, they're taking me trousers off!

GEORGE FORMBY, *I See Ice*

6

Settle by your fireside,
pick up your Radio Times:

BRITISH RADIO COMEDIANS

Many music hall entertainers of the thirties may have failed to make their mark in talking pictures, but some of them at least secured more regular employment on the radio, and are just as affectionately remembered for their unseen fireside fooling as are their colleagues who had to be viewed at the local Odeon or Palace of Varieties. The devoted researcher may even find something on film of Bransby Williams's monologues, or Owen McGiveney's quick changes, or the crazy pianist Herschel Henlere who produced out of his grand piano everything from toy dogs to strings of sausages. Kardomah filled the stage with flags; Wilson, Keppel and Betty could never count the times they had performed the eccentric sand dance which they called *Cleopatra's Nightmare*. Forsythe, Seamon and Farrell were zany transatlantic musicians who provided their own programme of musical variety. Even Dante the Magician, who had his own touring magic revue, eventually appeared on celluloid with Laurel and Hardy in *A Haunting We Will Go* (and for once stole the show from them). George Robey made a host of unamusing silent films, and in *Variety Jubilee* recorded his Peeping Tom song 'I Stopped, I Looked, I Listened'. There is celluloid, too, of the Ganjou Brothers and Juanita, acrobatic dancers who pretend to be made of porcelain, and of Teddy Brown, the fat man at a xylophone.

It is however to the radio archives that one must go for Harry Champion singing 'Any Old Iron', for Harry Hemsley with his convincing gallery of unseen children ('What did Horace say, Winnie?'); for the diminutive Wee Georgie Wood (his younger rival Jimmy Clitheroe can be seen with George Formby in *Much Too Shy*); for pianists Semprini and Charlie Kunz and Billy Mayerl; for ballad singers Talbot O'Farrell and Cavan O'Connor and Josef Locke and Monte Rey; even for ventriloquists Saveen and Arthur Brough. Horace Kenney, an apparently elderly gent with a quavering voice, was, though never seen, an unforgettable 'trial turn':

MANAGER: What kind of parts have you played?
KENNEY: I've played all kinds, sir.
MANAGER: Have you ever played leads?
KENNEY: Yes, sir. Leeds, Sheffield, Manchester . . .
MANAGER: No, no. Leading parts.
KENNEY: Yes, sir.
MANAGER: What in?
KENNEY: *The Face at the Window.* I was the face. Every time I showed my face, someone committed a murder.
MANAGER: After seeing your face, I can well understand it. What other leading parts have you played?
KENNEY: In *Sons of the Desert*, I was a camel. At least, I was the head and front legs.
MANAGER: And you call that a leading part?
KENNEY: Well, it was the leading part of the camel, sir.

Kenney was a radio regular. So was Cyril Fletcher, who used a silly voice to recite silly poems called 'Odd Odes', ranging from 'Dreaming of thee, dreaming of thee' to 'As they followed the 'orrible bloody trail across the blasted 'eath'. Fletcher was also an early exponent of the shaggy dog story, one of his wartime favourites going something like this:

There was this lonely hotel on the moors, see, and one night a very pretty Wren came along wanting a room, so the manager said he'd gladly open up a corridor on which there were just two rooms, and she could take her pick. So she did, but unfortunately there were no locks on the doors. And a little later, along came a Flight Command Lieutenant, and he wanted a room, so he took the other one. And still later, along came a Lance Corporal on the same errand, and the manager said we're full, but you can sleep on top of the billiard table, which was just off the corridor where the other two had rooms. So they all went to bed, and next morning they all came down to breakfast. The Wren was first, and the waitress asked her would she like porridge or cornflakes. And she said cornflakes. And then in came the Lance Corporal, and the waitress asked him the same question, and he said porridge. And finally the Flight Lieutenant arrived, and the waitress said porridge or cornflakes, and he said cornflakes. Which all goes to prove that the greater proportion of personnel in the armed services prefer cornflakes to porridge for breakfast . . .

Jimmy James and Dave Morris, both heavyweight regional comics with a zany style which went well on Blackpool Pier, were popular on radio, as was Norman Evans, even though part of the fun with his 'Over the Garden Wall' act was to see his grotesque dame make-up complete with bosoms which kept slipping. The wall over which he gossiped in his broad Lancashire tones, gurning* as he did so, sometimes disappeared so that he could be visiting a sick friend and offering conversation which was clearly of little comfort:

> You're not looking too well, are you? I brought you some flowers . . . I thought if I was too late they'd come in handy, but I see you're still here . . . I tell you what: it's a very awkward bend at the top of your stairs to get a coffin down . . . Ee, I'm glad I've been able to get along to cheer you up. Still, you never know, do you? I mean, there was Mrs White, it was nobbut last Thursday, you know, she was doing nicely, just like you are, and all of a sudden she started with spasms round the heart – went off like a flash of lightning. They're burying her today.

Never top of the bill, but regular favourites on radio variety programmes, were Murray and Mooney, whose format could hardly be simpler: Murray started a serious monologue, and Mooney interrupted it.

MURRAY: Ladies and gentlemen, a little monologue entitled: The Stake.

> There's a job to be done,
> We must cut out the fun
> And stick to our task, one and all . . .

MOONEY: I say, I say. Do you know who's in the navy?
MURRAY: No, who?
MOONEY: Sailors.
MURRAY: I don't wish to know that, kindly leave the stage.

> There's a job to be done . . .

MOONEY: Pardon me, what is the title of this recitation?
MURRAY: The Stake.
MOONEY: I see. Have an onion?
MURRAY: What for?
MOONEY: To go with the stake.
MURRAY: Oh, please leave. My apologies, ladies and gentlemen.

> There's a job to be done,
> We must cut out the fun –

MOONEY: What's the difference between a stoat and a weasel?
MURREY: I have no idea.
MOONEY: A weasel is weasily distinguished.
MURRAY: What about a stoat?
MOONEY: A stoat is stoatally different.

---

* Gurning: a West Country term for pulling funny faces, especially swallowing the nose with the lower lip.

MURRAY: Ohhh!

MOONEY: Do you know the best way to stop fishbones sticking in your throat?

MURRAY: No?

MOONEY: Eat liver.

This kind of act never went out of fashion. Only the other day I heard on the radio a fragment of comedy as follows:

I call my house Lautrec.
– Why's that?
Because it's got two loos.

In the late thirties and early forties there were scores of radio cross-talk acts, including Collinson and Dean, Dave and Joe O'Gorman, Clapham and Dwyer, the separate duos of the Crazy Gang, and Nat Mills and Bobbie, who varied the dose by their extremely plaintive delivery:

MILLS: Ladies and gentlemen . . .

BOBBIE: Ladies and gentlemen . . .

MILLS: We have come here tonight

BOBBIE: We have come here tonight

MILLS: To tell you . . .

BOBBIE: To tell you . . .

MILLS: Here, wait a minute, wait a minute. We can't both talk together, can we?

BOBBIE: No.

MILLS: Well, let's get on with it!

Silly asses were very popular, even with the working classes: on radio, for instance, Claude Hulbert and his wife Enid Trevor were top favourites:

CLAUDE: I want to tell you a very pathetic story.

ENID: I hate pathetic stories. I like something thrilling – exciting – mysterious. Don't you know any ghost stories?

CLAUDE: Oh, rather. I know an awfully good one, about a farmer who lived miles out in the country, and every night he used to go to bed at a quarter past ten, and wake up in the morning and go out and inspect his stock; but one morning he got up as usual and a terrible thing happened – there wasn't any!

ENID: Wasn't any what?

CLAUDE: Milk!

ENID: Milk! What has that to do with a ghost story?

CLAUDE: Oh, I thought you said a goat story.

ENID: Ghosts, spirits, apparitions. You know what an apparition is, don't you?
CLAUDE: Oh, certainly. It's a person who lives in Paris. A Parisian!

Then there was Claude Dampier, a tall, gangling, buck-toothed fellow who always sought inspiration from a never-seen Mrs Gibson. His wife Billie Carlyle didn't seem to mind, even when he was nearly banned from the BBC for saying that he must rush off to squeeze Mrs Gibson's oranges. Claude didn't often use *double entendre*: the following was more typical of his act:

CLAUDE: I have to go now. Mrs Gibson's moving house, and I promised to take her eleven mice and three rats.
BILLIE: Whatever for?
CLAUDE: Well, she has to leave the place in exactly the same condition as she found it! -

An unusual double act was that of Murgatroyd and Winterbottom, a tag concealing the identities of two comedians very well known in single harness as Tommy Handley and Ronald Frankau. Together, on radio only, they indulged in high-speed patter absolutely smothered in puns:

That sounds fishy to me.
– Don't worry, I know my plaice.
Say that again, I'm a bit hard of herring.
– Don't strain yourself, it'll give you a haddock.
Now, kipper civil tongue in your head . . .

and so on. Their introductory refrain remained standard:

Here's a song to introduce us,
If our gags are old, excuce us,
Anyway, please don't abuce us,
Or the BBC won't uce us,
    Then we'll sob.

Some folks think our jokes just punny,
Others' eyes with tears get runny
We don't care if they think us funny
Providing that they pay us money
    For the job.
Sing tra la la.
Why tra la la?
Folk singers always do.
Sing hey, sing hey, sing hey, hee, hi ho hugh.

Another popular double act comprised musical entertainers rather than comedians, but Flotsam and Jetsam kept it light even if their material was usually sung rather than spoken:

> We'll tell you our names so that no one forgets 'em:
> I'm Flotsam. – He's Flotsam.
> I'm Jetsam. – He's Jetsam.
> We broadcast news bulletins – in verse Flotsam sets 'em;
> To the bass notes of Jetsam –
> It's Jetsam who gets 'em.
> Flotsam and Jetsam, for your approbation
> Will now sing a souvenir of the Royal Coronation,
> For all of our listeners,
> And for anyone who lets 'em –
> Yours very sincerely . . . Flotsam and Jetsam.

Elsie and Doris Waters came to fame almost accidentally: their Gert and Daisy act, two easy-going cockney ladies who made topical comments on the world about them, arose from amateur nights and

ELSIE AND DORIS WATERS. Still recognizable in 1975, 'Gert and Daisy' congratulate their brother Jack Warner, who has just been made an honorary Doctor of Letters.

graduated to concert party appearances before becoming beloved of the BBC. You could hardly have called them stand-up comics at all, for they just chatted:

> GERT: Ain't it lovely, Daisy, living next door to one another? Here we are in our gardens, chatting away . . .
> DAISY: With only a fence between us.
> GERT: What do you mean? You've never had no offence from me.
> DAISY: Give your 'ead a good shake, Gert. Your brain's got knots in it. Yes, you weren't half lucky to get in there. Nice little place. A bit small, though. Sort of place where if you got mumps you might get summoned for overcrowding.
> GERT: Oh, I don't mind its being small. It's the drains I mind.
> DAISY: Oh, we've never had no trouble with them.
> GERT: Never had no trouble with the drains?
> DAISY: No, we ain't got any . . .

Elsie and Doris had a brother, Jack Waters, who came to fame rather later than they did, as Jack Warner. He was amiable as they were, and in later years, as Dixon of Dock Green, assumed the role of national comforter, but on radio and screen he went in for character comedy rather than stand-up gags, first coming to fame in the wartime *Garrison Theatre* where he held the show together with banter between himself and 'my little gel', and with the reading of letters from his 'brother Sid' at the front. The letters were supposedly heavily censored, which was why Jack came to be billed as Jack 'Blue Pencil' Warner. His other catch-phrase was 'Mind my bike!' In fact he was always ready to tour the halls and clubs with a stand-up act of his own, which included Maurice Chevalier impressions and jokes very much at variance with the image he normally generated:

> Cross-breeding's all the rage these days, isn't it, lady? Do you know what you get if you cross an elephant with a prostitute? A bloody great tart that does it for buns! The other day I met a friend of mine who was coming down the street limping. I said what happened to you? He said well, it's me hobby, isn't it, it's this cross-breeding. You see, I crossed a crocodile with a budgerigar. I said, what on earth did you get? He said I don't know its name, but it bit me leg off and said aren't I a pretty boy?

Another astonishingly popular radio double act was that of Arthur Askey and Richard Murdoch, who just as the war started were at the top of the tree in *Band Waggon*, a weekly ragbag of songs and sketches in which, by courtesy of their scriptwriter Vernon Harris, they lived in a flat at the top of Broadcasting House, together with Lewis the goat,

Basil and Lucy the pigeons, Mrs Bagwash the charlady and her daughter Nausea. The scripts would not now reproduce with any effectiveness, being dependent on repetition, topical allusions and such catchphrases as 'Ay theng yow!' ('I thank you') which took the nation by storm; but they could be regarded as the start of situation comedy, a subject which belongs in another chapter.

Many of the favourite BBC comedy artists were not so much gagmen as humorists. Mabel Constanduros was simply the voice of dear old Grandma Buggins; Suzette Tarri was the ageing cockney lady fond of a drop of Guinness but afraid of being left on the shelf; and Mrs Feather (Jeanne de Casalis) was a dithery upper-class dame forever at the end of a phone:

Hello, hello? Supervisions, Operations, Aberrations? Hello, who is that? Engineers? You again? Why are you tinkling my bell every two minutes? Two hours ago you told me I was in working order, and I've been as dead as mutton ever since. I mean to say, this can't go on. First you put me

JEANNE DE CASALIS, in one of her rare cinema excursions, takes tea with a heavily disguised Arthur Askey in *Charley's Big-Hearted Aunt*.

right, then you put me wrong again. Here am I, trying to pluck a duck in the pantry, and every two minutes I have to run in here because my bell's being tinkled. You're testing the line? Well, give it up, it's not worth it. It's been an invalid for years. And another thing, why is that man of yours still up a pole outside my bathroom window? I haven't been able to have a bath for two days. Mr Feather doesn't like it at all . . .

Stainless Stephen was an ex-schoolmaster ('stainless' because he came from Sheffield) who decided that the way to fame was to speak all punctuation:

Somebody once said inverted commas comedians are born not made full stop. Well, slight pause to heighten dramatic effect, let me tell my dense public (innuendo) that I was born of honest but disappointed parents in anno domini eighteen ninety something full stop. Owing to my female fan following the final two digits must be left to the imagination, end of paragraph and fresh line.

A little of Stainless went a very long way, but most people could giggle occasionally at Gillie Potter, a parsonical type who appears to have been invented by the BBC. In a voice highly suited to psalm-singing, he told of events in the imaginary English village of Hogsnorton, and especially in the Grange, where Lord Marshmallow holds sway, 'standing resplendent upon a rich fireside rug embellished with the Turkish symbol for good luck, being a double circle containing the holy letters GWR.'* Sometimes the Potter act took the form of an essay read by himself:

So soon as St Andrew's Day is over, and the Scotsman has hung up his haggis till Hogmanay, we are happily at the end of all the annual antics of our multifarious foreigners, and the natives of England can concentrate on Christmas. With that sound sense which is born of extensive economic experience, we English usually postpone the purchasing of presents for our dear ones until we have some evidence that the dear ones have done some present purchasing themselves. This is a policy largely responsible for that rushing out after the reception by the last post on Christmas Eve of a pair of bedsocks from Aunt Bessie, and the having hurriedly to decide between the air gun and the chocolate giraffe which constitute the sole remaining stock of the only shop still open . . .

Potter almost, if not quite, brings us to A. J. Alan, the piping storyteller of the BBC's pre-war days, who included elements of both

---

* The joke was that in the forties they would be primarily recognized as meaning Great Western Railway.

GILLIE POTTER, your reporter from Hogsnorton, a radio favourite of the forties.

Potter and Robert Benchley in his diffident way of recounting an improbable tale. Eric Partridge, in fact, has held him to be the originator of the shaggy dog story, but that would be an investigation in itself. Enough has surely been said to indicate that radio had plenty of humour of its own, apart from providing a convenient means of keeping stage and film performers before the public when they were not working in their primary media.

JACK WARNER: Do you know what the policeman said when he came home and found his wife in bed with three men? – 'Allo, 'allo, 'allo!

7

I'll bet you eight to five
that we meet Dorothy Lamour:

AMERICAN FILM COMEDY
1930–1945

The thirties and early forties were undoubtedly the sublime period of American film comedians, for one could not have had a more receptive audience than one which for so long had been restricted to silence, and now felt itself emancipated, with the world its comic oyster. Besides, it took at least ten years for all the best jokes, plus infinite variations on them, to be told; and laughter was the best medicine in that depression-ridden decade.

In a real sense, Stan Laurel and Oliver Hardy were not only the supreme example of thirties laughter, but also the historical link with the silent age. As graduates *cum laude* of the Hal Roach All Stars, they sailed confidently into the new era, masters of both styles. Indeed, when they remade some of their silent comedies with sound, both versions seemed equally valid. Most of their beloved gestures and gimmicks had been perfected in silent days – Stan's vivid cry, head scratching and instinctive magic, Olly's tie twiddle and camera look – but sound gave them a more realistic rapport with the other characters who were so essential to their suburban world: suspicious wives and policemen, angry neighbours, dizzy dames, stern bosses.

Nobody loved them but the public, people used to say about Laurel and Hardy, and it was one case where the punters knew best. Of course Stan and Olly were silly fellows who wouldn't have lasted long in the real world: one couldn't imagine them negotiating a deal, or fixing a fuse, or fathering children. But there was something in them of all of us: they encapsulated, perhaps, all the foolishness of which human beings are capable. We never exactly recognized *ourselves* in them – of course not – but we were bound to have an uncle or cousin or friend who reminded us of one or the other. When in the seventies Dennis Potter

LAUREL AND HARDY, as themselves for once, meet their mentor Hal Roach.

wrote a television play called *Blue Remembered Hills*, all about children but with the parts played by grown-ups, it seemed to offer nothing new because Laurel and Hardy had done it forty years earlier. That was the secret of their comedy: they were not merely innocents, but children in a grown-up world. They reacted not as men but as ten-year-old boys, and that was why they were funny; yet when they played their own kids in *Brats* they weren't funny at all, any more than children being tiresomely naughty are funny. Nowhere is this essential childishness of Stan and Olly better demonstrated than in *Sons of the Desert*, where as men of apparent substance they spend one evening a week at an exceedingly foolish male club of the Masonic type, where the Exalted Ruler conducts a final locked-hands sing-song:

> We are the Sons of the Desert,
> Having the time of our lives . . .
> Healthy and strong,
> Doing no wrong,
> Taking good care of our wives (God bless them).

Stan, Olly's next-door neighbour, is almost in tears when Olly persuades him that they must both swear to attend the forthcoming annual shindig of the Sons in Chicago; as he says, if he didn't ask his wife's permission, he wouldn't know what she wanted him to do. In the event, however, it is Olly who is embarrassed when he announces his intent, for his wife throws at him almost every piece of pottery in the house. With childlike glee, Olly concocts a scheme: he must pretend to be ill, in order to receive doctor's orders to 'go to Hawaii'. Astonishingly, since the arrangements are left in the hands of Stan, who has spent the previous reel eating wax fruit and now brings a horse doctor to diagnose Olly's supposed ailment, the scheme works. But instead of lying low at the convention, the boys can't resist frolicking on the streets during a parade, and are thus observed at a newsreel theatre, to which their wives have repaired in a state of shock, having just heard of the sinking during a typhoon of the ship on which the errant husbands were supposed to be travelling from Hawaii. The retribution which falls upon the deceitful Olly, who continues past the point of no return to spin a web of improbable lies, is swift and terrible; but for Stan, who is a good boy and tells the truth (after a flood of tears), the rewards are goodies to eat and drink, even a cigarette, and a cosy place before the fire in a silk dressing gown.

The films in which they have wives are almost always successful, especially when one of the wives is Mae Busch.★ Fed up with the encroachment of the bachelor Stan upon her marriage, she walks out on Olly at the beginning of *Their First Mistake*, and there ensues the oddest scene in which the two comedians lie on Olly's bed, doing every infantile thing but suck their thumbs as they vaguely contemplate a problematical future:

> STAN: What's the matter with her, anyway?
> OLLY: Oh, I don't know. She says I think more of you than I do of her.
> STAN: Well, you do, don't you?
> OLLY: We won't go into that.
> STAN: You know what the whole trouble is?
> OLLY: What?
> STAN: What you need is a baby in your house.
> OLLY: Why, what's that got to do with it?
> STAN: Well, if you had a baby . . . and it would keep your wife's mind occupied . . . you could go out at nights with me . . . and

★ In later years Jackie Gleason used to make fun of the name ('the ever popular Mae Busch') but she was a highly professional comic artist.

LAUREL AND HARDY as Stan and Ollie. Los Angeles must have been full of wet holes for Ollie to fall into. The film is *Angora Love*; when they remade it as *Laughing Gravy*, the goat became a dog.

> she'd never think anything about it. All your troubles would be over.
> OLLY: You know, I think that's a pretty good idea.
> STAN: You bet your life it's a good idea. You know, it's a well-known fact . . . that all the happiness in the house . . . when you have a baby . . . and there's a wife, and you, and the baby . .. it's a well-known fact. I've read about that.
> OLLY: I'm beginning to think you're right.
> STAN: You bet your life I'm right. You know, I'm not so dumb as you look.
> OLLY: You bet your life you're not. – What do you mean, you're not so dumb as *I* look?
> STAN: Well –
> OLLY: Come on.
> STAN: Where are you going?
> OLLY: We're going to adopt a baby.

And, this being Cloud Cuckoo Land, they do. Just like that. Like Olly, we won't go into the element of homosexual relationship between the pair of them; no audience in the early thirties would in any case have put an evil construction on the fact that they often shared a bed. Oddly, it even added to their innocence, without really explaining the need they had for each other. There is a splendid moment during the Masonic meeting in *Sons of the Desert*, when the Exhausted Ruler (as Stan calls him) announces that the strong must always support the weak, and Olly gives Stan a meaningful look which he shares with the audience. But Olly needs Stan too, if only to boss around, to pass on the contemptuous treatment which Olly's wife hands out to *him*. Somehow their friendship survives through thick and thin, and despite everything there are moments when they smile on each other, or sing together, or even put their feelings into words:

STAN: What's for breakfast?
OLLY: For breakfast, Stanley, we have coffee, and we have beans.
STAN: Boy, you sure know how to plan a meal.

Even when Stan does the worst he can to Olly, which is considerable in terms of collapsing houses, exploding gas ovens and demolishing walls, Olly just dusts himself off, gazes indignantly into the camera, and comes back for more. Almost the nearest he gets to protest is in *County Hospital*, when he is trussed up in traction after a fall, and Stan comes to visit. 'I brought you some hard boiled eggs and some nuts,' Stan announces. (His pockets hold salt and pepper, too.) Olly can scarcely believe this, but while he is violently inviting the audience to share his exasperation, Stan's attention has passed to an iron weight which in curiosity he picks up from the floor. The cable from it happens to run up over a pulley and supports Olly's plaster cast leg, which now violently descends on the examining doctor. Startled, but still holding the weight, Stan promptly falls out of the window, thus hoisting Olly upside down to the ceiling. We should not take for granted the inventiveness, the timing and the sheer physical dexterity involved in such moments; nor should we forget that the incidents all spring from character, which is why these gentle, absurd people are still so beloved nearly sixty years after their heyday.

Though viewers not under their spell may aver that Stan and Olly were always the same, examination will show that this is not true. In spirit, yes, they were middle-aged suburbanites, one fat and one thin; Stan was meek and mild, Olly full of self-esteem. But they kept us constantly surprised. There were Stan's tricks which Olly could never equal: the earsie-eyesie-nosie routine, the flicking of his thumb into flame, the pulling down of the *shadow* of a window blind. There were the elaborate falls to which Olly's elaborate pride must inevitably lead. There were grotesque physical jokes, and googly dialogue, and songs and dances, and chases and laughing acts. Considering the speed with which the Laurel and Hardy films were made, they still seem amazingly professional and subtly timed, especially in the complex tit-for-tat routines with their escalating comic violence based on custard pies or boiled rice or the items available in a grocery store. If you think it's impossible to make a comic ballet out of shin-kicking and trouser-ripping, see *You're Darn Tootin'*; and if you doubt that twenty minutes of pure fun can be derived from the attempts of two Christmas tree salesmen to make a deal with one householder, then *Big Business* (in which the householder in question is our old friend James Finlayson) must be the film for you. But it scarcely matters where you start. Half a dozen films into the *oeuvre*, you're bound to be converted. The boys never fail. (Well, almost never.)

In the early thirties, Stan and Olly had practically no competitors. There were other talking comedians who were well liked, but none who were loved. Of the double and treble acts, Bert Wheeler and Robert Woolsey had a fair run, but never lived up to the promise they apparently showed in the lost films *Rio Rita* and *Dixiana* (both 1929). Wheeler, who later had a small theatre named after him in New York's Dixie Hotel (not one of the Big Apple's more salubrious meeting places), was genial, excitable and somewhat dumb, rather like a British radio character of ten years later, Sam Scram in *Itma*. Woolsey was loud, sardonic and bespectacled, a businessman type with a cigar perpetually dangling from his lips. During the first eight years of the thirties they made for RKO twelve comedies, and the best adjective applicable to any was tolerable. They had titles like *Half Shot at Sunrise, Hips Hips Hooray, Caught Plastered* and *Mummy's Boys*, and they mixed in cross-talk with farce, none of it memorable.

The Ritz Brothers (real name Joachim) were a different matter. Basically a cabaret act, the three of them relied less on dialogue than on funny noises, gestures and disguises. They might variously appear as Peter Lorre, the Frankenstein monster, Captain Bligh, Napolean, Ted Lewis, or Dr Jekyll and Mr Hyde, and more than likely they would do so on roller skates. Some people adored them, some hated them; what was impossible was to ignore them: especially Harry, who was always in the centre because he pulled the funniest faces. For a couple of years from 1937 they were more than welcomed at Fox, and made a number of

WHEELER AND WOOLSEY have not revived well, but in the thirties they made a lot of people laugh. Here in *Mummy's Boys* Bert Wheeler is the one peeping out from behind a sarcophagus which looks suspiciously like himself.

top-budgeted extravaganzas. Then, right after *The Three Musketeers*, one of their best, something happened: either they became hard to handle, or Darryl F. Zanuck changed his mind. The next Ritz movie, *The Gorilla*, ran only 63 minutes and was a patent programme filler. Soon they were out, and although Universal put them under contract, they were used only as a threat to Abbott and Costello (just as Gloria Jean was to Deanna Durbin), and the movies they made were something worse than awful. It was back to the cabaret circuit for the Ritzes, but scarcely an unhappy ending since they were Las Vegas toppers till the end of their lives. In the mid-seventies, when only a couple of them were left, Mel Brooks did announce that his *History of the World* would be compered by Harry Ritz as the Farting Man; but the movie when it came out was bad enough without that.

The term 'physical comedy' could scarcely be better described than by the work of the Three Stooges, who between 1934 and 1958 made 190 two-reel comedies for Columbia. Their name denotes their original status, for they went to Hollywood as fall guys for a hard-boiled comedian called Ted Healy, with whom they can be seen in the Joan Crawford–Clark Gable musical drama of 1933, *Dancing Lady*. He thought he could do without them, but managed only a few supporting roles before he died in 1937. They, under long-term contract to Columbia, went from strength to strength, and although the critics always frowned on them, they now enjoy at least cult status for their always professional approach to their work, even though that work involved a great deal of violence (poking of eyes, banging of heads) made more acceptable by funny noises on the sound track. One of their early shorts, *Men in Black*, actually won an Academy Award in 1934, as had Laurel and Hardy for *The Music Box* a couple of years earlier, but after that, the Stooges had to be satisfied by the enthusiasm with which Columbia kept renewing their contract; for in the sticks, a Stooges comedy on the bill drew as many crowds as a Frank Capra feature. The titles tell almost all: *Ants in the Pantry, A Pain in the Pullman, An Ache in Every Stake, Violent is*

THE RITZ BROTHERS seem here to be rehearsing for the ballet, so stand back for disaster. The film, *The Goldwyn Follies*, is the one in which they sing the memorable *Hey, Pussy, Pussy*.

THE THREE STOOGES, Curly, Moe and Larry, intending no good to Vernon Dent in an early thirties short.

the Word for Curly, ★ *The Pest Man Wins, Some More of Samoa, In the Sweet Pie and Pie*. The Stooges might produce groans, but never yawns.

In the judgement of posterity, they lasted too long. Curly Howard left the act through illness in 1947, and somehow his various replacements never quite hit the spot. Yet the Stooges went on reworking their old situations, with diminishing enthusiasm, right through the sixties: they even made a few quite awful features.

To mention the Marx Brothers next is to move from the ridiculous to the absurd, from irrefutably lowbrow to quasi-highbrow. The Marxes were just as zany as the Stooges, and sometimes just as physical, but they disarmed all critics by giving the impression that either they or their scriptwriters had read a few books. Harpo certainly had, though on screen he didn't talk at all, only chased girls, whistled messages when danger threatened, performed visual gags (such as burning a candle at both ends), and played the harp. Brother Chico's instrument was the

★ This title parodied a current movie, *Valiant is the Word for Carrie*.

THE FOUR MARX BROTHERS, suitably labelled in *Monkey Business* (1931). They are Harpo, Zeppo, Chico and Groucho.

piano, which he attacked in an inimitable trigger-fingered style. He chased girls in private life, and played a lot of poker; on-screen he acted as interpreter for the others (he was the only one who could understand Harpo's whistled messages), affected a fake Italian accent, and wore a strange crumpled hat which once caused Groucho to mutter: 'I don't normally mind being insulted, but I resent it from a character whose head comes to a point.' Groucho, he of the stooping walk and the painted moustache, was the really literate one, but on-screen he translated his literacy into quips and insults. (Taking a man's pulse: 'Either he's dead or my watch has stopped.' Welcoming a wealthy sponsor: 'Ah, Mrs Rittenhouse, won't you . . . lie down?' Stuffing a handkerchief into a prisoner's mouth: 'This is the best gag in the picture.') There is a scene in *Monkey Business* when he runs into a lady's stateroom and hides in her wardrobe. Bewildered, she knocks and asks: 'What are you doing in there?' Groucho opens the door and ogles her: 'Nothing. Come on in.' My favourite line of all is from *Duck Soup*: 'Remember, men, we are fighting for this woman's honour, which is probably more than she ever did!'

Groucho also sings, on occasion, in a whining monotone which at least gets the words across. In *Horse Feathers*, as the world's least likely college president, he lopes into the stage at Commencement, rolls his eyes a few times, and launches into a song describing his policy of prohibition:

> For years before my son was born
> I used to yell from night till morn
> Whatever it is, I'm against it.
> And I've been yelling since I first commenced it,
> I'm against it!

In *Animal Crackers*, as guest of honour at a country estate, he is brought in on a litter, as befits a man just back from dangerous African exploits:

> CROWD: Hooray for Captain Spaulding, the African explorer!
> GROUCHO: Did someone call me Schnorrer?
> CROWD: Hooray, hooray, hooray!

His most famous song, perhaps, is 'Lydia the Tattooed Lady', from *At the Circus*:

> Lydia, oh Lydia, oh have you met Lydia,
> Lydia the tattooed lady?
> She has eyes that men adore so,
> And her torso even more so;
> Lydia, oh Lydia, that encyclopiddia,
> Lydia the queen of tattoo . . .
>
> She once swept an admiral clean off his feet;
> The ships on her hips made his heart skip a beat.
> He's an admiral now, in command of that fleet!
> You can learn a lot from Lydia!

It will have been discerned by newcomers to the subject that the Marx films are not models of plot, of character or of sentiment. The format is simply to shovel in as many gags and specialities as possible. There is always, for instance, a scene in which the sharp-witted Groucho is outsmarted by Chico's devious illogic, as in the 'sanity clause' bit ('There ain't no Sanity Clause') from *A Night at the Opera*'s contract-tearing scene, or this less remembered badinage from the shipboard saga, *Monkey Business*:

THE THREE MARX BROTHERS, fourteen years later in *A Night in Casablanca*.

CHICO: I come up to see the Captain's bridge.

GROUCHO: I'm sorry, but he keeps it in a glass of water while he's eating. Would you like to see where the Captain sleeps?

CHICO: Aw, I already saw that. That's da bunk.

GROUCHO: You're just wasting your breath, and that's no great loss either. Some sailor you are!

CHICO: You bet I'm a fine sailor. My father was a-partners with Columbus.

GROUCHO: Columbus has been dead four hundred years.

CHICO: That's what my mother said about my father.

GROUCHO: Let me explain to you about Columbus. Take a look at this globe.

CHICO: That's Columbus Circle.

GROUCHO: Columbus sailed from Spain to India looking for a shortcut.

CHICO: You mean a strawberry shortcut?

GROUCHO: I don't know. When I woke up, there was this nurse taking care of me.

CHICO: Whatsa da matter, couldn't the nurse take care of herself?

GROUCHO: You bet she could, but I found that out too late.

Finally there are spectacular elements depending on finely timed and edited visual comedy. In *Duck Soup*, the musical numbers and the war sequence; in *Horse Feathers*, the football game; in *A Night at the Opera*, the cabin scene and the wrecking of the performance; in *A Day at the Races*, the medical examination and the horse race; in *At the Circus*, the gorilla on the trapeze, and stately Margaret Dumont being fired from a gun; in *Go West*, the chopping up for firewood of a train on the move. Still, the essence of Marxism is for most people Groucho, whether for his outrageous puns ('You go Uruguay and I'll go mine'), his unquenchable libido ('Excuse me while I brush the crumbs out of my bed, I'm expecting company'), his way with an insult ('Why don't you bore a hole in yourself and let the sap run out?'), his surrealism ('What is it has four pairs of pants, lives in Philadelphia, and it never rains but it pours?'), or his aim to create anarchy, never better expressed than when he takes over the management of a hotel:

> GROUCHO: Now, the first thing we're gonna do is change all the numbers on all the rooms.
> CLERK: But sir, think of the confusion!
> GROUCHO: Yeah, but think of the fun!

Or perhaps one should say that the essence of Marxism is Groucho's writers, who through the years included such wits as George S. Kaufman, Morrie Ryskind, Arthur Sheekman, S. J. Perelman, Frank Tashlin, Bert Kalmar and Harry Ruby. They, for sure, are the unsung heroes of the Marx Brothers Appreciation Society.★

A more fundamental vein of zany humour was mined by a vaudeville pair called Ole Olsen and Chic Johnson. From 1930 on they made sporadic attempts to infiltrate Hollywood, but without real success until Universal bought up the film rights to their madcap Broadway revue *Hellzapoppin*. That adroit director H. C. Potter filmed it rather slickly in 1942, and although the studio insisted on the addition of a plot and a love interest, Olsen and Johnson were allowed not only to treat these somewhat cavalierly but to include most of the in-jokes and comedy schticks which had made the stage show such a hit. The film begins in Hell ('That's the first time a taxi driver ever went straight where I told him'), and ends, Hell having turned out to be a film studio, with an assistant director being shot full of holes out of which water sprays when he next takes a drink, despite his assertion that 'I always wear a bullet

---

★ One has almost forgotten to mention the Marx Brother named Zeppo, but then so did everyone else, including the scriptwriters; which is why he left the act in 1933.

From the left, CHIC JOHNSON and OLE OLSEN; then Martha O'Driscoll,
Walter Catlett and Gloria Jean. The film is *Ghost Breakers*, one of their less
successful follow-ups to *Hellzapoppin*.

proof vest around the studio.' Hugh Herbert wanders through in a
succession of disguises, and does his woo-woo chuckle at the audience.
('I'll be home for tea, Mom, have meat.') In between there is a
putting-on-a-show format at a country house party, and the show is
eventually sabotaged for reasons which may conveniently be forgotten,
but is a hit because the chaos makes a hard-boiled critic laugh. In
between whiles the projectionist gets the film upside down and in
reverse; Indians gallop through on their way to another set; a love song is
interrupted by a slide asking Stinky Miller please to go home; a woman
repeatedly stalks through yelling 'Oscar!'; a meek little man keeps
looking for 'Mrs Jones', until the small bush he is carrying has become a
tree and has to be brought in on a truck; Olsen and Johnson become one
person when the top half of the first and the bottom half of the second are
made invisible; and Mischa Auer, Martha Raye, the Frankenstein
monster and a bear are also involved. The whole is sufficiently slickly
packaged to have become a classic of crazy comedy. Hollywood
however could find no further adequate use for Olsen and Johnson, no

longer young and never beautiful; their three subsequent films varied from bad to you must be joking, and the sad decline which followed must have been ironic in view of their immense Broadway popularity over the years when each night they bestowed a final blessing on the audience:

> May you live as long as you want.
> May you laugh as long as you live.

Other double acts of the period need not detain us long. Burns and Allen found their greatest success in television, and will be mentioned in a later chapter on that subject. Thelma Todd and Patsy Kelly made a few two-reelers for Hal Roach in the early thirties, as later did Thelma Todd and ZaSu Pitts. Bobby Clark (he of the painted spectacles) and Paul McCullough, although they are pleasantly remembered in some quarters, made no real impact. In the forties, one might whisper the names of Wally Brown and Alan Carney, noisy pratfall artists of a few 'B' pictures, but then our survey of comedy teams must pause except for – and there is no way of staving off the evil day any further – Bud Abbott and Lou Costello.

It may be that Bud and Lou have been unjustly derided simply because they made a lot of money during the wartime years when standards were low, and because according to recorded history they were not very sensible or sympathetic people to know. The fact is that millions of people bought tickets to see them, and came back for more, during the first five years of the forties when they were Universal's top drawers; and then, after an unwise attempt to change their images, they managed another seven years of only gradually declining success, starting with *Abbott and Costello Meet Frankenstein* in 1948. They also put fifty-two half hours of their best stuff on television, all of which adds up to quite an *oeuvre* to pick over. Eager researchers will find that the mass is smaller than it seems, because they repeated themselves shamelessly: the basis of their success was perhaps a dozen crazy routines from vaudeville, where they started, and each of these turned up again and again, lightly disguised, with Bud always the slightly unsympathetic straight man, the bullying feed who never gets a funny line, and Lou the nervous, stuttering, babyish clown who finishes up holding the sticky end of all Bud's plans. The most famous of their routines is 'Who's On First', in which Bud describes a baseball game with players called Who, What, When and I Don't Know, and Lou has no idea what he is talking about. As performed, it is a small miracle of professional timing, but my own

ABBOTT AND COSTELLO IN SOCIETY? A more outrageous idea could scarcely be conceived.

favourite, perhaps because it has a touch of surrealism about it, is 'Fliegel Street', which for some reason was changed to 'Beagle Street' when it turned up (quite irrelevantly) in *Abbott and Costello in Society*. A friend of theirs who runs a hat shop has asked them on their way to return a pack of straw hats to the Susquehanna Hat Company in Beagle Street. This simple request leads to five minutes of escalating insanity, from the minute they hit the sidewalk:

> LOU: Where's Beagle Street?
> BUD: I don't know. We'll ask somebody.
> LOU: How much did you say these hats were?
> BUD: Seven fifty apiece.
> LOU: How do I look with a seven fifty hat on?
> BUD: Kind of spiffy. Now, don't get them dirty.
> LOU: Let's go.
> BUD: Be careful.
> LOU: Beagle Street, huh?
> BUD: Beagle Street. We'll ask somebody. Here, ask this fellow where Beagle Street is.
> LOU: Okay. Excuse me, can you tell me where Beagle Street is?
> MAN: Sorry, buddy, I haven't got a dime.
> LOU: Who's asking you for money? I'm only asking you where Beagle Street is.
> MAN (*suddenly aggressive*): Do I know where Beagle Street is? Of course I know where Beagle Street is. Do I look like I just got off a boat? Is there a tag on my lapel saying I just came from Ellis Island? Of course I know where Beagle Street is. I was born and raised on Beagle Street. My brother was born on Beagle Street. Do you know my brother? What right have you got to go around talking about my brother? I'll have you understand my brother is one of the finest boys that ever walked in shoe leather. My brother was an honor student in school. Go ahead. Say something nasty about my brother. Say something like he shouldn't get a parole.
> LOU: I'm just asking you where Beagle Street is. A common ordinary citizen just asks another fellow where Beagle Street is. I gotta deliver these hats to the Susquehanna Hat Company.
> MAN: Susquehanna Hat Company!
> LOU: Leave go of me!
> MAN: Is that a Susquehanna hat?
> LOU: Yeah.
> MAN: You know who makes these hats?
> LOU: How should I know?
> MAN: Child labour. Little girls – thirteen, fourteen years old. Little girls with curls down to here. They work fourteen hours a day. They work in a sweat shop all day long. Here's what I think of a Susquehanna hat. (*He takes the one from Lou's head and punches a hole*

through it.) And look at it. Look at that band. Imitation leather. Just like paper. And look – ow!

LOU: Whassa matter?

MAN: You stuck a wire in there for me to cut my finger. That's the worst thing I ever saw. You tell your Susquehanna Hat Company that's what I think of it! *(The man jumps on the hat and departs.)*

BUD: Well, you know what that's gonna cost you. You broke one of Dan's hats. Seven dollars and fifty cents.

LOU: All I did was put a hat on my head. *(He does so again.)* Did I ask the guy to take it off? All I asked was the way to Beagle Street.

BUD: It's the way you ask. Try this lady coming along.

LOU: Excuse me, lady, could you tell me the way to Beagle Street?

WOMAN: Beagle Street. Oh, why did you have to remind me of Beagle Street? My husband was killed on Beagle Street. Do you hear? *(She shakes him.)* My husband was killed on Beagle Street.

LOU: I mean – I mean – I dunno what I mean. All I want is to get to the Susquehanna Hat Company.

WOMAN: The Susquehanna Hat Company! Is that a Susquehanna hat? That was the kind of hat my husband was wearing when he was killed. And he wouldn't have lost his life if he'd been wearing a good hat, when the safe fell out of that fifteen storey building. But no! He was wearing a hat like this one! *(She grabs it and rips it apart.)* Oh, that's the cheapest – the worst grade of straw I ever saw! Oh, my husband's dead, he's dead! *(By now she is swiping Lou with the remnants of the hat.)*

LOU: He ain't dead, lady, he's hiding! *(The woman rushes off in tears.)*

BUD: Now listen. Just a minute. That's two hats you've broken. Do you know how much you owe Derby Dan? Fifteen dollars.

LOU: Fifteen dollars?

BUD: Yeah. And stop insulting women.

LOU: Look, all I asked her is where was Beagle Street.

2ND WOMAN *(passing by)*: Beagle Street. Don't ever mention that name. I can't stand it. Beagle Street! *(Anticipating the inevitable, Lou hands her a new hat. She tears it in pieces and departs. Lou holds the hat box protectively and looks up and down the street.)*

BUD: Now, just a minute, hold that still.

LOU: Take back the hats.

BUD: Nonsense. Just go on down there and find out where Beagle Street is.

LOU: How much do I owe Dan now?

BUD: Twenty-two dollars and fifty cents.

LOU *(putting on another hat)*: I'm gonna try just one more.

BUD: Well, be careful with that one. Will you, please?

LOU: Okay, I'll ask another guy. I'll ask anybody, I don't care. Hey, mister, could you please tell me where Beagle Street is?

2ND MAN *(bursting into tears immediately)*: Beagle Street. Don't ask me where Beagle Street is. I was walking along minding my own business and a safe fell from a fifteen storey building – and killed me!

LOU: A safe fell fifteen floors and fell on your head and killed you?

2ND MAN: Yes.

LOU: Then if you're dead, there's no use asking you the way to the Susquehanna Hat Company.

2ND MAN *(becoming maniacal)*: Susquehanna Hat Company! That's the hat I was wearing the day I was killed! *(He seizes Lou's hat and destroys it.)* I'm sorry . . . I think I've broken your hat.

LOU *(inspecting the remains)*: You *think* you've broken it?

2ND MAN: Yes.

LOU: This is the fourth Susquehanna hat I've . . .

2ND MAN: Susquehanna Hats! *(He begins breaking up the crockery on display outside Luigi's shop, where they are standing.)*

LUIGI: What you doing? You trying to ruin my place? Help! Police!

COP: What's going on here?

LUIGI: This big fellow, he hit the little fellow, my friend, and began breaking up my things.

COP: Come on you, you're going with me.

2ND MAN: You can't take me to jail. Oh, no. I'm dead. You can't take me to jail. *(But he goes.)*

LUIGI: He's crazy. Now, what can I do for you?

LOU: Luigi, how can I get to the Susquehanna Hat Company?

LUIGI: Susquehanna Hats! *(Luigi takes an axe and is breaking up his own shop as the scene fades out.)*★

It will be observed that, having once started his partner on the way to doom, Bud Abbott has little to do in this routine; but it is enough for the audience to sense his smart-ass presence, to know that Lou will get no help from that quarter. It is the same in 'Slowly I Turned', which is a variation on 'Fliegel Street'. The pair have been cast into an Arabian jail cell with a mad-eyed giant, who is quiescent until someone mentions the dreaded word 'Pocomoco'. Then what comes back to him is an old battle in which he tore the nearest person apart. 'Slowly I turned . . . step by step . . .' And of course the nearest person this time is Lou.

Abbott and Costello came to prominence almost by accident. Their first Hollywood appearance in *One Night in the Tropics* was nearly a flop, and their second, *Buck Privates*, was a hoary army comedy which devoted far too much time to its romantic subplot. It coincided however

---

★ The film adds a coda not in the original act. When they reach their apartment there is just one hat left. 'I think I'll just try the last hat on,' says Lou. Abbott sighs: 'What excuse are we going to give to the Susquehanna Hat Company?' Costello explodes: 'Susquehanna!' and begins breaking up the furniture.

with the national state of nerves about the war, which made recruiting a subject the nation was happy to laugh away, and within months Bud and Lou were making more money for Universal than anybody since Deanna Durbin at her height. Aided by their longtime writer John Grant, and backed by musical talent such as the Andrews Sisters, Ella Fitzgerald, Marion Hutton and Ted 'Is Everybody Happy?' Lewis, they ambled their way through a dozen lackadaisical shows in which the best laughs often came from Lou's range of expressions when threatened by the villains of the piece. In *In Society*, Thomas Gomez gives them some parting advice, to the effect that if they don't follow his wishes he can see in his crystal ball 'two plumbers floating down the river . . . and one of them is a fat little guy'. Meaningfully he takes his leave, but Costello has a puzzled look. 'The joke is on him. I can't swim.'

Displays of proletarian ignorance are also surefire laugh-getters, as when snooty butler Arthur Treacher, mistaking them for bona fide guests of his master, shows them to a swank bedroom and offers advice:

ABBOTT AND COSTELLO. The boys clearly don't like what Thomas Gomez sees in his crystal ball.

BUTLER: You have a very rigorous schedule here. You bathe at ten,
   you brunch at eleven, and you tea at two.
LOU: Hm. I also have a very rigorous schedule. I washbasin at eight, I
   doughnut at nine, I pinball machine at ten, I hamburger and
   onions at eleven, and I bicarbonate of soda at twelve.
BUTLER: That settles everything.
LOU: It certainly does.

Lou Costello could evoke gales of laughter merely by looking sheep-
ishly at the camera, by being coy with women, or by admitting that he
had been 'a baaaad boy'. Best of all, he was easily scared, as when
stranded with his partner in a wax museum where Bud proposes just
momentarily to leave him alone while he looks for a light:

LOU: I've got just two words to say to you.
BUD: What's that?
LOU: Hurry back.

You couldn't conceive of comics better suited to their time, the
footling forties. Nor can you think about them in the same breath as Stan
and Olly, or Chaplin, or Keaton, or even W. C. Fields, because they
were only gagsters, never people. If they had seriously tried to improve
themselves, their films might have had more than historical interest, for
when they paid attention to the job in hand they were good pro-
fessionals. As it was, they didn't know how to handle their careers or
their considerable fortunes, except by losing the latter at the racetrack,
and one of the aptest stories told about Lou never reached the screen.
Every Christmas he embarrassed his Beverly Hills neighbours by having a
bigger and better garden display, with an illuminated Santa Claus on his
roof, moving reindeer on his lawn and moving pictures on his side wall,
all of which caused bevies of sightseers from downtown. A young
comedian called George Gobel was one of the neighbours: he put a card
on his door reading:

MERRY CHRISTMAS!
SEE OUR DISPLAY ACROSS THE STREET

The following year, Lou moderated his display.
   Single comedians in Hollywood movies of the thirties were innumerable, especially if you include the singing entertainers like Al Jolson and
Eddie Cantor. Jolson, the epitome of Jewish brio, isn't remembered as a
comedian, but he needed material to cement his songs together, and the
story goes that he never minded where he got it. Not only did he steal

AL JOLSON (left) and EDDIE CANTOR: friends in public, but deadly professional rivals.

from other shows, he then had his lawyers send the doubly aggrieved star a letter threatening reprisals if he continued to steal from Jolson. The fact is that everybody accepted Jolson's ego as part of his act. His rivals didn't mind that he billed himself as 'the world's greatest entertainer', though one or two eyebrows must have been raised when he followed Caruso on a charity bill and told the audience 'You ain't heard nothin' yet!' His keen competition with his peers was well known, and he guyed it in an album cut in the forties, part of whose preamble was as follows:

> People are always asking me, Jolie, when you going to play the Palace? And I say, I'll tell you the first time I'm gonna set foot in that building, it'll be when Eddie Cantor and Groucho Marx and George Jessel are all on the bill. And I'm gonna buy out all the tickets for the first show, and sit in the middle of the third row and say: Slaves, entertain the king!

Jolson was the first star of talking pictures, and though his movie career quickly faltered, he settled in California anyway. Eddie Cantor, who was also Jewish and also sang in blackface, started his movie career earlier, and had a slower build-up but a longer time at the top. Still, one can imagine his regret, in the later age of film biographies, that *The Eddie Cantor Story* did not do one tenth of the business of *The Jolson Story*. Cantor wanted to be depicted as a family man and a nice guy, whereas Jolson hadn't minded being shown as a man who would sacrifice everything for applause. Besides, Cantor's voice and personality were lighter than Jolson's: he was effervescent rather than overwhelming, the milksop who finally got the girl by a kind of artless guile rather than bravado, as did Britain's George Formby. One of his successful vehicles, *Whoopee*, was taken from a play called *The Nervous Wreck*, and in it he sang the song with which he was always associated, rolling his eyes and lowering his voice on the last line of each verse.

> Every time I hear that dear old wedding march
> I am rather glad I have a fallen arch.
> I have heard a lot of married people talk
> And I know that marriage is a long long walk.

EDDIE CANTOR singing his famous number *Whoopee*, recreated for the 1944 film *Show Business*.

Some people say that marriage means romance,
But I prefer a picnic or a dance.

Another bride, another June,
Another sunny honeymoon.
Another season, another reason
For making whoopee.

She calls him Toodles, and blinks her eyes.
She bakes him strudels, and makes him pies.
What is it all for? It's so he'll fall for
Making whoopee . . .

He hasn't got much money, six thousand dollars per,
Some judge who thinks he's funny
Says, You'll give eight to her.
He says: Now judge, what if I fail?
The judge says: Budge right into jail . . .
You'd better keep her
You'll find it's cheaper
Than making whoopee.

Cantor had an inimitable way of capering around the stage while clapping his hands and rolling his eyes, and each of his movies had a song paced at this tempo, from 'Keep Young and Beautiful' in *Roman Scandals* to 'Having a Patriotic Time' in *Thank Your Lucky Stars*, a wartime effort in need of propaganda uplift:

Thank you for your cordial invitation, Mrs Jones
But with night club life we're through;
Non-essential spending bumps inflation, Mrs Jones,
So here's what we're planning to do:

We're staying home tonight, my baby and me,
Having a patriotic time.
I've got my income tax return to hurdle,
And she'll be saving mileage on her girdle.
Don't want to roam tonight – we're snug as can be,
Hoping the phone will never ring.
While I sit in my slippers and munch a piece of fruit,
She'll iron out the wrinkles in my victory suit.
We're staying home tonight, my baby and me,
Having a patriotic time.

According to the semi-autobiographical 1943 movie *Show Business*, Cantor was already singing in this vein while entertaining the hospitalized troops during World War I:

I don't want to get well, I don't want to get well,
I'm in love with a beautiful nurse . . .

Cantor was an original, and when Sam Goldwyn allowed his contract to lapse he went into radio, a medium for which, with his small clear voice, he was perfectly suited.

Warner Brothers was not normally thought of as a comedy studio, but in the early thirties it issued two farces a year starring Joe E. Brown, an amiable chap with a big mouth through which he emitted foghorn noises. He had been before arriving in Hollywood a circus clown and a baseball pitcher, and his vehicles took advantage of this varied experience, setting him in action situations requiring a good deal of physical dexterity. Most of the stories assigned to him had previously been filmed by the same studio as silents, often with Edward Everett Horton. They had neither wit nor style, but Brown was well liked, and his films sat happily on either side of a double bill. *The Hottentot, Six Day Bike Rider, Elmer the Great, Sit Tight, Earthworm Tractors* and *Wide Open Faces* were typical, but Brown was not out of place as one of the rude mechanicals in *A Midsummer Night's Dream*, and in later years he was Captain Andy in the 1951 *Showboat* and the eccentric millionaire who insisted on marrying Jack Lemmon in *Some Like it Hot*. In the later thirties Paramount matched his trademark with a big-mouthed young woman called Martha Raye, but she proved too strident to have wide appeal, and like Judy Canova, another lady with a corncrake voice, she fell from favour rather quickly. Oddly enough both of these ladies were partnered with Joe E. Brown, Raye in *Pin Up Girl* and Canova in *Chatterbox*.

The war years on the American home front were a fertile breeding ground for strident lady comics. Judy Canova and Martha Raye were trying to outvoice each other; Virginia O'Brien was a popular MGM speciality whose nasal voice and deadpan features made a mockery of romantic lyrics; and the grotesquely horse-faced and double-jointed Cass Daley was always good for a few astonished laughs as she twisted herself into unbelievable anatomical complications. She sang, too, after a fashion; in *The Fleet's In* she was the vocalist for Spike Jones's madcap version of 'Cocktails for Two'. (He introduced her as 'an osteopathic soprano – she sings in all the joints'.) The same film brought to popular attention a more fetching blonde who seemed entirely unable to keep still. Her name was Betty Hutton, and her delivery of 'Arthur Murray Taught me Dancing in a Hurry' made her a star. She was next seen bearing most of the burden of *Star Spangled Rhythm*, a Hollywood studio comedy in which she even volunteered to be part of Walter Dare Wahl's old burlesque mime act. (Three people, two of whom are trying to give a leg up to the third, find themselves in a limb-locked jumble with their hands apparently welded together.) Hutton went to the very top of the ladder within a couple of years – she was Preston Sturges's tragi-farcical heroine in *The Miracle of Morgan's Creek*, and Texas Guinan in *Incendiary Blonde* – but by the end of the decade the public had had enough of her, and her career fizzled out like a damp firework. Perhaps she simply didn't fit the post-war mood.

Ten years before Betty Hutton, there was Mae West. One does not think of Mae primarily as a singer, but she recorded enough ditties of her own composition to fill a long-playing record, and pretty near the knuckle they are too, as anyone can testify who has marvelled at the *double entendres* of 'I Like a Guy who Takes his Time'. Her career had spectacular ups and downs. In the early to mid-thirties she was credited both as the sole saviour of Paramount Pictures and as the reason for the formation of the Legion of Decency. Her sauciness, her ability to size up a man as a sexual equal, and her home-made wisecracks made her a

BETTY HUTTON. In the forties, she came and went like a skyrocket. Here in *Incendiary Blonde* she sings *Row, Row, Row*.

MAE WEST

Sure,
she's a lady!
You can tell by her
walk that she's got
class! Say, when this
cattle queen makes up
her mind to it, nothing
is going to stop her
from being a lady...
even if it kills her!

Adolph Zukor presents

"GOIN' TO TOWN"

Mae crashes society . . . struts right into the best places
and dares 'em to throw her out! Just wait until you
hear her sing grand opera! You'll roll in the aisles!
A Paramount Picture...Directed by Alexander Hall

MAE WEST. She still got top billing, but by 1935 she was on the skids so far as
Hollywood was concerned.

household word, though some of her best-known jests never reached
the screen. ('Say, is that a gun in your pants pocket, or are you just
pleased to see me?'; 'A hard man is tough to find'; and 'I wouldn't let that
guy touch me with a ten-foot pole.') Then, as with Al Jolson, over-
familiarity bred contempt. The sight of her corseted within the new
moral constraints which impeded Hollywood after 1933 was absurd: she
could only be funny in a smoking-room atmosphere. She seemed
suddenly old-fashioned and unamusing, and was forced to return to the
stage, to repetition of her former glories, and to premature semi-
retirement. For all that, she had changed the borderline of the permiss-
ible. Her tragedy was that of a pioneer.

Mae was forty when she appeared in her first film. Her role in *Night After Night* is small, but it is the only thing anybody in the audience was likely to remember. Mae, overdressed to the hilt, saunters into a night club and checks her wrap. 'Goodness,' remarks the girl behind the counter, 'what beautiful diamonds!' 'Goodness,' says Mae, with an eye towards heaven, 'had nothing to do with it.' The line – her very own – later became the title of her autobiography.

Thus simply did a sub-Broadway sensation of the twenties, whose name was whispered among women and sniggered at between men, conquer the then family medium of talking screen. Mae's reign was brief, but she did slip in a couple of corkers. *She Done Him Wrong* was a version of her play *Diamond Lil*, set in the Bowery of the nineties. The mere use of the original title had been considered too provocative, but Mae packed into the 62-minute running time most of the play's laugh lines, including her invitation to the young hero played by Cary Grant: 'Whyncha come up sometime, and see me?' She also remarked that 'It takes two to get one into trouble', and offered these words of wisdom: 'No gold-digging for me. I take diamonds: we may be off the gold

MAE WEST wooed by W. C. FIELDS in *My Little Chickadee*. It was a valiant comeback, but both former stars were now reduced to the status of cult figures, and only nostalgia carried them through.

standard someday.' Of her script for *I'm No Angel* she told the press, 'It's about a girl who climbed the ladder of success, wrong by wrong', and varied this with, 'This girl lost her reputation, but never missed it.' The movie itself contained such gems of *double entendre* as 'I'm no angel, but I've spread my wings a bit', but is best remembered for two splendid moments. At the beginning, Miss West is a fairground hula dancer, performing her gyrations to persuade a crowd of men to buy admission to a tent show. As the ruse works, and she slips off screen, she utters the one scornful word: 'Suckers!' Many thought it was Mae's real estimate of her audience, the same audience which had flocked to see her plays *Sex* (which according to the *New York Herald Tribune* won 'a high mark for depravity and dullness') and *The Drag*, which dared to speak of homosexuality. ('The cops says these guys is fairies.') Later, having shooed off two of her persistent and troublesome beaux, she relaxes in a cloud of feather boas onto her chaise longue and utters to her black maid the immortal bored command: 'Beulah, peel me a grape.'

Two years at the top were followed by a decade of decline, as Mae's audiences were both bewildered and indignant at the increasing moral tone imposed on their favourite wicked lady. She was always good copy for the press, letting them know of lines she had been forced to delete, such as 'I wouldn't lift my veil for that guy.' She had an apparently inexhaustible fund of near-epigrams:

> Sex and I have a lot in common. I don't want to take any credit for inventing it, but I may say, in a manner of speaking, that I have rediscovered it.

> It isn't what I do, but how I do it. It isn't what I say, but how I say it, and how I look when I do it and say it.

> Men are my hobby: if I ever got married, I'd have to give it up.

> It's not the men in your life that counts – it's the life in your men.

> Snow White and the Seven Dwarfs would have made twice as much money if they'd let me play the lead.

> Virtue is its own reward, but it's no sale at the box office.

> It's hard to be funny when you have to be clean.

By the early forties she had well and truly worn out her welcome in Hollywood, and returned to the stage, touring the world with her established favourites but adding new curtain speeches:

Diamond Lil is all mine, and I hers. In my modest way I consider her a classic. Like Hamlet, sort of, but funnier.

I'm glad you like my Catherine the Great. I like her too. She ruled thirty million people and had three thousand lovers. I do the best I can in two hours.

It is difficult to imagine in what movies Mae could have appeared during her maturing years. Her characters, all of them light caricatures of herself, were ill-suited to an age of increasing realism. Gradually she realized that audiences would not accept her carrying the whole burden of a show, and contented herself with the role of television guest star, as in the sitcom *Mr Ed*. She played herself as a prospective buyer of the hero's house. 'Come in, Miss West,' gushed Connie Hines, 'I've heard so much about you.' 'Yeah,' drawled Mae, 'but you can't prove a thing.'

Like all ancient monuments, Mae came to be revered in her old age. It may have been a mistake for her to appear at eighty in the notorious *Myra Breckinridge*, but her scenes as a casting agent were the only tolerable element of this execrable picture, and as usual she provided her own lines. Asked by the cops to buy a ticket for a charity event, she assents lasciviously: 'I've always adored policemen's balls.' Arriving at her casting agency, she finds a queue of strapping young stallions awaiting her inspection. After surveying them frankly, she murmurs to her major domo: 'I'm feeling a little tired today. *One* of these fellows'll have to go home.' And having admitted the first candidate to her inner sanctum, she is impressed:

> My, you're a tall boy.
> – Yes, ma'am, I'm six feet, seven inches.
> Let's forget about the six feet and concentrate on the seven inches.

One can't help admiring her spirit, but alas there are times when even the best of us should retire to cultivate our gardens. One shivered to hear that at the age of 87 Miss West, financed by two misguided millionaires, would return to the screen in a version of her twenties play *Sextette*. The result is hard to watch: luckily few people watched it.

Imitations of the corncrake accent of W. C. Fields have for half a century been so widespread that he is now in danger of seeming an empty cliché, especially since Rod Steiger's dismaying impersonation in a shoddy 1976 film, *W. C. Fields and Me*. Although booze finally got to him, he was until the mid-thirties a first-rate comedy star of stage and screen, an accomplished juggler, and a fairly determined literary man. (See *Fields for President*, a collection of his journalistic scraps.) He was also, when in the mood, a most ingratiating sympathetic actor, as is evidenced by his heartwarming Mr Micawber in the 1935 *David Copperfield*. All these facets, however, were long overshadowed by the act he put on of misogyny and misanthropy, an act which provided enough copy to keep him a household name throughout the world, even in the houses of people who never saw his movies. When asked how he liked children, he replied: 'Parboiled.' Having spent several filming days being upstaged by Baby Le Roy, he spiked the infant's milk with gin, then stalked around pointing at the dormant baby star and yelling: 'The kid's no trouper!' When asked by a young lady journalist why he never drank water, he replied succinctly: 'Fish fuck in it.' He assured a horrified Beverly Hills neighbour that he would go on shooting the birds in the trees over his lawn until they learned to shit green. Gradually, however, this belligerence mellowed into the character he assumed in his last and best remembered films, ramshackle affairs made for a long-suffering Universal. Now misanthropy was restricted to the growled asides of a fuddled man always behind the eight-ball, ducking from the world's attacks and incapable of settling down to an honest day's toil without the solace of alcohol in the Black Pussy Cat Café. This is the shiftless, exasperated, idealistic, henpecked rhetorician which in *The Bank Dick* Fields created for himself under the name Egbert Sousé ('accent *grave* over the e'*): His aspirations as a conniver are cancelled out by the fact that he is a sucker for the first smooth-talking trickster who comes along. In this case it is one J. Frothingham Waterbury (Fields's addiction to funny names was as acute as that of Preston Sturges) who sells him a bill of goods about being forced to dispose at a give-away price of five thousand shares in the Beefsteak Mine at Leapfrog, Nevada. He would sooner sell his old grandmother's paisley shawl, but needs must when the devil drives. The con man weaves a web of dreams about the blessings of wealth, including a country estate with a stream flowing through it, and ice cold beer at one's elbow.

Egbert promptly sows the seed in the ear of his prospective son-in-law Og Oggibly, a timorous bank clerk:

EGBERT: Og, my boy, I've got you set for life. I don't hang about these bars for nothing. I just met a poor fellow who's in trouble.

---

* Students of Fields may assume that part of the joke was the fact that it's really an *accent égu*.

W. C. FIELDS, daringly cast as Micawber in *David Copperfield*, gave the role all he had, and almost stole the picture from young Freddie Bartholomew.

There's something the matter with his grandmother's paisley shawl. He has five thousand shares of stock in the Beefsteak Mines and you can buy them for a handful of hay.

OG: Hay?

EGBERT: Ten cents a share. You've heard of the telephone company: they sold for five cents a share. If five'll get you ten, ten'll get you twenty. Beautiful home in the city. Upstairs and down. Beer flowing through the estate. Fishing – trees – a man comes up from the bar and dumps three thousand four hundred and sixty dollars in your lap for every nickel invested, says sign here, and disappears through the waving fields of alfalfa . . . You don't want to work in this bank all your life. You've gotta take a chance. Take it while you're young. My uncle who was a balloon ascensionist jumped out of the basket one day, three and one-half miles in the air. He took a chance on landing on a load of hay.

OG: Gosh! Did he make it?

EGBERT: No, and that's my point. He waited too late in life. Had he been a younger man, he would probably have made it. So don't wait too long. Don't make Myrtle a young man's slave. You want her to be happy, don't you?

OG: Yes, but I haven't the money. Of course, my bonus comes through in four days. Seven hundred dollars.

EGBERT: It's fate! You aren't one to die and leave your wife and children paupers! Borrow the seven hundred from the bank: you can pay it back when your bonus comes up. You're not a jobbernowl, Oggie!★ You're not a mooncalf! You're not a luddy duddy!

OG: Well, I've never done anything like that before . . .

EGBERT: Tell me, my hesitant friend – how does the bank make its money? By taking the customer's money and lending it out, that's what. That's what you're doing, and instead of paying it back in thirty or sixty days, you're paying it back in five days. My boy, I already feel that we own this paltry bank!

The effect of this discourse depends partly on Fields's nasal, orotund delivery, but there is enough character there for the audience to want him to succeed despite his petty deceptions, if only to spite the household of wall-to-wall women who make his life a misery. He does succeed, by a chapter of accidents, but not without a few tense moments when a surprise visit is paid by the bank examiner, J. Pinkerton Snoopington, played by the inimitably prissy Franklin Pangborn. Egbert's solution is to lure him into the Black Pussy Cat:

EGBERT: Do you ever take a little libation?

SNOOPINGTON: Well, I seldom drink – but perhaps for sociability's sake.

EGBERT: That's as good a reason as any. What's your pleasure?

★ One wonders how Fields came by this word, an archaic Elizabethan synonym for 'blockhead', scarcely used since John Marston's late 16th-century *Scourge of Villanie*.

SNOOPINGTON: A rye highball with plenty of soda. Make it light.
EGBERT *(winking at barman)*: A rye highball and poultice. By the way,
   has Michael Finn been in today?
BARMAN *(taking the point)*: No, but he will be.

When allowed to write his own scripts, Fields hid behind crazy pseudonyms like Otis Criblecoblis, Charles Bogle and Mahatma Kane Jeeves. Of the last, he explained that it had nothing to do with Orson Welles, but derived from the many English high society plays he had sat through with gritted teeth. Someone, he alleged, was always coming in and saying to the butler: 'M'hat, m'cane, Jeeves.' By the time he settled down to Hollywood affluence, Fields was a complex character, though at heart still a vaudeville performer, used to applause and hungry for it. He built into his films the old routines – the golf game, the dentist, the pool shark, the porch – but they were subject to diminishing returns, and his lasting popularity came from the ability of the mean old man he portrayed to encompass the failures of all his fans: their rage against the world, their stoic toleration of lesser beings, their partiality for some form of sweet release, their vague appreciation (through rose-tinted glasses) of the greater things of life. Through all this seeped the essential vein of malevolence: in the title *Never Give a Sucker an Even Break*; in the character names Larson E. Whipsnade and Filthy McNasty; in the scene from *It's a Gift* (possibly his best film) in which he leads a blind man into traffic. There also sometimes surfaces his real fear of death, which he called 'the old man in the bright nightgown'.* But always there is a touch of Micawber, the man who phlegmatically suffered the vicissitudes of life in the constant expectation that something better was about to turn up.

Fields of course was an alcoholic, who enjoyed the company of others similarly afflicted: Errol Flynn, John Barrymore, John Decker. His last starring film, *Never Give a Sucker an Even Break*, is an alcoholic's dream. The plot (which he wrote on the back of a postcard and for which he was paid 25,000 dollars) has him travelling by skyliner, from the open balcony of which he manages to drop a bottle of whisky. Unhesitatingly he plunges after it, and lands safely on top of a mountain where dwell the monstrous Mrs Haemoglobin and her daughter Oulietta, who, having

* When about to be lynched in *My Little Chickadee*, he was asked if he had a last request. He had: 'I'd like to see Paris before I die.' When this sally was met with jeers, he added: 'Philadelphia will do.' In fact he always hated the city of brotherly love because it gave his juggling act a bad reception. But his preferred epitaph was: 'On the whole I'd rather be in Philadelphia.'

never seen a man before, falls passionately in love with the unexpected visitor. Need one say more, except that we have recounted the portion of the story which makes most sense? For the rest, it's a matter of watching the star wince as line after line fails to work.

In retrospect it was inevitable that someone would try to team Fields and Mae West. Both presented characters at some remove from reality; both were vaudeville performers who had grown up in the school of hard knocks; both were scornful of the world through which they passed. Universal tried the combination in 1940, in *My Little Chickadee*, but the stars proved strange and uncomfortable bedfellows, going through their own routines without much reference to one another, so that the film fell flat. One must admit also that the script was lacking in several departments: it lacked wit, it lacked pace, it lacked finesse, it lacked suspense, it lacked logic and it lacked plausibility. Oddly enough it might work better today, with an audience conditioned to revere its giant talents, than it did in 1940, and certainly there are moments of greatness to snatch as they pass, like Fields's recollection, when he recognizes an old bartender friend, of an incident in their past:

> FIELDS: I was tending bar on the lower East Side. A tough paloma by the name of Chicago Molly comes in. We had lunch on the bar that day consisting of succotash, asparagus with mayonnaise and Philadelphia cream cheese. She dips her mitt into this melange. I was yawning at the time, and she hits me right in the mouth with it. Well, I jumps over the bar and knocks her down.
> BARTENDER: You knocked her down? I was the one who knocked her down.
> FIELDS: Oh yeah, yeah . . . you knocked her down . . . but I was the one started kicking her. *(To a bystander:)* Ever kicked a woman in the midriff with corsets on?
> BYSTANDER: No. I can't recall any such incident.
> FIELDS: Nearly broke my big toe. Never had such a painful experience.
> BYSTANDER: Did you ever see her again?
> BARTENDER: Yeah, she came back the next night and beat up the both of us.
> FIELDS: Yeah, but she had another woman with her . . .

This is the film for which Fields wears a tall felt hat with an extra wide band, and it gives added shiftiness to his scenes at the card table, as his eyes glint from side to side under the brim. 'Is this a game of chance?' enquires a would-be player. 'Not the way I play it, no,' murmurs Mr Fields. It is sufficient warning.

He even, for a few seconds, manages to treat the formidable Miss West as a stooge. 'Flowerbelle Lee,' he coos on being introduced, 'what a euphonious appellation. Easy on the ears and a delight for the eyes. May I kiss your symmetrical digits?' 'Help yourself,' mutters the helpless Miss West. He does, adding: 'May I avail myself of a second helping?' But while submitting to his badinage Flowerbelle has this Cuthbert J. Twillie sized up: a glance at his luggage tells her that he is a man of no substance. But he has an answer for that: 'I'm travelling a little light. The country is fraught with marauders.'

Miss West gets her own back in the bedroom scene when, having married Mr Fields for convenience, she substitutes a goat for herself in his bed. Her advice to the animal is: 'Just keep your mouth closed and let him do the talking.' It takes Fields quite a while to detect the substitution. 'Have you changed your cologne, dear?' he enquires. Thereafter Fields and West meet occasionally, for plot purposes, but seldom mingle before parting at the end with an exchange of catchphrases as they pass on the stairs: 'Why dontcha come up and see me sometime?' asks Mr Fields. 'Yeah, yeah,' says Miss West, not meaning it. 'I'll do that, my little chickadee.'

A little-remembered comedian of the thirties is Arthur Lake, who played very little besides the harassed husband, Dagwood Bumstead, in the *Blondie* series. Lake was a close friend of William Randolph Hearst, and visitors to the magnate's 'castle' at San Simeon, the model for Xanadu in *Citizen Kane,* wil find the kitchen demonstration based on Lake's choice of menu for a day in 1938; but his movie persona was so limited that one thought of him more as an animation than as a living person. This may be a tribute to the skill with which he steered his accident-prone suburbanite through an escalating series of domestic and business mishaps; one remembers a single image, brow furrowed and hair parted in the middle, but Lake certainly brought that image to perfection.

Fred Allen and Jack Benny and Bob Hope were all stars of radio before Hollywood beckoned, household names whose fictional characteristics and retinue of supporting players were as familiar around everybody's house as the foibles of Uncle Bill and Auntie Mabel. Between them and their writers the sitcom (= situation comedy) was formalized, and television is still suffering from it;★ but they had other ambitions. Fred Allen's were not fully realized. A little baggy-eyed and dyspeptic to be a film hero, even a comic one, he made sporadic forays into the movies

★ See ch. 11.

but none was enough to give him a following, and the best of his films, *It's in the Bag*, was more like a reunion of old radio gags and personalities than a movie in its own right. Basically a remake of the Gogol story about a fortune hidden in one of a set of chairs, which had already been a George Formby vehicle and would later surface again with Mel Brooks, it launched the bewildered but never browbeaten Mr Allen on a lunatic journey of discovery, and included a splendid routine in which he and his family decide temporarily to give up their search and attend a movie house outside which the commissionaire is promising 'immediate seating'. Inside, they are jostled from aisle to aisle until they find themselves out on the pavement; when they protest, they are told that although there are no seats downstairs, they should try the balcony. Up there it is the same story, so they complain to the manager that there are no seats anywhere, yet a man outside is offering immediate seating. 'Oh, that's Joe!' roars the manager, breaking into uncontrollable laughter. It is the kind of comic nightmare with which most of us are only too familiar.

Jack Benny does a guest spot in the film as the possible owner of one of

IT's IN THE BAG. A reunion of former vaudevillians trying to earn a living as a barber shop quartet. Fred Allen, Rudy Vallee, Victor Moore, and . . . Don Ameche? How did *he* get there?

the chairs, and plugs his comic reputation for meanness. On entry to his apartment Allen is required to check his hat with a girl who obviously expects a tip, and when Allen admires Benny's tie it is promptly removed, wrapped up, and sold to him for 'the same as I paid for it two years ago'. Elsewhere the humour takes on a surrealist quality. Robert Benchley appears as the inventor of a mousetrap which requires the mouse to climb up steps, fall into a beaker of water and drown. (Someone comments: 'It all seems rather complicated.' 'I thought you'd see it my way,' he replies.) John Carradine plays a sinister organ-playing lawyer. Jerry Colonna is a psychoanalyst in need of psychoanalysis. When Allen becomes a singing waiter, his colleagues turn out to be Don Ameche ('I ran out of inventions'), Rudy Vallee ('I ran out of megaphones') and Victor Moore ('After fifty years of chasing women I ran out of breath').

All this agreeable malarkey explains why Fred Allen never became a star comedian in the movies. He was the straight man, always leaving the laugh lines to other people, except when he could soft sell the audience with topical comment, as he did at the beginning of all his radio shows:

> California is a great place . . . if you happen to be an orange. The only time a native Californian will admit it's raining is when he steps out the front door and goes down for the third time. When I was in Hollywood, it rained so hard the Brown Derby shrunk three sizes. The water got so deep you couldn't tell Veronica Lake from any side street, and Walter Pidgeon started looking like Donald Duck.

In addition to the sitcom element Allen's shows would sometimes contain interviews with passing celebrities, and Allen's style was similar to that of Johnny Carson in later years. When he hosted Captain Knight with his pet eagle Mr Ramshaw, Allen commented that 'all I know about an eagle is enough to keep away from one. I am a man who hears no eagle, sees no eagle and speaks no eagle.' Still, he admitted, he wouldn't mind having Mr Ramshaw's claws in his contract.

Allen's much publicized feud with Jack Benny was carefully staged by the pair of them: the ruder the insults, the more the audiences laughed. Benny, too, seemed to leave most of the laughs to other people, and told few jokes, but he was a man whose silences were funny: once you were accustomed to his character, you could imagine his stony glare as he desperately thought up a retort to whatever insult had been handed out by his cast of regulars. One of his most famous lines was based on his meanness and a pregnant pause:

JACK BENNY. Continuing his derided film career, he took his radio cast with him to make *Buck Benny Rides Again*. People laughed at the time, but the film isn't revived.

> GUNMAN: Your money or your life! *(Silence.)* I said, your money or your life!
> BENNY *(angrily)*: I'm thinking it over!

Benny was happy to belittle himself. His first radio show in 1932 began as follows:

> Ladies and gentlemen, this is Jack Benny talking, and making my first appearance on the air professionally. By that I mean that I am finally getting paid, which will be a great relief to my creditors.

By the fourth programme the introduction had become:

> This is Jack Benny talking. There will now be a pause for everybody to say 'Who cares?'

When he wasn't belittling himself, he was being swollen-headed:

> Hello, everyone, this is Gentleman Jack talking, America's representative youth. The Beau Brummel of the air. And by my own consensus of opinion, a pretty swell guy.

Age was another useful source of humour: even in his seventies, Jack always gave his age as thirty-nine, and it always got a laugh. So did the refusal of his black chauffeur Rochester (Eddie Anderson) to treat him with any deference. They were still getting laughs out of that on a reunion show when both were old men:

> BENNY: Rochester, would you see who that is, ringing the bell?
> ROCHESTER: Massa Benny, we don't do dat no more!

From the early days Jack mooned about his prospects in Hollywood, and of course everyone put him down, including his wife Mary Livingstone:

> MARY: Gee, Jack, I think you'll be just swell in pictures. There's always room for another Boris Karloff.
> JACK: But I'm not a Karloff, Mary.
> MARY: No, but you certainly bore us.

Soon even Benny's daughter was kidding her old man's supposed meanness. After a violin recital her instrument was admired. 'Yes,' she said, 'it's an heirloom. Great-grandfather passed it on to grandfather, grandfather passed it on to my father, and my father sold it to me.'

When a few of the movies had been released, it was Jack who kidded them, and in truth, although decently made and scripted, they seldom rose to the occasion, for his throwaway technique was simply not bravura enough for the big screen, and it wasn't enough to replay all the gags about his being a vain, violin-playing old skinflint. The one exception was *To Be or Not to Be*, in which Ernst Lubitsch coaxed out of him not merely a real performance, but one of the funniest performances in screen history. Still he is letting other actors get the laugh lines, but he achieves a manner of shocked composure which remains funny after forty years of repeated screenings. As Josef Tura, the self-styled 'great, great Polish actor', he moves unhurriedly down-stage each night to perform the title soliloquy, only to see an airforce officer in the third row leave his seat for the purpose of making love to Tura's wife in her dressing room. In his subsequent entanglements with the Gestapo, Benny treads with impeccable ease the borderline between comedy and suspense, and he also looks good in tights. What more could one ask?

Benny appeared for the benefit of newspapers to feud not only with Fred Allen but with the rising Bob Hope, who was Benny's equal on the air and whose film career had a more clearly marked upward pattern. Hope's advantage was a more go-getting image: you could just about imagine him getting the girl, though he seldom did when Bing Crosby was around. (In *Road to Utopia*, Hope does marry Lamour, but their son grows up to look like Crosby. 'We adopted him,' explains Hope to camera.) Yet the picture of Hope which most people took to their hearts – and he was among the world's top stars in the early forties – was that of the callow coward who sometimes became foolhardy and then won through almost by accident.

In his early films – *The Big Broadcast of 1938, Some Like it Hot, Never Say Die, Give Me a Sailor* – you see a smart-ass comic who talks too much, a Milton Berle with poorer jokes. But *Thanks for the Memory*, though only a quiet domestic episode, was a modest success: he and Shirley Ross sang the theme song with disarming simplicity, and it became his signature tune for the rest of his life.

It was *The Cat and the Canary* which created a new comedy star. The 1922 spooky house thriller had been filmed more than once before, but this version was perfectly cast and elegantly photographed; what's more, there was a subtle switch in the leading character. On stage, the leading light comedian (Henry Hull in the stage original) played a horse doctor, a nervous equivocator who had to get laughs with such lines as: 'I have felt better, but on the other hand I have felt worse', and 'The sky didn't look any too good when I came in, but on the other hand, it may be all right by tomorrow.' Bob Hope was allowed to transform this into something resembling himself, and his very first appearance, when he is being canoed by a taciturn Indian through a dark and sinister swamp, establishes him clearly as the breezy personality heard every Sunday through fifty million radio sets:

> HOPE *(gulping at the sight of alligators)*: I'm not really frightened, I'm just naturally nervous. Eating in restaurants all the time, playing Chinese chequers . . . besides, this is my very first sea voyage . . .

THE CAT AND THE CANARY. With this modest comedy-chiller Bob Hope leaped into the top league . . . but the advertising people don't seem to have known that he was a comedian.

> You look like the jolly type, Clarence. Do you like jokes? You don't mind if I ramble on, it kinda takes my mind off the malaria germs. Anyway, here's one. A farmer had a cow, see, but he couldn't afford to feed it alfalfa, so he fed it sawdust. He sure saved money all right, but he had a lot of trouble getting the splinters out of the milk. Splinters, milk, don't you get it?
> GUIDE: Mm. Me heard um last year. Jack Benny program.

Five minutes later, having arrived at the mouldering ancestral home, Hope is asked by a nervous spinster: 'Don't these big empty houses scare you?' 'Not me,' he answers, 'I was in vaudeville.' And when to the question, 'Do you believe that people come back from the dead?' he answers, 'You mean like Republicans?', another Hope trademark is established, that of topical references outside the plot.

In 1940 *The Ghost Breakers*, a kind of reprise with variations of *The Cat and the Canary*, firmly fixed Hope as megastar and national kidder. ('Basil Rathbone must be throwing a party,' he remarks during a thunderstorm.) A year later he was playing himself, or at least a Hollywood star afraid of loud noises, in the army farce which seems mandatory for every comedian. Hope's was called *Caught in the Draft*, and an added character element was an attempt at romantic braggadocio which during the war years was seen as an admirable quality in every red-blooded American, though in Hope's case it only meant that his pretensions were bound to get punctured sooner or later.

The script of *Caught in the Draft* was devised as a series of one-liners scattered around the meagre premise that Hope was to be conscripted and end up a hero. ('Me in the army? I even jump when somebody cracks his knuckles.') 'Every night a different dame,' his agent quips. 'Yeah,' sighs Hope. 'I wish they'd do something about February.' Suddenly he sees a pretty girl. 'What a bundle,' he mutters, ogling her: 'she looks like Dorothy Lamour with clothes on.' (In-joke: she *is* Dorothy Lamour, in one of her rare non-sarong roles.) His subsequent romantic approach is both unusual and ineffective:

> HOPE: Pardon my left hand. The right hand is paralysed. Signing too many autographs. I'm sorry I'm not doing one of my love scenes today. You'd be thrilled. When I do a hot love scene, the camera perspires.

CAUGHT IN THE DRAFT. Hope the star, generously sharing the laughs with Eddie Bracken and Lynne Overman.

LAMOUR: How exciting.
HOPE: Yes, I've toasted many a leading lady.
LAMOUR: Oh, you're wonderful.
HOPE: Well, I'm a sort of Madeleine Carroll with muscles.
LAMOUR: Really.
HOPE *(to make-up man)*: More blood. Make me braver.

In 1940 also, Hope enjoyed his first teaming with the amiable crooner
Bing Crosby in a somewhat flatulent comedy called *Road to Singapore*.
This starting point for a famous series came about by accident. The
script was one of many routine efforts churned out by studio writers for
artists under contract, who just occasionally said 'No'. The thumbs
down in this case was given by Burns and Allen, and the script was
retailored for Fred MacMurray and Jack Oakie, who then became un-
available because other pictures were delayed. Finally someone had the
brainwave of capitalizing on the radio popularity of Crosby and Hope,
both known for good-humoured banter rather than wit; and since the
given setting was the East Indies, what could be more natural than to
pop in the sarong queen, Dorothy Lamour? Plus a few songs, of course.

Road to Singapore unspools tediously. There is none of the really zany
comedy which came later, none of the confidentiality with the audience,
none of Crosby's plotting to involve his partner in ever more dangerous
schemes. In this one it is Hope who has the ideas, such as they are, and
both leading men come across rather unsympathetically, Hope as an
impecunious limpet attached to Crosby's totally irresponsible rich boy
with a wanderlust. They do play patacake, which is to say that they go
through a distracting slap hands routine before punching into the
villains for a donnybrook, and that's a joke carried through the series
(except that in one case the villains punch first, and Hope exclaims:
'They saw the movie!'), but on the whole *Singapore* is a studio-bound,
soporific and rather stupid enterprise.

Road to Zanzibar is not all that much better, though it does establish
Crosby as the callous comic mastermind, and there are a few crazy jokes
as they trek through the jungle (when Hope has to wrestle a gorilla, and
the sight is so painful that Crosby has to avert his eyes, a *Censored* sign
obliterates the scene), but one really had to wait for *Road to Morocco*
before the series found its comic feet. Here within the first ten minutes
the wanderers are lost in the desert ('This must be the place where they
empty all the old hour-glasses'); a camel spits in Hope's eye (it really did);
Hope appears in cameo as the ghost of his own Aunt Lucy and makes
jokes about Columbia's current hit *Here Comes Mr Jordan*; and a catchy
song (sung from the camel's back) is filled with alienation-effect gags:

We're off on the road to Morocco . . .
This taxi is tough on the spine.
Where we're going, why we're going, how can we be sure?
I'll lay you eight to five that we meet Dorothy Lamour . . .
We're off on the road to Morocco . . .
Hang on till the end of the line . . .
For any villains we may meet we haven't any fears:
Paramount will protect us, 'cause we're signed for five more years.
We certainly do get around;
Like a complete set of Shakespeare that you buy in the corner drugstore for a
    dollar ninety eight, we're Morocco bound.
Or, like a volume of Omar Khayyam that you buy in the department store at
    Christmas time for your cousin Julia, we're Morocco bound.

When later on Hope turns into a monkey, and the camel says 'This is the screwiest picture I was ever in', we recognize the influence of *Hellzapoppin* and the Marx Brothers. (Almost concurrently, in *Go West*, Groucho was gagging an engine driver and assuring the audience 'This is the best gag in the picture.') But their audiences were minorities compared with those of Hope and Crosby, from whom any lunacy was accepted with grateful thanks by international war-weary audiences:

> HOPE: Fine thing! First you sell me for two hundred bucks. Then I'm
>   going to marry the princess. Then you cut in on me; then we're
>   carried off by a desert sheik; now we're gonna have our heads
>   chopped off.
> CROSBY: I know all that.
> HOPE: Yeah, but the people who came in in the middle of the picture
>   don't.
> CROSBY: You mean they missed my song?

Road to Utopia is undoubtedly the wackiest Road of all, even to the extent of having an inset Robert Benchley make inane comments on the action. ('This, folks, is a device known as a flashback.') When our heroes are stokers on an Alaskan steamship, their conversation is interrupted (another borrowing from *Hellzapoppin*) by a gentleman in evening dress, wanting to know the way to stage seven; and while they travel by dog sled across the Yukon wastes, Hope comments that a mountain ahead looks like bread and butter. Crosby shakes his head – his partner is going barmy – but the mountain then lights up with the Paramount halo of stars, so that Hope can say triumphantly, 'That's bread and butter to me!' There is also a classic Hope line. Pretending to be a tough western gunfighter, he makes the mistake in the saloon of ordering lemonade. Fifty pairs of eyes look up, and he is quick to correct himself: 'In a dirty glass!'

BOB HOPE in the *Road* films was always the patsy for Bing Crosby. Here in *Road to Zanzibar* he has even agreed to glide through the air unaided by machinery; but as the song says, Paramount will protect him.

The remaining three Roads are in descending order of interest – the end of the war, and the world's realization of the hard road it must tread towards reconstruction, made crazy comedy seem more than slightly immoral – but the Crosby-Hope byplay continued on radio and television until both men were in their seventies. With the end of the forties, however, Hope's grasp of top box-office returns grew slacker. The old West proved a useful setting for his tenderfoot antics in *The Paleface, Fancy Pants* and *Alias Jesse James*, but between these pleasant frivolities he showed an uncomfortable urge to play Hamlet, or at least Damon Runyon. Then he was a rather lugubrious Jimmy Walker in *Beau James*, and in *The Facts of Life* he even committed adultery with Lucille Ball. His vehicles of the sixties showed a lumbering attempt to come to grips, variously, with sex, sentiment, young people, babies and old burlesque situations; they all failed, and it was too late to resurrect the farcical coward which the world had known and loved. The movie audience virtually gave up Hope, but he and his barrage of scriptwriters remained in demand by the American forces all over the world, and he became not only the favourite of presidents but the most travelled comedian of all time, while his television specials kept him among the richest men in

America. Still, unlike Benny and George Burns, who at eighty were still pretty close to the top of their form, the middle-aged and elderly Hope was often a somewhat forlorn figure, a mechanical wisecracker lost without his idiot board, but capable of being wound up for a special event such as the Oscar ceremony, which he compered for many years.

As early as 1944 Hope's place in the heart of America was being challenged by Danny Kaye, a multi-talent from Broadway. Good-looking and zany at the same time, Kaye was put under contract by Samuel Goldwyn after his immense personal success on Broadway as the madcap photographer in *Lady in the Dark*, and launched in a series of Technicolor extravaganzas backed by Virginia Mayo and the Goldwyn Girls. They – films and girls – have worn patchily, but in the late forties Kaye seemed incapable of putting a foot wrong. He benefited, too, from a live season at the London Palladium, during which he seemed to light up the dreary streets of post-war London like a rocket, and even became a crony of George Bernard Shaw. The accolades were too many and too great, and he suffered in their afterglow. By the mid-fifties he was out of fashion, and the scripts being offered to him were threadbare, so he contented himself thenceforth with occasional stage appearances, some

DANNY KAYE, wowing 'em in the cinema foyer as he goes through the famous credit routine in *Up in Arms*.

musical dabbling, tireless work for UNICEF, and a TV series which failed to set the Hudson on fire. In his sixties a morose quality seemed to set in: the man adored by millions had become somehow unsympathetic. Luckily his best years on film, the years when he seemed capable of any achievement, when his voice and body did exactly what he told them to.

Up in Arms was perhaps no more than a rollicking recruiting poster vaguely based on Eddie Cantor's *Whoopee*, but Kaye did get to play a nervous wreck and to perform his cinema lobby speciality when he parodies some of the absurd technical credits which even then were being perpetrated upon a bored public. *Wonder Man* was in the 'Topper' vein and nearly perfect, with Kaye as a mild twin trying to lose the dominant personality of his murdered brother's ghost. He also gave us 'Otchi Tchornya' as sung by a Russian baritone with hay fever: its hilarities are impossible to convey in print. In *The Secret Life of Walter Mitty*, an enormous box-office hit of its day, he was hampered by a slow-moving script encumbered by seven dream sequences, but slipped in a fashion show impersonation of a top French couturier:

> I'm Anatole of Paris,
> I shriek with chic:
> My 'at of the week
> Caused three divorces,
> Six runaway 'orses . . .
> I'm Anatole of Paris:
> The 'ats I sell
> Make people yell
> Is that an 'at or a two-room flat?

Alas, a very flat period followed, during which his writers fell back on remakes. *The Kid from Brooklyn* was Harold Lloyd's *The Milky Way, A Song is Born* was Gary Cooper's *Ball of Fire, On the Riviera* was Maurice Chevalier's *Folies Bergère*, and all were better the first time round. A version of Gogol's *The Inspector General* was an interesting departure, but not a successful one. *Hans Christian Andersen* was too sugary, despite its hit parade songs; *Knock on Wood* turned out as routine comedy-thriller stuff. A Kaye film was no longer an event, and in the unremarkable *White Christmas* (a remake of *Holiday Inn*) he took second billing to Bing Crosby and did little of interest. The only remaining highlight came in 1955, but by then it was too late: the public had virtually written Kaye off. Still, *The Court Jester* remains a great pleasure thirty years later, both as a Robin Hood spoof (with Basil Rathbone more or less resuming his old Guy of Gisborne role) and as the nearest Americans ever got to the spirit of British pantomime. Within fifteen minutes Kaye has exhibited almost all his talents. Two pretty good songs; a senile impersonation ('Who are you?' – 'Pretty good, thank you'); some playing with words ('Did you hear what the Duke did with his dirk in the dark to the Doge?'); snatches of various languages; a little slapstick; a little dancing; a touch of romance; and a few sharp snatches of dialogue such as the following:

> KAYE: What I want to do is get in, get on with it, get it over with, and get out. Get it?
> RATHBONE: Got it.
> KAYE: Good.

The Court Jester is fun all the way, and has several climactic routines, one of which, based on confusing instructions, has a venerable Hollywood history. It began with Eddie Cantor in *Roman Scandals* ('the pellet with the poison's in the pullet with the parsley'), and appeared again in Preston Sturges's script for *Never Say Die*, when the hero about to fight a

THE COURT JESTER. Danny Kaye and the midgets sing 'They'll Never Outfox the Fox'.

duel was told 'There's a cross on the muzzle of the pistol with the bullet, there's a nick on the muzzle of the pistol with the blank.' In *The Paleface*, also starring Bob Hope, the action was a western showdown, and the instructions varied as follows:

> He draws from the left, so lean to the right. There's a wind from the east, so lean to the west. He crouches when he shoots, so stand on your toes.

In *The Court Jester*, the concept has expanded into a scene of marvellous confusion, as Griselda the friendly witch warns Hawkins (Kaye), who is going to joust with the villainous Griswold, that she has arranged to help him by poisoning his opponent's formal drink. Hawkins, quivering in his armour, is already nervous enough without this bewildering information:

> GRISELDA: Griswold dies as he drinks the toast. I put a pellet of poison in one of the vessels.
> HAWKINS: Which one?
> GRISELDA: The one with the figure of a pestle.
> HAWKINS: The vessel with the pestle.
> GRISELDA: Yes, but you don't want the vessel with the pestle. You want the chalice from the palace.
> HAWKINS: Don't want the vessel with the pestle. I want the . . .
> MAID JEAN: Chalice from the palace.
> HAWKINS: Hmm.
> GRISELDA: It's a little crystal chalice from the palace.
> HAWKINS: Does the chalice from the palace have the pellet with the poison?
> GRISELDA: No, the pellet with the poison's in the vessel with the pestle.
> HAWKINS: The pestle with the vessel.
> MAID JEAN: The vessel with the pestle.
> HAWKINS: What about the palace from the chalice?
> GRISELDA: Not the palace from the chalice. The chalice from the palace.
> HAWKINS: Where's the pellet with the poison?
> GRISELDA: In the vessel with the pestle.
> MAID JEAN: Don't you see? The poison is in the vessel with the pestle.
> GRISELDA: The chalice from the palace has the brew that is true.
> MAID JEAN: It's so easy. I can say it.
> HAWKINS: Then you fight him.
> GRISELDA: Listen carefully. The pellet with the poison's in the vessel with the pestle. The chalice from the palace has the brew that is true.
> HAWKINS: The pellet with the poison's in the vessel with the pestle. The chalice from the palace has the brew that is true.

MAID JEAN: Good man.

GUARD: Sir Giacomo – into your armour.

HAWKINS (moving forward alone): The pellet with the poison's in the vessel with the pestle. The chalice from the palace has the true that is brew. Er, brew that is true. The pellet with the poison has the true that is brew. The chessel with the passle . . .

GUARD: Hurry, hurry.

HAWKINS: The pellet with the pestle's in the vessel with the poison. The palace from the chalice has the brew that is blue. No. The pellet with the poison's in the pissel with the pessel. The pellet with the parcel's in the cellet with the classel. The plassel with the plessel. The blessel . . .

GUARD: Come along, his majesty's waiting.

HAWKINS: I've got it. I've got it. The pellet with the poison's in the vessel with the pestle. The chalice from the palace has the brew that is true. Right?

GRISELDA (returning): Right. But there's been a change. They've broken the chalice from the palace.

HAWKINS: They broke the chalice from the palace?

GRISELDA: And replaced it with a flagon.

HAWKINS: A flagon?

GRISELDA: With the figure of a dragon.

HAWKINS: A flagon with a dragon.

GRISELDA: Right.

HAWKINS: But did you put the pellet with the poison in the vessel with the pestle?

GRISELDA: No. The pellet with the poison's in the flagon with the dragon. The vessel with the pestle has the brew that is true. Just remember that.

HAWKINS: Yes. Thank you very much.

Meanwhile Griswold's aide, having overheard some of this conversation, informs his master, and the two combatants approach the joust in the same dire state of confusion . . . by which time the audience, when I first saw The Court Jester, was in urgent need of medical attention.

For comparison with this tongue twister, we should note an old Dion Titherage sketch, long the property of Britain's Cicely Courtneidge which was taken over by Beatrice Lillie and used by her, quite irrelevantly, in one of Bing Crosby's lesser known thirties comedies, Dr Rhythm. It is worth looking up for its own sake, because Bea Lillie's screen appearances are rare, and because in it she is partnered by the ineffably prissy Franklin Pangborn. Let us call it Double Damask. Miss Lillie enters a department store, makes a beeline for the haberdashery, and confronts the nearest assistant with a demand for two dozen double

BEATRICE LILLIE performs the Double Damask sketch in the company of that perpetual prissypants Franklin Pangborn.

damask dinner napkins. His momentarily surprised request for a repetition of the order throws her into a spooneristic tizzy, and their inability to understand each other drives him to seek help:

> ASSISTANT *(indicating him)*: Here is our Mr Peters, Madam. Perhaps if you asked him –
> SHOP-WALKER: Can I be of any assistance, Madam?
> MRS SPOONER: I'm sorry to say it, but your assistant doesn't appear to speak English. I'm giving an order – but it might as well be in Esperanto for all he understands!
> SHOP-WALKER *(with a superior air)*: Allow *me* to help you, Madam. You require?
> MRS SPOONER: I want two dazzen dabble drummusk dinner napkins.
> SHOP-WALKER *(starting)*: I beg pardon, Madam?
> MRS SPOONER: Good heavens, can't *you* understand?
> SHOP-WALKER: Would you mind repeating your order, Madam?
> MRS SPOONER *(pulling herself together)*: I want two dazzen –
> SHOP-WALKER *(interrupting)*: Two dozen.
> MRS SPOONER: Didn't I *say* two dozen?

SHOP-WALKER: You said 'dazzen', Madam – but I understand what you mean. Two dozen – in other words, a double dozen.

MRS SPOONER *(relieved)*: That's it. A duzzle dubben of dabble dum-musk dinner napkins.

SHOP-WALKER *(smiling as one would to a child)*: Pardon me, Madam. You mean a double dozen of dummel dabbask dinner napkins.

ASSISTANT *(helpfully)*: Double damask, sir.

SHOP-WALKER *(coldly)*: I *said* 'double damask'. *(To* Mrs Spooner.*)* It's danner nipkins you require, Madam? . . .

ASSISTANT: You'll excuse me, sir. You mean two dummen dabble dimmick dizzy napkins.

MRS SPOONER: I don't want dizzy napkins at all! I want two dizzle dammen dussack –

SHOP-WALKER: No, no! Two dazzle dummen dizzick –

ASSISTANT *(excited)*: Two *dozen*, sir! Two dozen dimmel duzzick –

MRS SPOONER *(staggering, wildly)*: Two damn dizzy duddle dimmer dapkins!

SHOP-WALKER: Madam, please, *please*! Your language!

MRS SPOONER: Oh, hell! Give me twenty-four serviettes!

We near the end of our account of American comedians who had reached their apogee in Hollywood by the mid-forties. But we should not forget those who primarily laboured, like Laurel and Hardy and the Three Stooges, in short subjects. In my young days, given feature attractions of equal merit, the cinema one finally patronized might well be decided from the category board, and my choice would almost always fall on the one which allotted sixteen or seventeen minutes to the antics of Leon Errol or Edgar Kennedy. Kennedy was a bald, heavily built, irascible fellow, who with his brother Tom had been one of the Keystone Kops before turning director and scriptwriter as well as actor. Between 1931 and 1948 he appeared for RKO in 103 short comedies in which he portrayed a suburban family man, harassed by a silly wife and a no-good brother-in-law. Edgar always intended to do the most sensible thing, but often ended up in a devastated house because his latest do-it-yourself idea had gone sadly wrong. His trademark, apart from using 'Chopsticks' for a signature tune, was his famous 'slow burn': when things went wrong he would fume silently, spreading his stiff fingers wide as he passed a hand over his face in speechless mortification before finally exploding with wrath. For most of us he was one of the family; and we could equally have welcomed Leon Errol, an Australian who had trained as a doctor before going to America, where by devious routes he became a Broadway staple in the Ziegfeld Follies. He was well over fifty when he settled in Hollywood, where he made innumerable feature appearances but was most at home in his 98 two-reelers, also for

LEON ERROL, in *Mexican Spitfire Out West*, steals a scene or two from Donald Woods and Lupe Velez.

RKO. In appearance he was short, bald and wiry, with legs apparently made of rubber, the flexible mainstays of his drunk act. His usual guise was that of a much married man who in the course of a night on the town had to conceal glamorous ladies from the gaze of his suspicious wife; his shorts were French farces in miniature. In the *Mexican Spitfire* feature series, which was supposed to star Lupe Velez, he stole the show in the dual role of Uncle Matt and the yoke-shouldered English Lord Epping, all monocle and haw-haw. At seventy he was still playing such roles with enthusiasm, agility, and superb timing.

Another book should chronicle a score of comedy performers who were supporting actors rather than lead comics. Nervous Hugh Herbert with his constant exclamation which sounded like 'Woo woo'; Richard Haydn, fish mimic; pompous windbag Raymond Walburn; pratfalling William Demarest; self-effacing Roland Young; eccentric busybody Walter Catlett; cynical Lynne Overman; bumbling Nigel Bruce; rasp-voiced Lionel Stander; whimsical Cecil Kellaway; unctuous Eric Blore; game-for-anything Charles Winninger; explosive Donald McBride; fake Italian Erik Rhodes; popeyed aristocratic Russian refugee Mischa

Auer (né Ounskowsky); Willie Best, Bob Hope's scene-stealing black servant in *The Ghost Breakers*; effete Charles Butterworth; cuddly S. Z. Sakall; silently fuming Walter Abel; whiskery Andy Clyde; sneezy Billy Gilbert; lustful Jack Oakie; roly-poly Eugene Pallette; bombastic Jack Carson; bug-eyed Jerry Colonna; henpecked Charlie Ruggles and dithery Mary Boland. They were all part of the golden age of Hollywood comedians; they sent us no messages, but they certainly sent us fun. And perhaps Danny Kaye was summing them all up as well as himself when in the early eighties he came back to the London Palladium for a Royal Command performance and once again murmured confidences to the audience as he swung his legs over the footlights, no doubt remembering what once was and wondering why it couldn't have lasted a little longer.

FRED ALLEN: I love long walks, especially when they're taken by
    people I hate . . .

8

Interlude:

WHAT DID YOU DO IN THE WAR, FUNNY MAN?

Those of us who lived through World War II sometimes have the impression that every comedy film we saw found the villains turning out to be Nazi spies, routed in the last reel by the comedian who until then had behaved like an utter ass. It simply isn't true. There *were* examples of that genre, sure enough, but they were few, as indeed were comedies of any kind: it seems that such comedians as flourished at the time were mostly away fighting 'for the duration'.

The war was longer for Britons than for Americans, and we were closer to Adolf anyway, so it was perhaps natural that all our funny men should be eager to get into the fight even before it started. We have noted that *Old Mother Riley Joins Up* was released in November 1939, so that it must have been conceived at least before hostilities began. The same applies to a 1939 Sandy Powell effort, *All at Sea*, in which he accidentally joins the navy and catches a spy or two. As the new year started, Tommy Trinder was in the army in *Laugh It Off*. The first major wartime comedy however was *Let George Do It*, released in March 1940. This was smartly written and even more smartly produced: Ealing Studios had really got their act together, except in the small matter of timing. The plot was about Norway being saved from invasion; by the time the film came out, the country had been overrun and conquered, so that a rather embarrassed foreword had to be added. George Formby played a travelling bandsman who mistakenly arrives in Bergen instead of Blackpool, and is mistaken for a secret agent. Not only does he rout the local spy chief (Garry Marsh as an orchestra leader transmitting musically coded messages); he also has a dream in which he descends through the German sky to knock Hitler for six. (The film's American title was in fact *To Hell with Hitler*.) Would it had been so easy, George,

LET GEORGE DO IT. You may guess correctly that George Formby will eventually triumph over the wiles of Nazi spy Coral Browne and win the fair hand of Phyllis Calvert.

as it was for you in the film, tumbling from your harebrained adventures into the arms of Phyllis Calvert and fading out on your catchphrase: 'Turned out nice again, hasn't it?'

What the comics did very willingly during the war was appear in short government propaganda films which preceded the main feature. Arthur Askey lectured on the spreading of diseases through coughs and sneezes in *The Nose Has It*. In *Nero*, Alastair Sim and George Cole gave a little lecture on how to make a little coal go a long way. Basil Radford appealed to us not to waste rubber. Elsie and Doris Waters gave cookery hints. Robert Morley berated hoarders in *Partners in Crime*. Sydney Howard's blackout was a bad example in *Mr Proudfoot Shows a Light*. In *Yesterday is Over your Shoulder*, Robertson Hare explained about Government Training Centres. Stanley Holloway presented a new 'Albert' monologue in *Albert's Savings*: the accident-prone 'little lad' went off to buy National Savings Certificates. Alastair Sim again, in *Her Father's Daughter*, encouraged his offspring to take up war work. Fred Emney was the star of *Goofer Trouble*, neglecting to take cover during an air raid. In *Eating Out with Tommy*, Tommy Trinder extolled the virtues of a 'British Restaurant'. Jeanne de Casalis in *Fine Feathers* learned about a balanced diet. And Will Hay in *Go to Blazes* explained how to put out an incendiary bomb. All this kept the familiar faces before our eyes, but it remains surprising that in times so stimulating, no government department ensured that lighthearted feature films of high quality were there in abundance to make us laugh.

1940 was in fact the war's peak comedy year. Arthur Askey in *Band Waggon* exposed a pirate TV station being used by spies. Jack Buchanan in *Bulldog Sees it Through* exposed an armaments saboteur. Basil Radford and Naunton Wayne in *Night Train to Munich,* which must surely count as a farce, though an excellent one, helped Rex Harrison to outwit Nazi officers on a train speeding through Germany on the day war broke out. Spies lurked somewhere in *Somewhere in England*, but the film made so little sense that it hardly mattered. In *Under Your Hat*, Jack Hulbert chased spies to recover a stolen carburettor. Tommy Trinder in *Sailors Three* captured a German battleship. George Formby in *Trouble Brewing* stumbled upon a shipyard saboteur. And in *Gasbags*, the entire Crazy Gang, aided and abetted by Moore Marriott, ballooned across the Channel, assaulted Hitler, and burrowed their way back in a secret weapon. Perhaps, after all that nonsense, the realities of war became slightly boring; but in America hostilities had not yet started, and the first American fiction film which plainly took sides was Hitchcock's *Foreign Correspondent*, released during the summer. Even then, the Nazi villains were not named as such.

In 1941, British war comedies were down to four. In *The Ghost of St Michael's*, Will Hay caught a spy on Skye. *The Ghost Train* was rewritten for Arthur Askey so that the gun runners could become secret agents. (The detective half of the comedy characterization, previously played by Jack Hulbert with both aspects intact, was now given to Richard Murdoch.) *Old Mother Riley's Ghosts* concerned spies in a haunted castle, and *Inspector Hornleigh Goes To It* had Gordon Harker and Alastair Sim setting out in pursuit of black marketeers and catching, by way of a dentist sequence and a school sequence which would have intrigued Hitchcock, a ring of dangerous enemy agents.

By this time Hollywood had woken up to the comedy possibilities of war. Abbott and Costello had been drafted in both *Buck Privates* and *In the Navy*; so had Bob Hope in *Caught in the Draft*. All had been big grossers. By the end of the year Bud and Lou, in *Keep 'em Flying*, had even completed their tour of the armed services; but Laurel and Hardy's *Great Guns*, alas, was only a whisper in the realm of comedy, enlivened briefly by a 'magic' shot in which Stan walks across the screen carrying on his shoulder the front end of a long plank, then comes in also carrying the back end.

In early 1942 the Americans were recovering from the shock of Pearl Harbor, yet comedy propaganda vehicles were still few, even if one counts second features from the likes of Judy Canova, Joe E. Brown and the East Side Kids. In this unreal atmosphere it is hardly surprising that Lubitsch's satirical masterpiece *To Be or Not to Be*, with Jack Benny in top form outwitting the Gestapo in war-torn Poland, was thought to be in poor taste: it bore all too clearly the stamp of intelligent thought. More to the public fancy were Abbott and Costello, preventing radio broadcasts to a foreign power in a much rewritten *Rio Rita*, or band-leader Kay Kyser being inducted in *My Favourite Spy*. Best of a thin bunch was Bob Hope in *They Got Me Covered*, fighting a splendid Nazi in the shape of Otto Preminger, but it was far from the star's best.

Back in Britain we had little to crow about in Frank Randle's *Somewhere in Camp* and *Somewhere on Leave*, but Arthur Askey in *Back Room Boy* was better, catching Nazi spies in a Scottish lighthouse. (Nobody complained that the plot had already seen duty in *The Ghost Train*, *Oh Mr Porter* and *Ask a Policeman*.) Askey then went semi-serious in *King Arthur was a Gentleman*, becoming a war hero when he believed he owned King Arthur's sword; and something similar happened to Tommy Trinder, sabotaging enemy machinery in *The Foreman Went to France*. Luckily, they both recovered. In *We'll Smile Again*, Flanagan and Allen uncovered spies in a film studio; in *Gert and Daisy Clean Up* it was black marketeers, and in *The Balloon Goes Up* lady comics Revnell and West ('the long and the short of it') found spies on a barrage balloon site.

SOMEWHERE IN CAMP. Sergeant Harry Korris understandably unimpressed when Frank Randle says 'Aah!' The onlookers in braces are Dan Young and little Robbie Vincent ('Let me tell you . . .')

Best of the year, though not in brilliant form, was Will Hay: in *The Black Sheep of Whitehall* he uncovered spies in a nursing home, while in *The Goose Steps Out* he impersonated a Nazi spy and went to Germany, where in the film's best scene he instructed a class of Hitler Youth in giving the V sign to Hitler (the wrong way round, of course).

In 1943 Hollywood won by a short head. Bob Hope in *Let's Face It* captured a Nazi U-boat in Long Island Sound, and Red Skelton routed spies in *I Dood It*. In *Rookies in Burma*, Wally Brown and Alan Carney became the only comedians to escape from a Japanese prisoner-of-war camp; nobody else seems to have thought it a funny idea, though early in 1944, in *Up in Arms*, Danny Kaye, having been reluctantly drafted, was briefly captured by the Japanese. In *Make Your Own Bed*, Jack Carson found a radio station to be riddled with enemy agents, and Laurel and Hardy in *The Big Noise* quite accidentally rounded up a spy ring. (In *Air Raid Wardens* they looked after the home front with equal incompetence.)

Back across the water in 1943, George Formby was in the Home Guard in *Get Cracking*, a lively comedy which may have given *Dad's*

Army a few ideas. Gordon Harker in *Warn that Man* proved that you can't even trust a peer of the realm: he may be a Nazi spy in disguise. The film of Tommy Handley's *It's That Man Again* took place in a bombed theatre; *Old Mother Riley Detective* had the redoubtable dame catching black marketeers; Revnell and West were Land Army girls in *Up with the Lark*; at the end of the year George Formby was back catching navy spies in *Bell Bottom George*; and Arthur Askey ran an escort agency for lonely soldiers in *Miss London Ltd.*

It seems that by the middle of 1944 the industry thought we were so close to winning the war that it was unnecessary to laugh our way to victory. There were no major war comedies at all, and the only lesser example, *Dreaming*, touched very briefly on the subject and was far from Flanagan and Allen's best. As for 1945, there was only the Marx Brothers' *A Night in Casablanca*, in which the villains were *post-war* Nazis in hiding; while in Britain George Formby was seen in his last film, *George in Civvy Street*. The war was over. We seemed at the time to have joked our way through it; but it must have been mostly on radio.

GASBAGS. The Crazy Gang burrow into Germany, and Teddy Knox impersonates Hitler. Others in disguise: Naughton, Gold, Nervo, Allen, and Flanagan as Goering.

9

Nothing to laugh at at all:

POST-WAR BRITISH COMEDY
AND THE GRIP OF TELEVISION

They were grim times, those post-war austerity years. No food, no coal, and not much to make us laugh. Noël Coward, rebuked for laughing at the international situation in 'Don't let's be Beastly to the Germans', was allowed to laugh retrospectively at the decline of empire in his brilliant 1945 song performed by two befuddled elderly officers drinking themselves silly in the mess:

> Whatever became of old Shelley?
> Is it true that young Briggs was cashiered
> For riding quite nude on a push-bike through Delhi
> The day the new Viceroy appeared?
> Have you had any word
> Of that bloke in the Third?
> Was it Southerby, Sedgwick, or Sim?
> They had him thrown out of the club in Bombay
> For, apart from his mess bills exceeding his pay,
> He took to pig-sticking in quite the wrong way . . .
> I wonder what happened to him?

And by the time 1951 came along, nobody could reasonably object to his poking a little fun at the very idea of Britons spending millions on a Festival of Britain to cheer themselves up, at a time when there was still nothing to be cheerful about:

> Face the future undismayed,
> Pray for further Marshall Aid,
> Have the toast from Cavalcade
> Drastically rewritten . . .

It was indeed the beginning of the age of satire, but Britons were then so ill-attuned to the genre that Coward was considered merely irrelevant. What the nation needed was cheering up, and Coward showed no sign of being willing to perform that function, certainly not in his 1952 song for the *Globe Revue*:

> There are bad times just around the corner,
> The horizon's gloomy as can be:
> There are black birds over the greyish cliffs of Dover
> And the rats are beginning to leave the BBC . . .

None of the pre-war comedy stars was still around in the late forties, not at least in top recordable form, and it would be a long haul before they were replaced, if they ever were. There were comedy actors, of course, as opposed to comedians: Alec Guinness, for one, could not be ignored. But he wasn't a comic around whom a script was built: he was a serious actor who brilliantly played comic roles. So were George Cole and Alastair Sim and Margaret Rutherford, all of whom by 1951 we

THE HAPPIEST DAYS OF YOUR LIFE. With Alastair Sim and Margaret Rutherford billed, you could start laughing at this one while you were still in the queue.

were taking for comedians, taking them gratefully because there was no other obvious choice. *The Happiest Days of Your Life*, indeed, remains one of the funniest British comedies of all, vibrant with wit and professionalism from first shot to last. What of equal merit had we had from the *soi-disant* comics since the end of the war? Nothing from George Formby or Gracie Fields or Max Miller. Will Hay had died. So had Sid Field, whose second and last starring vehicle, *Cardboard Cavalier*, was a period extravaganza at least superior to his first, much vaunted super-production *London Town* which, although it preserved four of his best sketches, came at the audience like lumpy porridge. Field was a pleasing droll with mobile limbs and facial features, but when looking now at these sketches, rediscovered after 40 years, we have to wonder whether he was such a great comedian as was made out at the time. His photographer sketch is an accumulation of obvious campery, and the golf lesson makes rather elementary play, Abbott and Costello style, with the confusions attendant on such instructions as 'Make the tee', 'Address the ball' and 'Let's go'. The film did not help by presenting them without audience laughter, even though they were supposed to be part of a stage revue.

Nor were we likely to be grateful for such unschooled fragments as Sandy Powell in *Cup Tie Honeymoon*, or Frank Randle in a scarcely edited farrago called *Holidays with Pay*, or Hal Monty (supported by a young man called Max Bygraves) in *Bless 'Em All* and *Skimpy in the Navy*. As for Tommy Trinder, he was reduced to appearing in a cheapjack army comedy called *You Lucky People*, photographed through a lens with a flaw in it.

It was fortunate indeed for the good name of British laughter-making that this depressing period in the history of stand-up comedy was enlivened by the rise to international eminence of Ealing Studios, whose trademark between 1947 and 1953 introduced at least half a dozen undeniable classics in the field of theme comedy. The theme was usually that of the underdog winning out against authority, and there was seldom a single hero: these were stories of community and tradition, based on real backgrounds and factual situations, but elaborated almost to the point of fantasy by whimsical plot development and characterization. The little studio on Ealing Green, through its development in the hands of such predecessors as Associated Talking Pictures, had always been a reliable source of fun and frolic. It had produced most of the Gracie Fields and George Formby features, and the later extravaganzas of Will Hay and Tommy Trinder, and its present expertise was largely attributable to the wisdom and experience of

Michael Balcon, a British equivalent of Louis B. Mayer, with the taste of David O. Selznick.

Balcon was a benevolent despot, but everything that came out of Ealing was a genuine team effort. Writers were highly regarded, and the team which worked there as a literary repertory company included John Dighton, Angus MacPhail, Roger MacDougall and T. E. B. Clarke. On the directorial roster were Anthony Kimmins, Basil Dearden, Marcel Varnel, Walter Forde, Alberto Cavalcanti, Charles Crichton, Harry Watt and Robert Hamer. Through the forties one can trace early suggestions of the Ealing comedy which was to be: in the slick ensemble playing of *Saloon Bar* (1940), in the unspoiled village setting of *Went the Day Well?* (1942), in the social consciousness of *They Came to a City* (1944), in the upper-middle-class country milieu of *Dead of Night* (1945), in the cameraderie between classes of *The Captive Heart* (1946), in the low-life East End community of *It Always Rains on Sunday* (1947). It was however not *until* 1947 that the first full-blown 'Ealing comedy' arrived.

This was *Hue and Cry*, directed by the ill-starred Henry Cornelius (after this happy beginning he died a few years later while still in his forties) from a script by T. E. B. Clarke. Here was a starkly realistic setting, the bombed East End of London, but on to it was grafted the most whimsical of plots: ignorant teenage boys uncover a group of criminals operating through subtle changes in the stories written for a boys' paper by an eccentric old recluse. (This key cameo was contributed by Alastair Sim, a perfect Ealing type who astonishingly made no further films for the studio.) The ingenuity of the contrasts involved proved as close to a new concept of comedy as the critics needed to laud the effort to the skies; and as a result of their encouragement there emerged from the same team two years later a second London bombsite comedy called *Passport to Pimlico*. This enterprising lark set itself up as a cheerful protest at the continuing so long into peace of wartime restrictions: the plot pivot was the discovery (by explosion) that part of London belonged to ancient Burgundy and was therefore not subject to post-war rationing. The twists and turns were a bit convoluted for some, and need explaining to audiences forty years later, but there was no doubt of the warmth accorded to the film's freshness and to its familiar cast including Stanley Holloway, Sidney Tafler, Raymond Huntley, Naunton Wayne, Basil Radford, John Slater and Margaret Rutherford.

Almost simultaneously Ealing released *Whisky Galore*, remote in setting, simple of story and abounding in pictorial style: it concerned the devices adopted by crafty Scottish islanders to prevent authority finding

out about their stealing of whisky from a wreck. There was an inimitably wry, tongue-in-cheek quality about this little film. My favourite
line covered a shot of umpteen children running one by one from a
crofter's cottage. 'The islanders,' comments the off-screen voice, 'are a
people of few and simple pleasures.' Of a mainly Scottish cast Jean
Cadell, Gordon Jackson, Morland Graham, Duncan Macrae and John
Gregson stood out, with Basil Radford and Catherine Lacey maintain-
ing the stiff upper lip of the British.

As though to establish the versatility of Balcon's boys, there appeared
in the very same month as *Whisky Galore* the wildly untypical *Kind
Hearts and Coronets*, a Victorian melodrama rewritten as a comedy of bad
manners in the style of Saki. Ealing never attempted anything like it
again, and its aristocratic subtleties were not entirely to the public fancy,
but at least the studio brought them off in high style. Dennis Price as the
wronged avenger gave his only classic performance, and Alec Guinness
in the cameo roles of all eight victims firmly fixed his claim to a star
career.

Anti-climax was inevitable. The next, eagerly anticipated Ealing
product was a drably disappointing multi-drama called *Train of Events*,
the next Guinness comedy a slight affair called *A Run for your Money*,
about Welsh football fans on the spree in London. *The Blue Lamp*,
however, though a pale imitation of Hollywood's *The Naked City*, had
plenty of the kind of humour and sentiment which the man and woman
in the street could appreciate, and was a box-office smash, apart from
launching Jack Warner on a twenty-year television career as 'Dixon of
Dock Green'. Still, it seems odd in retrospect that nearly two years
passed between *Kind Hearts* and the next Ealing comedy to be critically
favoured. This was *The Lavender Hill Mob*, which appeared in June 1951
and was considered a comic masterpiece, despite the censor's imposition
of an ending in which the delightful amateur bank robbers get caught.
Guinness's addition of a bulge to his neck and years to his age was the
kind of performance that attracts awards, though Stanley Holloway in a
showier part was no less memorable.

More obviously satirical, and indeed a cinematic *tour de force*, was *The
Man in the White Suit*, which emerged less than two years later. A
rejuvenated Guinness played victim rather than protagonist in this
skilful fable about a man who invents an imperishable cloth and is made
to wish he hadn't. Memory puts him behind the sound effects and the
cameo roles, notably those played by Cecil Parker, Ernest Thesiger,
George Benson and Henry Mollison. The critics proclaimed an instant
classic, but the public would have preferred something broader.

Ealing had remained a provider of 'straight' films – *The Overlanders, Scott of the Antarctic, Where No Vultures Fly* and *Mandy* were all theirs – and it did not take long for the critics to start dismissing the comedy genre they had 'discovered' as nothing very new. The turning point, in fact, came as early as 1953 with *The Titfield Thunderbolt*, not only the first to be graced by colour but which with hindsight may seem the best Ealing comedy of all. I remember the eager anticipation of the crowds which packed the Odeon Leicester Square for the press show, and the shrugs of disappointment afterwards from the professional scribes. 'Old hat,' they said. Yet *The Titfield Thunderbolt* has an immense variety of virtues to display, not least its affectionate and detailed description of a rural England which even now obstinately refuses to disappear. Here were the vicar, the bishop, the barmaid, the poacher, the commuter and the young squire, all joining forces to prevent their local railway line from being axed, and despite some reliance on formula plotting the tale rose to several exciting and amusing climaxes, abetted by sterling performances from George Relph, Godfrey Tearle, Gabrielle Brune, Hugh Griffith, Naunton Wayne, John Gregson, and Stanley Holloway as the local wealthy toper who finances the enterprise because on a private railway he can drink all day. 'Here's to our two magnificent generals,' he toasts: 'General Gordon and General Booth.'

Now, however, the short Ealing comedy boom was virtually over. The studio was to continue for three more years in full production before being gobbled up by MGM and having its premises sold to the BBC, but those years produced more misses than hits: *The Square Ring, Meet Mr Lucifer, The Love Lottery, Touch and Go, The Rainbow Jacket.* Certainly *The Maggie* was half OK, but *The Magnet* was not. *Lease of Life* was a gentle tragedy built from Ealing's normal comedy ingredients; *The Night My Number Came Up* seemed at the time an uneasy departure into the land of dreams; *Out of the Clouds* was appalling by any standard. *The Cruel Sea* touched epic quality, but *Dunkirk*, another war story, was nowhere near it. I have never understood the affection felt in some quarters for *The Ladykillers*, which seems to me a clumsy and obvious black comedy lumbering on well beyond its natural length; and the last Ealing comedies of all, *Barnacle Bill* and *Davy*, are pale shadows of the studio's classic form. The period's best film in the Ealing style was *Father Brown* with Alec Guinness, and that was made for Columbia by an independent company. Michael Balcon would have been proud of it.

When cinema audiences had no further use for the Ealing comedy spirit, and when the studio had lost the knack of generating it, it was transferred more or less intact to television, where it has remained ever since: ironically, cinema versions were later made of the series which delighted most television viewers. 1986's *Langley Bottom* series, though not an unqualified success, amiably tried to recapture the village life of *The Titfield Thunderbolt*. But in the fifties, when television techniques were cruder, it seemed appropriate to revert to the styles of Formby and Hay: thus *Whacko* with Jimmy Edwards (film version, *Bottoms Up*), thus Peggy Mount and David Kossoff in *The Larkins* (film version, *Inn for Trouble*), thus *The Army Game* (film version, *I Only Arsked*), a very obvious barrack-room comedy which was transmitted live from the stage of the Chelsea Palace. Eric Sykes, who wrote his own stuff, pleased a nation with simple domestic goings-on, as did George Cole with the middle-class inanities of *A Life of Bliss*. *Bootsie and Snudge* at least added a touch of fantasy to its picture of life in a London club, and one felt that Alfie Bass and Bill Fraser, graduates from *The Army Game*, were comic creations of some resilience, who like Abbott and Costello (if not Laurel and Hardy) could have survived exposure against a variety of foreign and historical backgrounds. But for whatever reason, the opportunity was missed. With rather more certainty, 1961's *The Rag Trade* brought comic style and spirit into its peep behind the scenes of a dressmaking establishment, and *Our Man at St Marks* provided a light-hearted but convincing image of a suburban parish (as did *All Gas and Gaiters* of a bishop's palace). *The Likely Lads* was certainly the first British comedy to be set in urban Northumberland, and its heroes, James Bolam and Rodney Bewes, became household words.

Through the decade one remembers with pleasure *Never Mind the Quality Feel the Width*, about the incompatibility of a Jewish and an Irish tailor; *Doctor in the House* and various sequels, from the films; and the resonant low life of *On the Buses, The Dustbinmen, Nearest and Dearest* and *Steptoe and Son*, which last was Galton and Simpson's rewriting of Hancock (see p. 211) and Sid James after Hancock left them for what he mistakenly thought were better times. This was low comedy aimed at the *Sunday Times* set, as were the 'new generation' classroom antics of *Please Sir*. All classes in the end warmed to them, as they did for different reasons to the impeccably observed wartime nostalgia of *Dad's Army*, in which a gaggle of senior citizens had the acting time of their lives as a platoon of the incompetent but indomitable Home Guard. And Wendy Craig weathered several changes of status and title in a series of domestic comedies which began with *Not in Front of the Children*. It is notable that none of these sixties comedies had anything at all to do with the swinging London which was then preoccupying tourists, film-makers and journalists; also that six of the nine series mentioned in this paragraph were rewarded with feature film versions which did ex-tremely well in cinemas that would certainly not have financed the original concepts. Television had become a starmaker.

The seventies brought still more domestic comedies: *Father Dear Father* was upper class, *Happy Ever After* and *Bless This House* lower-middle. Old age had its fling in *Last of the Summer Wine* and *For the Love of Ada*, while Ronnie Barker in *Open All Hours* was a lustful shopkeeper knocking sixty. But a touch of sophistication had crept into such shows as *The Liver Birds*, and *Yes Honestly* and *A Man about the House* and *The Lovers*, and the farce of *Love Thy Neighbour* had a point or two to make about race relations. (Britain's first black show, *The Fosters*, turned up in 1976.)

As befits a country with music hall traditions, ribaldry was not neglected. The department store farce *Are You Being Served?* looked after that, with its insistence on jokes about effeminacy and ladies' knickers, and a strong element of camp crept into *It Ain't Half Hot, Mum*, detailing the wartime Indian adventures of an army concert party. Even slapstick was catered for, in the curious *Some Mothers Do Have 'Em*, in which Michael Crawford teetered on ladders as the intolerably accident-prone wimp Frank Spencer. Low life was back in *Porridge*, a clever prison comedy with Ronnie Barker as an old lag, and *Rising Damp*, which starred Leonard Rossiter as a wily slum landlord; both took a sour look at life. Rossiter also served in *The Fall and Rise of Reginald Perrin*, as a frustrated middle-aged commuter. Further up the social scale, *The Good Life* gave an edge to its contrast of a self-sufficiency couple with their well-heeled neighbours. Newish ground was broken by *To The Manor Born*, with Penelope Keith as a bankrupt landowner forced to inhabit the lodge while the main property is taken over by a *nouveau riche* tradesman. Arthur Lowe had several lucky strikes as intolerant senior citizens, better as the absent-minded *Potter* than as the priest in *Bless Me Father*. Elaine Stritch was the strident American in London, taught a few tricks by her butler, Donald Sinden, in *Two's Company*, and Sinden also appeared with Windsor Davies in a comedy of antique dealers, *Never the Twain*. Coming into the eighties, perhaps the sharpest of all sitcoms was *Yes, Minister*, whose comic account of doings in darkest Whitehall was supposed by many to be close to the real thing.

Zany comedy is never far away from the British. In the fifties, Anthony Newley wrote and appeared in a valiant failed attempt called *The Strange World of Gurney Slade*. The influence of the radio Goons filtered through into such series as *Idiot Weekly Price 2d*, *At Last the 1948*

Show and *A Show Called Fred*, and *That Was the Week That Was* gave it further impetus, preparing the way for *Monty Python's Flying Circus* and *Not the Nine o'Clock News*. And if all sitcoms grew franker with the years, the zanies just grew ruder.

Success in British television comedy is as much a matter of good luck as of good management. All the above comedies suffer commercially by comparison with their more prolific American counterparts, which are scheduled in batches of twenty-six and thirty-nine. Such long seasons may be exhausting for all concerned, but at least they establish the concept. British programme controllers, with the honourable exception of Lew Grade, have always thought timidly in sixes and sevens, and in terms of cancellation if a show does not catch on immediately. Only at the BBC have comedies like *Hi De Hi* and *'Allo 'Allo* been given a chance to recover from their early doldrums, and if there is one thing to be learned about British audiences, it is that though they may not much care for a concept on first acquaintance, they welcome it back like an old friend. But still the British treat comedy as a cottage industry, and are content to remain influential in America by selling formats rather than programmes. Thus *Home to Roost* appears in the US, with other actors, as *You Again?*; *A Man about the House* as *Three's Company*; *George and Mildred* as *The Ropers*; *Till Death Us Do Part* as *All in the Family*; and *Porridge* as *On the Rocks*. Having set up such *doppelgänger*, British creative talents prefer to pass on to something else rather than drive even the finest of formats into the ground. Only thirteen episodes of *Fawlty Towers* were ever made; *Steptoe and Son* struggled up to forty; *The Army Game* reached 153. That's still a long way behind Lucille Ball, who in her three long-running series, not counting the one she began in 1986 at the age of seventy-five, reached 479.

This cursory survey of British television comedy has left British cinema thirty-odd years behind. Let us return to the very early fifties, when less than one family in a hundred had a set in the living room.

As the fifties established themselves in British cinema, we were offered what looked like the first new low comic for aeons, Ronald Shiner, who starred as the sergeant in *Reluctant Heroes* and the spiv in *Worm's Eye View*. Shiner of course had long been familiar as a cockney supporting actor, and that is exactly what he remained even when billed above the title. The strain especially showed when he was handed a reworking of some other star's script. He was expected to be Jack Hulbert in *Up to his Neck* (*Jack Ahoy*) and Will Hay in *Top of the Form* (*Good Morning Boys*), and he simply couldn't manage to be either. Not that he had any strong

competition, unless one counts Norman Wisdom, who had a remarkable box-office run *faute de mieux*. Producer Hugh Stewart devised for
him an extremely trying set of comedies in which the ex-paperhanger
and window cleaner, who played even more gormless than George

NORMAN WISDOM, of whom Penelope Gilliat wrote that he specialized 'in a
kind of bashfulness verging on mental deficiency'.

Formby ever knew how to be and was addicted to the singing of sentimental songs instead of funny ones, fell off ladders and down laundry chutes for ninety minutes before landing in the girl's lap at the fadeout. Even Mr Wisdom seems to have tired of this routine, for in 1961 he tried a twenties Wodehouse comedy, *The Girl on the Boat*, and was all at sea in it; then in 1969, apparently from desperation, he turned up in an independent sex farce called *What's Good for the Goose*. This cooked his own goose with a hitherto astonishingly loyal public, and apart from a few television appearances his career at the top was over. It is not a career which can be reviewed with admiration: even his very first film gag, in which he seems to be riding in an open Rolls but is in fact astride a bicycle on the other side, was borrowed from Harold Lloyd.

Wisdom was Britain's only copperbottomed box-office comic success of the fifties. Frankie Howerd had a spluttering run which never really ignited; along the way he played Bottom in Shakespeare and Lurcio in *A Funny Thing Happened on the Way to the Forum*; the latter led to the television series *Up Pompeii*, to which he was ideally suited because of his confidential way with the audience. Tall, with a pudding face and hair which looked too uncontrolled to be unreal, he worked a natural stammer into his act, with results sometimes so jerky as to be exasperating to those only anxious to hear the gags:

> So I said – no, listen – it was Tuesday, I think, or was it last Wednesday – oh, it isn't fair, you're laughing – mmm – terrible weather we've been having, isn't it, missus? I went to this doctor, you see – well you have to, don't you? We all get our twinges, you know . . .

and so on. When he recently cited two doctor jokes as among his standards, and actually got down to telling them, they turned out to be so old as probably to have been circulating before he was born:

> It was my turn in the surgery, but the nurse said do you mind if this lady goes in before you, she's in terrible trouble, her legs are stuck together. And there she was, poor dear, hobbling along, joined above the knee. So what could I do, I let her go in. She wasn't in there a minute, and came out right as rain. I was amazed! So when I went in, I said how did you cure that woman so quickly, the one with her legs stuck together? He said legs stuck together? She just had two legs down one knicker! – So when I went out she was there waiting for her bus. All right now, I said. She said yes, I must be off home to my children. I said how many have you got? She said sixteen. I said sixteen, that's an awful lot, you don't want to have any more than that. She said don't worry, I won't, not now I've got my hearing aid. I said what's your hearing aid got to do with it? She said well,

I've always been deaf, and at night in bed my husband would say are you going to sleep, or what? And I'd say what? and that's how I came to have sixteen children!

At one point in the early sixties Howerd became the darling of the intellectuals, but that fashion waned, and apart from *Up Pompeii* his best work was probably in his first film *The Runaway Bus*, where he had Margaret Rutherford to play against. Howerd however takes pleasure in decrying it as a cheapie, saying that they set the whole story in fog so that they wouldn't have to build any sets; and there may well be some truth in that.

Benny Hill, almost as camp as Howerd, starred in an Ealing film called *Who Done It?*, but his personality did not have the comic strength for a feature film and henceforth he appeared only in supporting roles or bits. He was at his best on the West End stage and in what became an immensely long series of television specials. Their schoolboy smut – they ran like one comic postcard after the other, with plenty of girl-ogling and trouser-dropping in between – unexpectedly in the seventies

FRANKIE HOWERD, whose hair seems not long for this world, has the asset of co-starring with Margaret Rutherford in his first film *The Runaway Bus*.

made him a star in America, where the Puritan tradition was just waiting
to be broken by someone so giggly, sly and English. But more of that in
a later chapter.

The fashion in the early fifties was for turning leading men into
comedians: Dirk Bogarde in the *Doctor* films, Kenneth More in *Gene-
vieve* and *Raising a Riot*, Donald Sinden in *An Alligator Named Daisy*,
John Gregson in *Value for Money*, David Tomlinson in *Castle in the Air*.
(Conversely there were several failed attempts to turn Stanley Baxter,
an extremely clever comedian and impressionist, into a leading man.)
Alastair Sim, George Cole, Joyce Grenfell, Margaret Rutherford,
Richard Wattis and Colin Gordon formed a more genuinely comic
repertoire in such films as *Laughter in Paradise*, *Innocents in Paris* and the *St
Trinians* saga (which delved rather too singlemindedly into such unpro-
ductive veins as spivs, horse doping and comic Arabs). Peggy Mount
emerged from provincial repertory in 1956 as a stentorian mother-in-
law prototype in *Sailor Beware*, but despite its immense authority her
appeal quickly wore thin.

Light satire emerged through the Boulting Brothers in three funny
pieces, before they lost their touch. *Private's Progress*, despite a meander-
ing story line and some unnecessary touches of melodrama towards the
end, confirmed what everybody knew to be true about army scroung-
ing and malingering; *I'm All Right Jack* did the same in spades for the
trade unions, with its carefully plotted confrontation between capital
and labour. (Peter Sellers was magnificent as never again in the role of
Kite,.the communist shop steward, who sighed when he thought of
Russia: 'All them cornfields, and ballet in the evening.') *Brothers in Law*
then cocked a mischievous snook at the legal profession.

These films had created in Ian Carmichael a new innocent abroad. The
victim of every army dodge in the first film, in the second he was the
very picture of ineptitude as he applied for an executive trainee job in a
confectionery factory and absently placed his bowler hat on the enrob-
ing belt, watching in horror as it came out covered in chocolate and
studded with candied fruit. But by the time the Boultings went gunning
for the Church of England in *Heavens Above*, this characterization was
out of favour, and he was relegated to a bit part while Peter Sellers did
what he could (which wasn't much) with the naïve but earnest vicar who
causes the kind of hoo-ha which rises above satire into fantasy. These
Boulting comedies, all catnip at the box office, built up a family of
supporting comic players who were henceforth instantly familiar: Irene
Handl, Liz Fraser, Terry-Thomas, John Le Mesurier, Cecil Parker, Sam
Kydd, Eric Sykes, Bernard Miles, Peter Jones, Victor Maddern, Ken-

neth Griffith, Miles Malleson, Thorley Walters, Reginald Beckwith, Geoffrey Keen, Eric Barker. Hovering above the title, usually, but with little to do, was Richard Attenborough as foil to the hero, the know-all who watches his friend's sticky progress with a sympathetic shake of the head.

Meanwhile the Rank production outfits, aiming for the funnybone rather than the little grey cells, found the predicaments, amorous and medical, of young doctors to be a rich and unending source of revenue, especially when James Robertson Justice as Sir Lancelot Spratt was around to bark at the young students and graduates. A high-water mark of laughter was reached in *Doctor in the House* when students were gathered round a patient, being instructed in how long should elapse before a wound stopped bleeding. 'You!' he snapped to an absent-minded Dirk Bogarde, 'what's the bleeding time?' 'Er, half past two, sir,' was the innocent reply.

The *Doctor* comedies were patchy at best: below this level, British comedy in the early fifties was fairly horrifying. Richard Hearne, an acrobatic farceur from the circus ring, played his whiskery creation Mr Pastry in a couple of knockabout farces for children. Someone called Dominic Roche surfaced briefly in a north country comedy called *My Wife's Lodger*, and was never heard from again. Norman Wisdom's stooge Jerry Desmonde unwisely assumed star responsibility for *Alf's Baby*, which may have had something to do with the fact that a few years later he committed suicide. Arthur Lucan ended his career in a sad piece called *Mother Riley Meets the Vampire*, co-starring a Bela Lugosi awesomely at the end of his tether. The team which was to become famous as the Goons – Peter Sellers, Spike Milligan, Michael Bentine and Harry Secombe – had in 1952 starred in a monstrosity called *Down Among the Z-Men*, and they were lucky that it did not kill their careers stone dead. Arthur Askey was back, in such semi-character pieces as *The Love Match, Ramsbottom Rides Again* and *Make Me a Million*, but he seemed strangely subdued compared with his television persona: in that medium he was still the same silly little man, proliferating new catch-phrases such as 'Before your very eyes' and 'These jokes are free for pantomime'. Tommy Steele was showing willing in *The Duke Wore Jeans* and *Tommy the Toreador*.

The decade was nearly over when an unsuspected new comedy series began, very cheaply and casually (and in fact not very well at all). Oddly enough it starred Bob Monkhouse, a patter comedian who was seldom seen on the big screen but on the small one, despite an unnervingly nervous manner, had three successful decades to come as quizmaster and

The *Doctor* series. None of the sequels was up to *Doctor in the House*, but they all set the turnstiles clicking.

talk show host. Seen today, *Carry On Sergeant* is a tattered ragbag of
ill-told army jokes, incoherent and seldom funny, but its box-office
returns confirmed that it gave the public of 1958 what was wanted, i.e.
familiar and accessible low comedy:

> Here's my excused-marching chit. My excused-webbing chit. Ex-
> cused handling-of-firearms chit. Excused boots chit . . .
> – Blimey. You're just a heap of chits.
>
> Your rank, soldier!
> – That's a matter of opinion.

And those are the *best* jokes in *Carry On Sergeant*. Unless you'd like to
hear the one about the soldier who has vertigo, and the sergeant tells him
vere to go . . .
   Carry On Nurse was better, but it overstressed the sentimental side of
the play on which it was based, which emerged again a few years later in
its own right as *Twice Round the Daffodils*. *Nurse* was simply a collection
of anecdotes about the patients in a general ward, and it ended with
Wilfred Hyde White having a daffodil stuck up his rear end.★ This seems
to have amused American audiences into convulsions, and was doubtless responsible for the increasing vulgarity which crept into the 'Carry
On' scripts from then on. *Carry On Teacher* certainly began in the blue
vein, as the gym mistress is questioned by school inspectors:

> Are you satisfied with your equipment, Miss Allcock?
> – Well, I've had no complaints so far.
> Do you find that mental relaxation always follows physical activity?
> – Oh, absolutely!
> And do you favour the Swedish method?
> – Well, I always say it's the same the whole world over!

By the time *Carry On Constable* emerged, a team had clearly been
formed. Kenneth Williams, Charles Hawtrey and Kenneth Connor,
who had been in the first three films, all had an element of camp about
their personalities, but they were now balanced by the gruff, no-
nonsense Sid James, the man with the dirtiest laugh in the whole wide
world. Almost his first words were an instruction to a constable:

> And look in on Mrs Bottomley at number 24. She complains of sus-
> picious activities at the rear of her premises.

★ In a later 'Carry On', Frankie Howerd as a patient waved away a nurse bringing
daffodils to his bedside. 'Oh, no, you don't,' he said: 'I saw that film!'

Then there was this exchange between a constable and one of several newly recruited policewomen:

> I know how to manipulate my truncheon.
> – That's a great comfort to us all, I'm sure.

Carry On Regardless wasn't much stronger on wit, as witness this scene in a pet shop:

> Got any blue tits?
> – No. This shop is centrally heated.

Carry On Cruising was the first in colour, but otherwise unremarkable except for its vacuous script:

> What's your job?
> – Typist.
> Shorthand?
> – No, both the same length.

> Hello, what's afoot?
> – It's that peculiar-shaped thing at the end of your leg.

> Why should I say it again, when you've already wheedled it out of me right here on deck?
> – I've never wheeled on deck in my life!

That was the end of Norman Hudis's tenure as scriptwriter: he went to Hollywood and was only occasionally heard from. Talbot Rothwell took over, and deciding what should go into the scripts gradually became a simple matter of what could be got past the censor. *Carry On Cabby* and *Carry On Jack* were disappointing by any standards; *Carry On Spying* was an adequate spoof on *The Third Man*; but *Carry On Cleo*, released in the wake of the dreadful Elizabeth Taylor *Cleopatra*, found full public acceptance and national newspaper attention: the 'Carry Ons' had become an institution.

> HENGIST: I plead for my life! I plead for mercy! I plead for forgiveness.
> ANTONY: What a miserable little pleader. Take him away.

> CAESAR *(eyeing a nubile slave)*: A nice little thing. Where did we capture her?
> BILIUS: At the settlement they call Bristol, my lord.
> CAESAR: I should have guessed.★

★ Foreigners should ask a friendly Englishman with a command of cockney rhyming slang to explain this one.

CARRY ON UP THE KYYBER. Peter Butterworth, Terry Scott, Charles Hawtrey and Roy Castle in heavy disguise.

CLEOPATRA: So you are the great Caesar.
CAESAR: You recognized me.
CLEOPATRA: I have seen your bust.
CAESAR: I wish I could say the same.

Two minutes later Caesar is going around complaining: 'Infamy! Infamy! They've all got it in for me!' It's that kind of movie.

Carry On Cowboy is the western spoof Hollywood should have made instead of *Blazing Saddles*. In the opening scene the local madam is looking down at the Rumpo Kid's gun, though her gaze could just possibly be elsewhere:

BELLE: My, you've got a big one.
RUMPO: In Texas, Ma'am, where I come from, we all got big ones.

Belle (Joan Sims) is not above borrowing a line from Mae West, as when Marshal P. Knutt rushes in and jams his revolver in her back:

KNUTT: Hold it right there.
BELLE: I hope that's your gun, marshal.

Nor in the next one, *Carry On Screaming*, are Abbott and Costello forgotten:

> Your name, please.
> – Doctor Watt.
> Doctor who?
> – No, Watt. Who's my uncle.

At this point the 'Carry Ons' changed distributor, and Rank (which seldom had a finger on the public pulse) thought it wise to dispense with the overall title. The public proved the unwisdom of this and the next two films were promptly reissued under the clumsy titles *Carry On Don't Lose Your Head* (about Sir Rodney Effing, alias the Black Finger-nail, and his fight to save the Duc de Pommfrit from Citizen Camembert) and *Carry On Follow That Camel*, a Foreign Legion skit about Sheik Abdul Abulbul, who worships the prophet Mustapha Leke. (The credits had become the funniest parts of any 'Carry On' extravaganza.) Phil Silvers was imported for this one, but he didn't help much.

The next fully fledged 'Carry On' was *Carry On Doctor*, starting an occasional series of 'bedpanoramas' compared with which the official 'Doctor' series was like reading Jane Austen by candlelight:

> I dreamed about you last night, Nurse.
> – Did you?
> No, you wouldn't let me.

> I keep myself fit and strong. You may not realize it, but I was once a
>   weak man.
> – Well, once a week's enough for any man.

(What was that Groucho Marx once said? 'I can't manage more than one gala day.') Frankie Howerd was the guest star here, but *Carry On Up the Khyber* (or *The British Position in India*) relied on the regulars to play such taxing roles as Sir Sidney Ruff-Diamond, the Khasi of Kalabar, Private Widdle and Bungit Din. *Carry On Camping* looked as though it had been filmed mostly in the rain, and the humour arose chiefly from campers getting in the wrong tents. A minor first – or perhaps not so minor considering that it came from Barbara Windsor – was a flash of above-the-belt nudity. *Carry On Again Doctor* testified to the popularity of its predecessor, but this medical specimen was rather too plotbound to be hilarious. By the time of *Carry On Up the Jungle* (1970) the team was starting to repeat itself ('That's a very big one you have there, isn't it, Mr Boosey?') and the entertainment resolved itself into a jungle reprise of *Carry On Camping*, with jokes which seemed to have been researched by Joe Miller:

> You would need to be very circumspect.
> – Oh, but I was, when I was a baby.

> I'm flabbergasted. My gast has never been so flabbered.

> Night draws on, you know.
> – Oh, how sensible of you to bring a pair.

The alternative titles given for *Carry On Loving* included *One Thing on Top of Another, It's Not What you Feel but the Way that you Feel It* and *Two's Company but Three's Good Fun Too*. The form, however, unusual for a 'Carry On', was that of a complex bedroom farce with little exterior action, and the *Monthly Film Bulletin* of the British Film Institute noted rather sniffily that 'the characters shy away like startled geldings from any practical manifestation of their ceaseless preoccupation with copulation.' The practical manifestation was to come, but not yet. *Carry On Henry* was a bit rougher – some characters were actually beheaded – but this Tudor romp still toyed with Topic A. Cromwell thinks of a new tax:

> CROMWELL: SET. Sex Enjoyment Tax.
> HENRY: Do you think they'd stand for it?
> CROMWELL: Stand for it, sit for it, lie down for it, what does it matter as long as we get the money?

Talbot Rothwell was still running through vernacular nicknames for naughty parts of the body:

> CROMWELL: You can't make a lot of money these days. At least while the going was good I got Hampton Court.
> HENRY *(absentmindedly)*: Very painful, that, getting your Hampton caught.

Henry suspects his equerry of dallying with the queen:

> ROGER: Certainly not, sire.
> HENRY: Your hand on it?
> ROGER: Not even a finger on it.

The film was subtitled *Anne of a Thousand Lays*, and its publicity slogan was *A Great Guy with his Chopper*. The foreword alleged that the story

Assorted CARRYING ON. Barbara Windsor about to pop her bra in *Carry On Camping*; Kenneth Williams and Hattie Jacques similarly occupied; Peter Butterworth, June Whitfield and Kenneth Connor carrying on abroad; Bill Maynard, Bernard Bresslaw and Sid James in *Carry On Matron*.

was based closely on a newly discovered manuscript by one William Cobbler: 'in fact, it is all Cobbler's.'

Carry On at Your Convenience was set in a lavatory factory (overseas title, *Carry On Round the Bend*), but did not much appeal to the public, so *Carry On Matron*, back on more fertile terrain, was rushed into production and cleaned up:

> Your last patient looked very upset, doctor.
> – I'm not surprised, I just told her she was pregnant.
> Was she?
> – No, but it certainly cured her hiccups.

Carry On Abroad was about a holiday package on the Mediterranean island of Elsbels, and degenerated into bedroom farce with collapsing walls. Clearly the production team had run out of ideas, but *Carry On Girls* was probably not the way to go, being the first 'Carry On' which the BBC refused to broadcast before 9 p.m. It was rather single-track-minded in its obsession with nudity, having it off and female wrestling, and the participants had begun to look a bit old for that kind of thing. *Carry On Dick* was better, a fruity romp past the legend of Dick Turpin, who in this version has an identifying mark on his male organ, resulting in a great many Bow Street Runners following him to the loo. Some of the gags were reminiscent of previous outings:

> He treats her shamefully, I hear. You'd never believe he was once a knight.
> – Tut tut. It's too much for a woman of that age.

Carry On Behind was a meaningless title for a yarn set in an archaeological dig. None of the principal regulars was employed on this one, and without them it wasn't the same, and certainly not so good. They were not, in fact, to return: Sid James died in the following year, 1976, and there were only two more 'Carry Ons' to go, neither of them at all notable except for failure. *Carry On England* was a crude and cheaply made army farce, full of leers rather than chuckles. The seaside postcards which had been the inspiration of the series were abandoned in favour of locker room smut, and filled with macho types who clearly did get what they wanted, which removed all the humour of frustration. Worse was to come: *Carry On Emmanuelle*, a send-up of sex films, was so badly made as to be an insult, and so lacking in jokes as to seem in worse taste than the porno movies which it painfully tried to parody. It was the twenty-eighth and last 'Carry On': a good run which should perhaps have reached the finishing post a little earlier.

The history of British comedy films since 1958, when the 'Carry Ons' began, is not exactly a tale of triumph, though it had its ups as well as its downs. 1959 boasted a couple of agreeable black comedies from producer Mario Zampi. *The Naked Truth* had Peter Sellers, Peggy Mount, Joan Sims and others agreeing to murder a blackmailer who was troubling them all, and *Too Many Crooks* was a romp about incompetent kidnappers who get mixed up with a funeral. *School For Scoundrels* took a fair shot at putting on screen the essence of Stephen Potter's 'Lifemanship' books. Rank remained up-market with *The Captain's Table* about life on a cruise linder; *Bachelor of Hearts*, about the life of a Cambridge undergraduate; and *Rockets Galore*, a pleasant but rather lame sequel to *Whisky Galore*. Even though it may not have been put to the best use, the comedy talent amassed in these films was considerable. Up at Elstree, Associated British kept its sights firmly below the waist. *Girls at Sea* was exactly what it sounds like, and *Follow that Horse* was about an animal which had swallowed a valuable microfilm and might reasonably be expected to excrete it. *The Navy Lark* was the first comedy for some time to be adapted from a broadcast series: it was a trend which would amplify throughout the coming decade.

Brian Rix and his farce crew from the Whitehall Theatre had been in cinematic evidence for some years, with *Reluctant Heroes, Dry Rot* and *The Night We Dropped a Clanger,* but they would never rival their Aldwych predecessors in style. *Dentist in the Chair* was intended as the start of a series to rival the 'Carry Ons', but it never got off the ground: one more feeble film and that was it. (Nobody can laugh at dentists for long.) *Watch Your Stern,* with Kenneth Connor, was a 'Carry On' in all but name. Two comedies with war themes were *Desert Mice,* about the problems of ENSA (Entertainments National Service Association, or Every Night Something Awful) in bringing song and dance to the troops in the western desert, and *Light Up the Sky,* in which Ian Carmichael, Benny Hill and Tommy Steele were somewhat ill-matched as guardians of a searchlight battery.

1961 brought a rash of forgettable comedies starring Leslie Phillips, an amiable fellow who could play silly ass, conman or upper-class twit, sometimes all three in the same movie. He also had a striking line in errant husbands; and if required, he could be a likeably incompetent professional man. He was everywhere: with Geraldine McEwan in *No Kidding,* with Bob Monkhouse in *Weekend with Lulu* (Lulu was a caravan trailer), with James Robertson Justice and Kenneth Williams in *Raising the Wind,* with Peggy Cummins in *In the Doghouse,* with Stanley Baxter in *Crooks Anonymous.* Later he would take over the 'Doctor' series from Dirk Bogarde. That year, too, there was a small outbreak of Spike Milligan, that unpredictable humorist who despite his popularity on radio as one of the Goons would on his own become a taste less easily acquired by the mass audience, which found him too wild and way out. He was in *Invasion Quartet* with John Le Mesurier, and on his own in quite a funny film called *Postman's Knock,* before his star waned. Cliff Richard, too, with a gang including Melvyn Hayes and Richard O'Sullivan, considered himself a comedian of sorts, and they made three top-grossing comedy musicals in a row (*The Young Ones, Summer Holiday, Wonderful Time*).

In 1962 Phillips and Baxter were still at it in *The Fast Lady* (she was a car). Coy titles of that kind were the rage in the sixties: *A Pair of Briefs,* with Tony Britton, was about married lawyers, and *The Iron Maiden,* with Michael Craig, was about a steamroller. Not many people cared: there had been too many inconsequential comedies of that sort. In the following year there were only three British comedies of any kind, apart

THE FAST LADY. Stanley Baxter can't stop, and Leslie Phillips can't stop worrying.

from the 'Carry Ons', which had clearly cornered the market, and in 1964 the mould was broken by the only entrant, *A Hard Day's Night*; but here it was director Richard Lester who was the comedian. (One more film, *Help!*, and the Beatles were played out as film stars.) So what had happened to British comedy? The only visible example in 1966 was *The Sandwich Man*, which won no prizes from anybody, and even that was devised by a man who had made his name in broadcasting, Michael Bentine.

Television, in fact, was now generating far more comedy talent than the cinema, which, not for the first time, failed to notice the ladder being removed from under its feet. If we go back to 1958, when the 'Carry Ons' started, we shall find that the funniest man in England, by common consent, was Tony Hancock, who was both too subtle and too unrestrainable ever to have fitted into the kind of visual comedy required for the big screen. Cinema comedians reflected almost none of the changes which were taking place in Britain between 1955 and 1963, the time when by order of Harold Macmillan we'd never had it so good;

according to Christopher Booker's fascinating account *The Neophiliacs*, the country was being born again with angry youth at the helm. Certainly in 1962 a television series called *That Was The Week That Was* changed the face of comedy for all time, and although David Frost was not by any means the only begetter of this return to satire, he is the figure most associated with it, and from time to time turned himself into a comedian as well as a probing interviewer, a compère and a game show host. To begin with very uncertain of himself, he 'rose without trace' (to quote Kitty Muggeridge) until he almost seemed to be running not only this country but America too, and his unctuous catchphrases, such as 'Thank you, good evening and welcome' were the most parodied in the world. The comedy which circulated around Frost and *TW3* was very different from any which had been previously offered to the British public. It was offered at *Sunday Times* level, and *Daily Mirror* readers had to understand it as best they could. It named names: *TW3* relentlessly pilloried the then Home Secretary Henry Brooke and transport minister Ernest Marples. It accepted sex as a subject for discussion, and bad language was not taboo (one *TW3* sketch consisted largely of the words

THAT WAS THE WEEK THAT WAS. A juvenile-looking quintet from 1962: David Frost, Roy Kinnear, Kenneth Cope, Lance Percival and William Rushton.

'bum' and 'knickers', just to get viewers into the mood; and it was quite prepared through humour to do some righting of wrongs. Here is an example of the kind of material used by David Frost in his *Frost Over England* series. Can anyone imagine its being put across by a music hall comedian of the previous generation?

> There was this train running through Poland. In one compartment were an old Polish lady, a young Polish girl, a Polish patriot and a Russian officer. The train went through a tunnel, and in the darkness there was the sound of a kiss, followed by a hard slap. When the train emerged from the tunnel, the Russian officer had one eye slowly closing, and a bleeding lip.
>
> The old Polish lady thought, how brave that young Polish girl is. She was kissed by the Russian officer but defended her Polish honour.
>
> The young Polish girl thought, how odd that the Russian officer should prefer kissing the old Polish lady to kissing me.
>
> The Russian officer thought, how unlucky I am. The Polish patriot kissed the young Polish girl, and she thought it was me.
>
> And the Polish patriot thought, what a clever Polish patriot I am. I kiss the back of my hand, hit the Russian officer in the face, and nobody says a word.

Another Frost gambit was to read supposed news items from a clipboard. In fact most of them were stolen from the long-running *New Statesman* column 'This England', which encourages readers to send in excerpts highlighting British eccentricity; but nobody seemed to mind hearing them again, and other comedians such as the Two Ronnies were quick to imitate the idea.

Another powerful satiric force had been provided in 1961 by a four-man stage revue called *Beyond the Fringe*, which poked fun at, among other things, the older type of churchman; Harold Macmillan; the plight of the aged; and the relationship of Benjamin Britten and Peter Pears. A long and brilliant section was devoted to debunking the patriotic spirit which had brought the country through World War II, and in particular to debunking propaganda films like *Target for Tonight, A Diary for Timothy* and *The Way to the Stars*, which had remained dear to the nation's heart.

It was against this background, of comedy being taken over by university graduates (Frost and the *Beyond the Fringe* team were all of this ilk), that Tony Hancock had risen to the heights, only to fall even more rapidly into the depths of alcoholism and an early death by suicide at 44.

He was a tragic figure, a man trapped by his own brilliance as well as his inadequacies; the world was simply moving too fast for him. Of course, those who die before their time often gain a reputation beyond their just deserts, and it may be that some of those watching in 1986 the BBC's long-awaited reshowing, following copyright problems, of a dozen selected Hancock half-hours, may have been quite puzzled by the adulation showered on the comedian since his death, especially if they knew that at the time he took the overdose he was a self-confessed failure with no hope of recapturing his former glory. What brought him down was a combination of drink, melancholy and megalomania, but the seeds of self-destruction had always been there. From the awkwardness of youth – and physically he was particularly awkward – Hancock had set his sights on power and fame; but as soon as he acquired them, by a mixture of hard work and lucky timing, he grew too big for his boots and abandoned the supports who had nurtured him and were as essential as his own talent to his popularity. His faithful foil Sid James, who was so much more than a stooge; his scriptwriters Galton and Simpson, whose easy dialogue, sharply tempered to the times, draw at least as many laughs on the printed page as can be gained from watching the recorded performances; all were deemed dispensable. It was Will Hay all over again. (Galton and Simpson, once dropped, rewrote the Hancock character as young Harold in *Steptoe and Son*, and enjoyed an equal success with it; then they too seemed written out, as though they had been born to record the follies of only one era, the one in which they were young.)

Revaluation of Hancock is not assisted by the poor quality of the black and white recordings which could be made from the old 405-line system, or by the quite dismal production standard of television comedy at that time. The camera was seldom in the right place, and the sets seemed likely to collapse at any moment: in *The Economy Drive*, when Tony and Sid return from holiday to find a pile of uncancelled bread outside the back door, that door clearly opens on to a blank wall. But one's main reservations are for Hancock's own performances, full of 'corpses' and unlearned lines, which scarcely befit top star status any more than does his tendency to laugh at his own jokes and then desperately glance to the camera in the hope that the audience would be doing some laughing too.

The image of Hancock survives all this. He started as an army entertainer (National Service), was seen doing mildly funny things in West End revues, then joined a company of supporting comics available to the BBC for its radio shows. He first became a nationally known

TONY HANCOCK. At the height of his celebrity as a master portrayer of the common man, the seeds of self-doubt were all too evident.

figure when cast as tutor to a ventriloquist's dummy in *Educating Archie*, and his catchphrase 'flippin' kids' was eagerly awaited in every edition. This led to a radio series of *Hancock's Half Hour* in which he and a gang (which included Sid James, Hattie Jacques, Bill Kerr and Kenneth Williams) exemplified the frustrations of London life in that indeterminate period of the late fifties, caught in confusion between the old England and the new. One episode in particular, in which none of them could think of anything to do on Sunday afternoon, became an instant classic. Hancock's character was that of the perennial groucher who felt entitled to a better life but never got it. His address was a ruinous house at 23 Railway Cuttings, East Cheam, and one gathered that he was something to do with the stage: he was always issuing veiled threats to Val Parnell, and on one occasion was booked by Sid to play *Henry V* at Giggleswick. When the show transferred to television, only Sid was retained as a brusque foil to Tony's meanderings. They lived together, Laurel and Hardy fashion, and Hancock now sported a Homburg hat and a black astrakhan overcoat, symbols of his delusions of grandeur and his aspirations to gentility. By the end of the half-hour he had inevitably failed at whatever challenge he set himself, and his comic disillusion gave comfort to millions who often felt as frustrated as 'the lad' himself. (Alas, Hancock's disillusion was acutely real and omnipresent.) The regular cast now consisted of familiar cameo players who in one way or another put him down: Hugh Lloyd as a librarian, Colin Gordon as a doctor, John Le Mesurier as a judge. One of my favourite episodes typified the British reaction in a first-class railway carriage to a garrulous bore who looks as though he ought to be further down the train:

> TONY *(to Sid)*: That man's a doctor.
> SID: Is he?
> *Doctor peers over the top of his paper at this.*
> TONY: He said to carry on with the wintergreen. Didn't you?
> DOCTOR *(leaning over to Tony)*: This is a first-class carriage, you know.
> TONY: I'm well aware of that. I've got a first-class ticket.
> DOCTOR *(disappointed)*: Oh.
> TONY: Oh yes, I always travel first class. Well, you have to when you're a star of the theatre. And it comes off tax. Yes, first-class me, all the way up to Leeds.
> DOCTOR *(sadly)*: You're going all the way to Leeds?
> TONY: Oh yes. I'm opening at Giggleswick tomorrow night.
> DOCTOR: Where?
> TONY: Giggleswick. I'm doing Henry the Fifth. A lovely part he's written for me. Once more into the breach, dear friends, once more, and fill up the wall with our English dead . . .
> DOCTOR: I am familiar with the play.
> TONY: Oh good. Perhaps you'd like to help me do my lines on the journey? It'll pass the time for us. I'll get the swords down and we can have a little run through.

Comparatively few laughs were provoked on TV by the episode which on audio cassette is the funniest of all. *The Reunion Party* finds Tony, fifteen years after the war, preparing a get-together for his old mates, long unseen:

TONY: It's not a question of clinging on to the past. It was the wonderful feeling we had in those days. A bunch of young chaps, thrown together from all walks of life, were joined together with a sense of purpose, mutual respect, and bound by a deep everlasting friendship that time will never erase.

SID: Well I don't know what sort of regiment you were in, mate, but it wasn't like that in mine. As soon as the shells started coming over we disintegrated. First bloke on the motor bike was off, never mind about the others.

TONY: Well it wasn't like that with us. It was one for all and all for one. Beautiful friendships were formed in those days, born in the heat of battle, and forged in the plonk bars of Cairo. Ah, you'll love them, Sid, they're a marvellous bunch of lads. The four of us, like quads we were . . . Smudger Smith, Ginger Johnson, Chalky White, and me.

SID: Kippers Hancock.

TONY: How did you know they called me Kippers?

SID: With your feet what else could they call you?

TONY: The condition of my feet in those days was quite different to what they are today. Chasing the Hun across Europe, that was what flattened these, mate. I collected these feet trying to make Britain a better place to live in, so don't let's have so much of it.

For some reason the Hancock most frequently recalled is *The Blood Donor*, but it was a poor performance: he had concussion from a car accident, and read his lines from cue cards, so that he never appears to be speaking to his fellow actors. He found this easier from then on than learning lines; it was the beginning of the end, despite the brilliant script:

TONY: Good afternoon, miss. I have come in answer to your advert on the wall next to the Eagle Laundry in Pelham Road.

NURSE: An advert? Pelham Road?

TONY: Yes. Your poster. You must have seen it. There's a nurse pointing at you, a Red Cross lady actually I believe, with a moustache and a beard – pencilled in, of course. You must know it, it's one of yours, it's next to 'Chamberlain Must Go', just above the cricket stumps. It says 'Your blood can save a life'.

NURSE: Oh, I see, you wish to become a blood donor.

TONY: I certainly do. I've been thinking about this for a long time. No man is an island, young lady. To do one unselfish act with no

thought of profit or gain is the duty of every human being.
Something for the benefit of the country as a whole. What should
it be, I thought. Become a blood donor or join the Young
Conservatives? But as I'm not looking for a wife and I can't play
table tennis, here I am. A body full of good British blood and
raring to go.

This short series, in which Hancock was increasingly bag-eyed and
flabby, often ill at ease without Sid James to play against, was the last he
could sustain. Its end coincided with a devastating interview by John
Freeman on 'Face to Face', and for the first time the public began to
wonder how long their comic idol could survive. When he next
appeared on television it was for ITV, in a night club series which
appalled his former fans. Meanwhile two films of which much had been
expected proved disastrous. *The Rebel*, about a suburbanite turned
fashionable artist, was all bluff and bluster, with the acid touch of Sid
James again much needed; *The Punch and Judy Man* was an attempt at
character study, an analysis of failure in a seaside resort. Anthony
Aloysius St John Hancock (many people had thought them his real
names) no longer seemed funny to anybody, and his personal idiosyn-
crasies made him virtually unemployable. It had been a short reign, but
it had put him into the history books, and nobody gloated when he
committed suicide in an Australian hotel. Hancock was a character we
all needed, because there is a Hancock, somewhere, in all of us. We had
lost part of ourselves.

Even when Hancock died, radio and television comedy had come a
long way from the immediate post-war years when the BBC was so
restricted by outmoded conceptions of good taste. The five subjects
which had to be most carefully watched were religion, royalty, physical
disability, colour and homosexuality. It was alleged that Frank Muir and
Denis Norden, when they joined the scriptwriting team of *Take It from
Here*, wanted in defiance to start one show with the line: ' "Christ," said
the queen, "that one-legged nigger's a poof." ' Other taboo subjects
were lavatories, immorality, honeymoon couples, fig-leaves, prostitu-
tion, commercial travellers, ladies' underwear and brass monkeys.
According to one source the joke that really got Max Miller banned
from the airwaves was the result of a wager. He bet that he could say a
certain four-letter word on the air; and he did, as part of a story about
taking an eye test and not agreeing with the optician. Said Miller: 'Every
time I see F, you see K.'

It was in this disturbed atmosphere that Muir and Norden had
originated *Take It from Here*, primarily as a vehicle for Jimmy Edwards,

though Dick Bentley and Joy Nichols (later June Whitfield) became equally popular. The wartime radio shows had stretched over into peace, but in one way or another were nearing their end, and the time was ripe for new development. Should it be towards a magazine format? Surely that had been exhausted by *Monday Night at Eight* and *Band Waggon* and *The Old Town Hall*. *Danger Men at Work* had aped the Marx Brothers, *Innocence is Bliss* had aped the 'Brains Trust'. *Hoopla* was basically a variety format with the same performers each week in charge of different 'stalls'. (Max Wall had grown into favour in this one, for his funny voices as he told tales of 'our shed' and ecstasized as follows: 'Oh, do let's have tea, with lashings of toast simply ooooozing with butter!')

Each branch of the services had taken part in a rotating Friday variety hour: the army one had become Charlie Chester's *Stand Easy*, the navy one settled into civilian format under Eric Barker, and the air force one survived as *Much Binding in the Marsh,* under the command of Richard Murdoch and Kenneth Horne. The theme tune of the last-named show was being hummed by the nation, and a particularly devastating verse was devised to coincide with the American communist scare:

> At Much Binding in the Marsh
> We're nearly always short of filthy lucre.
> At Much Binding in the Marsh

RICHARD MURDOCH and KENNETH HORNE, inimitable stars of *Much-Binding-in-the-Marsh*.

We play a lot of after–dinner snooker.
To get a brand new snooker set we've constantly been urged
And yesterday this very very startling fact emerged:
We've only got the colours left, the reds have all been purged.
At Much Binding in the Marsh.

Still the prevailing influence over any writers of radio comedy had to
be *Itma*, which had run for ten years from 1938 and done almost as much
as Churchill to raise wartime morale. It is difficult to explain exactly
why. The phrase *It's That Man Again* had originally been applied by the
press to Hitler, who in the early scripts was represented by a sinister spy
called Funf; but by the time the war started, *That Man* had come to mean
Tommy Handley himself, a figure of sympathetic authority persistently
harassed by all and sundry. This loose theme, if one can so dignify it,
was expressed in a torrent of puns, rapidly delivered to a barrage of
sound effects led by a door opening and closing to mark off each lunatic
visitor. There was Ali Oop the peddler: 'You buy nice dirty postcard,
very slimey, oh blimey.' There was Mrs Mopp the charlady: 'Can I do
you now, sir?' There was Sam Scram the useless factotum: 'Boss, boss,
sump'n terrible's happened.' There was Colonel Chinstrap the tippler:
'I don't mind if I do.' There was the salesman: 'I'll call again. Good
morning. Nice day.' There was the diver: 'I'm going down now, sir.'
There were many more: it sometimes seemed that every week Ted
Kavanagh, who in all exceeded 300 half-hour scripts, invented a new
catchphrase every week, and a character to go with it. It was all very fast
and very silly, and if you didn't catch a pun first time, you'd missed it.
The pacy signature tune, however, could scarcely fail to sharpen the
listener's attention:

It's That Man Again,
Yes, that man again,
Yes, sir, Tommy Handley is here.
Mother's pride and joy,
Mrs Handley's boy,
Oh, it's useless to complain:
When trouble's brewing,
It's his doing,
That man, that man again!

Actually the trouble was never Tommy's doing at all: he was only the
butt and the stooge, as later was the star of *Round the Horne*. But
Handley's genius was that he never stumbled over a single one of the
many complex puns invented for the occasion, and this skill coupled

TOMMY HANDLEY's fast patter made him an ideal radio comedian, but he could also hold his own on film, as can be seen from the feature version of *It's That Man Again*.

with his north-country amiability, guaranteed him a place among the immortals. Personally he is barely memorable, even from the film of *Itma* or its competent successor *Time Flies*.

So what were Muir and Norden to do? In the British tradition, they compromised. Their three-part show, divided by two musical numbers, started with microphone banter between the principals, à la *Hi Gang*. It followed with a routine sketch, which for most of the run was The Glums, a perfectly awful family of a type hitherto unseen, but which helped blaze the trail of situation comedy. And the third section contained a spoof of some imperishable movie genre: trouble at the mill, courtroom drama, epic. ('What dost thou?' said Antony to Cleopatra. 'I dust the sphinx,' she replied.) It was all quite brilliant, but borrowed, either from the cinema or from American radio, as were its contemporaries and successors *Ray's a Laugh, Meet the Huggetts, A Life of Bliss* and *Educating Archie*. Only with Hancock did the process begin to reverse itself.

As we have seen, it did not reverse itself successfully. The public declined to pay to see Hancock in films, especially when he was plainly on the skids. But a trend had been started. The ebullient Jimmy Edwards transferred in 1960, as *Bottoms Up*, his Muir and Norden television success *Whacko!*, starring himself as a schoolmaster somewhat more physical than Will Hay ('Wake up at the back, there!') and in the same year the diminutive Charlie Drake, who with his whining voice and slightly fantasticated persona, had been an unexpected TV success, hit the big screen in a tolerable piece called *Sands of the Desert*. Next year Edwards had another film hit with *Nearly a Nasty Accident*, a version of a TV play, and Drake hit the jackpot again with *Petticoat Pirates*. A failure was Dave King, who for a while had been England's Mr Television: after the chilly reaction to *Go to Blazes*, he retired for many years to lick his wounds before re-emerging as a character actor. But from that point on, every British film comedy that took money was derived from a TV original.

This was even true of Morecambe and Wise. They had worked the halls for years, but only television had made them stars. As it happened, although their films did well, none of them lingers pleasantly in the mind: the boys were used to timing their material according to the audience's reaction, and they never licked the problem of timing it for the camera. Still, they had twenty years at the top so far as television is concerned, and on the whole they deserved them. During their high peak they unashamedly plundered the work of Laurel and Hardy as well as Abbott and Costello, and indeed their first variety acts consisted of

ERIC MORECAMBE and ERNIE WISE made three not-very-successful efforts to become major film stars, but the audience that really adored them, regarding them as foolish uncles, was the armchair one at home.

sketches stolen directly from the movies by dint of notes hurriedly scribbled in the dark during a performance at their local north-country fleapit. But over the years they brought their double-act to a high pitch of brilliance, contriving always to make one think they were doing it off the cuff, for the very first time: their movements and interjections were so immaculately timed, and backed by a string of remarks which we only gradually came to accept as carefully rehearsed catchphrases. 'Get out of that.' 'You can't see the join.' 'He's the one with the short fat hairy legs.' 'Can I have the tea, Ern?' 'There's no answer to that.' By the time they became television favourites they were the Picassos of their profession, sending up each other and their guest stars from the moment of Eric and Ernie's first appearance in evening dress before the curtain:

> ERN: What's in the box?
> ERIC: He just gave it to me.
> ERN: Who?
> ERIC: Arthur Negligée. The antique expert in the next studio.
> ERN: You mean Arthur Negus.
> ERIC: Yes, I was watching his antique programme. Thought I might pick up a few jokes.
> ERN: You're not short of antique jokes.
> ERIC: Is that it?

ERN: The antique programme, Going for a Song.
ERIC: He sings as well? I didn't know that.
ERN: You're interested in antiques?
ERIC: You've seen the wife.

Sometimes their sketches rambled on too loosely to a disappointing lack of conclusion, but their visual gags and their lavishly staged musical numbers were always splendid. At their best they had no peers for producing laughs out of the least promising material. Eric always delivered the obviously funny lines: Ernie was the amiable straight man, nothing more, and if he seemed sometimes to lose his place, that was probably all part of the act. So was his determination to present to the audience a barrage of dreadful plays 'what I have wrote'. In these spoofs of every film genre one might think of, guest stars of quite astonishing eminence vied to make fools of themselves: Glenda Jackson as Cleopatra, Vanessa Redgrave as Josephine, John Mills escaping from yet another prison camp. A running gag for years was that Peter Cushing had never been paid for his appearance; he would pop in hopefully, or send pleading letters, and Eric would offer to get him a firewood round in lieu. Each show in a season would end with a variation on the same gag: the pixilated pair going out through strange doors, being upstaged by a massively bosomed lady singer or by a harmonica player whose time never came. Like all music hall turns Eric and Ernie had a signature tune: it was 'Bring Me Sunshine', and they certainly brought plenty of that to every house in the land, though for some reason they never succeeded in the States. When Eric died suddenly, after years of semi-convalescence from a heart problem, it was an occasion for national mourning. The loss was more marked because Ernie, bereft of his source of laughter, hung on as a not very sparkling host or panel game contestant. Without Eric, it became clear, he might never have got closer to fame than the end of Brighton Pier.

A major disappointment for Morecambe and Wise was their lack of success in films. They made three, but even apart from the problem of timing laughs for the camera, they found that on the big screen the times were out of joint for foolishness winning through against adversity. *The Intelligence Men* was slack and silly. *That Riviera Touch* picked up only with a stunt surfboard chase towards the end. *The Magnificent Two* found them floundering in the middle of a banana republic revolution, facing dangers which seemed rather too real to be funny. The final attempt, *Night Train to Murder*, finished up as a TV movie: after a couple of indeterminate reels it placed them in a spooky house facing the kind of cobwebby dangers which had effectively stimulated Bob Hope and Abbott and Costello. This time they sent up the material too relentlessly. Watching with a groan, as one joke after another fell with a dull thud, one wanted to tell them to go back and do it over . . . but by the time it was shown, Eric was dead. Still, for years almost without number they lit up all our lives with images of lively lunacy. I cherish most of all the moment when, opening an elaborate dance number, they stepped in debonair fashion down a mammoth staircase, the last wide step of which turned out to be a pit of water.

Benny Hill was a national figure even before Morecambe and Wise, and went on a great deal longer. His forte too was the one-hour television show, the holiday event when the audience was supposed to let its hair down. The difference was that the audience came to laugh *at* Benny rather than with him. Even behind his partiality for disguise, the real Benny Hill is an elusive figure, neither fish, fowl, nor good red herring: one recognizes the round face, the rounder body and the shy

BENNY HILL's simple-minded salute usually heralded a piece of comic-postcard ribaldry! The surprise was not that this went down well at home, but that he managed to conquer America with it.

look, but one knows nothing of the man inside. He almost never makes public appearances, and his rare interviews are full of macho jokes which one suspects to be at variance with his real nature. At the age of sixty he still seems to spend his waking hours scouring Joe Miller's gag book for wheezes and *double entendres* which can be crushed into his format of unrelated sight gags, doggerel verses and blue sketches. The public Benny, like another of that name, seems stuck at the approximate age of 39, simpering at the camera as he half-apologetically lets forth a barrage of dreadful puns and minor obscenities. Lately he has been accompanied by his own brand of Goldwyn Girls, known as Hill's Angels, who were rebuked by press and public alike for showing too much of themselves in the endless crotch shots favoured by the director (and presumably by Benny himself). The sum effect is 'dirtier' then Frank Randle ever dreamed of being, and made worse by the under-rehearsed air which usually prevails despite expensive film sequences. But these are the go-as-you-please eighties, and providing he moves nimbly enough Benny even gets away with a sketch about wife swapping which would have horrified the TV censors of twenty years ago (when the Eamonn Andrews talk show had to be taken off the air because the Earl of Arran remarked that his coronet had four balls and eight strawberry leaves, and Jimmy Edwards said that his would have more balls than that).

There is never any real sequence to the presentation. The girls are introduced as Miss Foam Rubber, Miss Unwed Mother of 1983 and Miss Ballcock. There is a saucy exchange with one of them:

> My boy friend calls me Dimples.
> – I don't see any dimples.
> You're not my boy friend.

There is a parade of howlers in schoolboy French:

La mer	Her horse
Je t'adore	Shut the door
Ouvrez la porte	Open the port
Coup de grace	Mow the lawn
Coq au vin	Pass

Then some one-liners:

She's so dumb she thinks a coolie is a quickie in the snow.

I'd love to see her in 3D. That's my hotel room.

A Mexican sketch is announced (but not performed) for the sake of its purported cast of characters, which includes a girl called Buenos Knockers and a hero called Señor (seen your) Willie. Moments of transition have silly riddles inserted as graffiti:

> Why do elephants have four feet?
> – Because they'd look silly with six inches.
>
> Why does Siberia have blizzards while
>   Britain has Bernard Manning?*
> – Siberia had first choice.
>
> Our water is safe for drinking, it's been
> passed by the health inspector.
>
> Women are like pianos: when they're
> not upright, they're grand.

One of these days Benny will surely get round to using the joke card which I once glimpsed in a London car's rear window: 'Save gas, fart in a jar.' Meanwhile he will content himself with playing both Cagney and Lacey in the same sketch (the former by use of an anamorphic lens which reduces his fat) and devising hoary quickies like the one with himself as an ancient Lothario who consults the doctor:

> It's my sex drive, doctor, it's too high. I want you to lower it.
> – At ninety two? You must be joking. It's all in the mind.
> That's why I want you to lower it.

Or the one about the ugly wife who rebukes her slovenly husband:

> What would the neighbours think if I ran about half naked?
> – They'd think I married you for your money.

Inevitably the end titles roll over a speeded-up chase in which members of the cast zoom over some country scene like demented buzzflies. It may leave the audience exhausted, but Benny is already collecting items for his next special.

The British having always had a partiality for blue humour, it might be thought that such elementary, alimentary stuff would not be exportable. Yet in the late seventies clever marketing made Benny Hill, edited down into half hour samples, the hit of American syndication, and soon

---

* Manning is a self-advertising comedian from the working men's clubs, and the butt of almost all his fellow comics. Whether this animosity is real has never been clear.

the puritan Yanks were yelling for more, like men suddenly released from bondage. It may not be going too far to attribute to Benny Hill the sudden emancipation of American sitcoms in the eighties, for instance in *Kate and Allie*, when the divorcée heroines, in order to qualify for reduced rent as one household, tell the landlady that they are lesbians, only to find that she is a lesbian too, and rather fancies one of them. He certainly must have something to do with the network acceptability of such a strident talent as Joan Rivers, a reconstituted Jewish princess with a Brooklyn accent, who swoons at the name of a guest celebrity but proceeds to put the most embarrassing questions. 'How would you rate your boyfriend, sexually, from one to ten?' 'How would you rate yourself?' On a recent English version of her so-called show, Christopher Reeve was encouraged to confess where and when he first experienced sex, while the diminutive sex therapist Dr Ruth Westheimer made clucking noises of appreciation. When Rivers turns the spotlight upon herself, however, we get no more than plainly fictional jokes about her dim husband Edgar: 'You know, last week he made love to me three nights before he realized I was out of town.' Nor is lavatory humour prohibited. Bob Monkhouse, appearing on Joan's show in return for her being on his some weeks earlier (how matey these TV folk can get when it says so in their contract), was encouraged to be even nearer the knuckle than is his norm. He related the tale of how he lurched out of a pub one winter night, full of beer, and couldn't find the Gents. So he was tempted to abandon his quest and write his name in the snow. 'Anybody who can dot the "i"'s has great self control, and the man who can cross the "t"'s is a master technician,' he quipped: 'And at least that's one thing you girls can't do.' 'Oh yes we can,' yelled Rivers, 'it just takes longer!' This on BBC2?

A television comedian of almost unclassifiable style was Tommy Cooper, who dramatically collapsed and died on the stage of Her Majesty's Theatre during a live broadcast. At the time most viewers thought the collapse was part of his act: Cooper's antics were totally unpredictable. He once turned up on *This is Your Life* to pay tribute to an actor whom he then claimed he had never met. Bulky of figure, but tall enough to carry it, he had a tendency to facial perspiration, and annoyingly gabbled his words so that the inane jokes were often obscured, but audiences still roared with laughter at the silly way he looked under the red fez which he always affected. He once walked on with an axe apparently embedded in his skull, and was generally fond of comic headgear. Appearing under the hat of an 18th-century naval officer, he would announce 'Nelson'; then, getting down to his knees, 'Half Nelson'. His speciality was the fumbling of magic tricks, through which he would ramble inconsequentially in a manner which was funnier than the material:

> I went out to dinner last night, ordered everything in French. Surprised everybody: it was a Chinese restaurant. I said to the waiter, this chicken's got one leg shorter than the other. He said, what do you want to do, eat it or dance with it?

He might even abandon a joke in mid-career and announce that his nose itched. You never knew with Tommy; but on the whole he added to the cheerfulness of the nation, and when he uttered his manic staccato laugh, most people felt bound to join in.

To return to the seventies: Benny Hill has failed on the big screen, so have Morecambe and Wise, so has Hancock. Reg Varney, star of TV's *On The Buses*, but a stand-up comic in his own right, is about to fail too, in *Go for a Take* and *The Best Pair of Legs in the Business*. Even Danny La Rue, female impersonator extraordinary (or so it seemed at the time) comes a cropper in *Our Miss Fred*. And after that the comedians, the chaps who tell jokes, seem to stop trying. Bruce Forsyth, another Mr Television of his day, and longtime host of *Saturday Night at the London Palladium*, never makes a film, apart from a couple of character cameos. Ken Dodd and Jimmy Tarbuck, likeable lads from Liverpool, make no films at all. Nor does Al Read, the Lancashire character comic who brought 'Right, monkey' into the language. Nor do any of the graduates of Granada Television's talent contest *The Comedians*: Charlie Williams, Ken Goodwin, Tom O'Connor, Mike Reid, the aforesaid Bernard Manning. Nor does Ted Rogers. So what do they do, these jovial uncles, as they inevitably wear out their initial welcome and their stand-up style goes out of fashion? They become quiz show hosts. In America this is a totally separate calling – one suspects that some of the most successful are generated from dynamos – but in Britain the quizzes and games provide eventide occupation for comedians who once stood centre stage at the London Palladium. Monkhouse on *Bob's Full House*, Forsyth on *Play Your Cards Right*, Rogers on *Three Two One*, Les Dawson on *Blankety Blank*, Tarbuck on *Winner Take All*, Leslie Crowther on *The Price is Right* . . . apart from the occasional one-man show, that's how they have to earn a crust in the eighties if they are not to fade into limbo like Norman Vaughan and Don Errol.

It was the television sitcoms which from the start of the seventies transferred with increasing inevitability to the big screen. The trend had in fact started as far back as 1955, when Peggy Mount and David Kossoff as *The Larkins* appeared in a film version called *Inn For Trouble*; but now the movie transfers came full flood. *Dad's Army* was a good one. The gentle humours of the elderly rude mechanicals of Warmington-on-Sea, who during World War II did what they could to safeguard Britain's white cliffs from the Hun, seemed almost Shakespearean in their British gentility; Mainwaring and Wilson and Pike were at least the equals of Justice Shallow and Ancient Pistol and Dogberry and Verges and Bottom the weaver. The vicar and the ARP warden were familiar types too, and the film found broader location possibilities than the TV series: there was one almost elegiac moment when a brigadier on a white horse is accidentally floated downstream on the centre section of a temporary bridge. Arthur Lowe, John Laurie, John Le Mesurier, Clive Dunn and Arnold Ridley (the now aged author of *The Ghost Train*) ensured that their images will long remain part of the history of British entertainment. Smooth film versions of the aforementioned *Up Pompeii* and *On the Buses* came next, and before 1971 was over crowds were flocking to *Please Sir*, a very modern version of Will Hay, with John Alderton as the

DAD'S ARMY. The opening sequence of the film version. John Le Mesurier, Arthur Lowe, Ian Lavender, Arnold Ridley, James Beck, John Laurie, Clive Dunn.

cheerful teacher of an East End school where the teenage pupils pay him no respect whatsoever. (The idea was derived from the film *To Sir with Love* which had starred Sidney Poitier, and which was itself a lighter update of *The Blackboard Jungle*; it would now transfer again to America as *Welcome Back Kotter*.)

1973 brought the first of two big screen transfers of *Steptoe and Son*, which as has been seen had developed from the Hancock character, now a dustman with romantic and literary ideas above his station, handicapped by a doddering but determined father who has lost his teeth but retained his sex drive, and is not above retrieving and consuming pickled onions which have fallen into the dirty water of his bath. This superficially disgusting odd couple had the nation in hysterics over forty or more television half hours – and anyone who does not believe that such material can produce classic comedy should watch for themselves the performances of Harry H. Corbett and Wilfrid Brambell – but in the case of the film versions the decision to make the dose even stronger and lewder had the result that it was barely palatable at all. *Bless this House* was a respectable version of an unremarkable domestic comedy in which Sid James passed the time when not otherwise occupied, but *The Alf Garnett Saga* was another instance of going too far in order to satisfy the supposedly tougher requirements of the cinema-going audience. The first film version of *Till Death Us Do Part*, the original of *All in the Family*, had shocked the nation in 1968, and by now the bigoted loudmouth from the East End was finding his welcome wearing thin, despite vigorous playing by Warren Mitchell and Dandy Nichols. But the ruderies were in line with more original films which had come up by the non-sitcom route, which generally involved some association with David Frost's spreading empire. *Bedazzled* (1968, with Peter Cook and Dudley Moore), *Every Home Should Have One* (1970, with Marty Feldman), *The Rise and Rise of Michael Rimmer* (1971, with Peter Cook), *Rentadick* (1971, with James Booth) were distressingly vulgar without being very funny, and the trend continued at least into 1977 when *Jabberwocky* was disowned by the highbrow critics who had begun by applauding such 'realistic' approaches to humour: as Michael Billington said in the *Illustrated London News*, 'the constant emphasis on blood, excrement, dismemberment and filth ultimately becomes rather wearing'.

For the Love of Ada (1972) was certainly gentler stuff, with Wilfred Pickles and Irene Handl as an elderly couple romantically attached, and *Ooh You Are Awful* was a Bob Hope-style chase comedy with a black edge, giving TV comedian Dick Emery an opportunity to don all the various disguises (including that of a sexually frustrated middle-aged woman) regularly found so hilarious by his fireside audience. Innocuous transfers in 1973 included *Never Mind the Quality, Feel the Width* (John Bluthal and Joe Lynch as Jewish and Irish tailors amicably at odds) and *Father Dear Father* (Patrick Cargill farcically frantic as a man beset by females). A blacker tone was adopted by *That's Your Funeral*, about incompetent undertakers, and a cruder one by *Nearest and Dearest*, a Lancashire romp with Hylda Baker and Jimmy Jewel (once of the comedy team Jewel and Warris, now on the way to becoming a character actor). *The Lovers*, too, had a strange style, with Richard Beckinsale and Paula Wilcox as prim north-country types attempting to lose their virginity: the style was what made it palatable to equally prim audiences.

A Man about the House and *The Likely Lads* were cleverly written series also innocently obsessed with sex: they both turned up as films, with added frankness and toilet jokes, in 1975. And that was almost the end of the TV transfer boom, during which filmgoers proved remarkably willing to pay for at the local Odeon what they had viewed gratis week after week at home. (The benefit to the historian is that the films will last longer, and look fresher, than some of the early tapes.) The trend did take a little while to fade away: *Are You Being Served* came to the big screen in 1977, and as late as 1980 we were being offered the dire *George and Mildred* and the pleasantly opened out *Porridge*, in which Ronnie Barker as a cherishable rogue makes prison life seem almost desirable. But the obsession of the British cinema with television was then over, for the increasing harshness of most new movies from Hollywood had resulted in a total split of audience: people who watched television no longer felt safe at the movies, and those teenagers who still wanted the raunchiness which the big screen now offered could only despise what they saw as the blandness offered by the box in the corner.

Meanwhile the multi-talented Peter Sellers, almost inevitably in a time hungry for laughter, went to Hollywood in a blaze of glory and publicity. From playing too hard, he promptly had a near-fatal heart attack, and was never the same man afterwards. After half a dozen erratic appearances in the mid-sixties he fell into the hands of Blake Edwards, a man of many talents, all minor; a writer-producer-director for whom excess was the norm. Together they made, among other extravaganzas, six *Pink Panther* films; but Sellers was good only in the first one. There, his accident-prone Inspector Clouseau was a secondary character; subsequently expected to carry the whole burden, he quickly became tedious, while grisly is the only word for the movie cobbled together from outtakes after Sellers' death. Funnier, in parts at least, was *The Party*, in which Sellers for a change played an accident-prone Indian, unwittingly causing chaos at a Beverly Hills shindig to which he has been unintentionally invited. By the end of this overlong comedy the house was wrecked, but the best remembered moment came when the cigar-chomping mogul, told that his wife has fallen into the pool, grunts: 'Get the jewellery.' Sellers, alas, was no Jacques Tati, and especially not when he lapsed into sentimentality.

The lunatic fringe remains to be dealt with, and I speak of the Goons on radio and of Monty Python on television. The Goons would almost certainly have looked too untidy in vision: their appeal was similar to that of *Itma*, with sound effects and funny voices offering just enough of a foothold for the audience to use its imagination. Of the original four, only Peter Sellers went on to become an international star, though his stature lessened as he took himself too seriously and one bad film followed another. Harry Secombe remained welcome at home, as much for his operatic voice as for his giggly humour. Spike Milligan became a law unto himself, often in evidence but seldom in order; and Michael Bentine occupied himself with visual gimmicks aimed mainly at children, such as a flea circus with invisible fleas. (In 1985 he turned up on a Bob Monkhouse show with a fast-moulting stuffed buzzard which urinated profusely all over the set.)

The Goons had originally, perhaps, been a reaction from the years of war and austerity, and their impetus was no more than an inclination to be silly. The comedians who hid under the group title 'Monty Python', however, usually had a point to make, though only they may have known what it was, and in the 'dead parrot' sketch and the Ministry of Silly Walks any meaning was lost in the laughter which greeted the antics on view. They often went pretty far, sometimes too far: one show about death was reviled and never repeated, and the dispute about their 1979 film *Monty Python's Life of Brian*, a cruel spoof on the life of Christ, still rages. *Monty Python's Meaning of Life* failed to reach a wide audience because of a revolting sketch in which self-indulgent gluttons in a restaurant finally explode over the scene in a sea of goo (Campbell's soup was used.) Their best film, *Monty Python and the Holy Grail*, disappeared without trace because of legal entanglements; a spoof of the Arthurian legend, it creates and maintains a remarkably dour atmosphere as background for some funny if violent jokes. Of the several Python talents, the immensely tall John Cleese has remained the most visible, through the television series *Fawlty Towers* (in which he played the incompetent but irascible owner of a seaside hotel) and the 1985 comedy

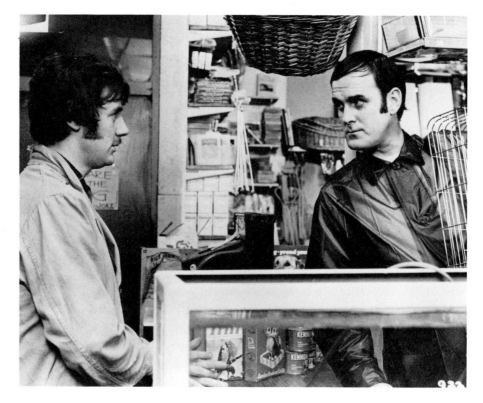

MONTY PYTHON'S FLYING CIRCUS. John Cleese (right) is dissatisfied with the parrot he has just bought from Michael Palin. It seems to be dead.

Clockwise, in which he adapts the Fawlty character into that of a mega-lomaniac headmaster driven berserk by frustrations which prevent him from accomplishing a simple train journey. (It sometimes seems that the only solution modern comedians can find for any of us is madness.) Michael Palin has moved in a gentler vein of semi-nostalgia, both in the TV series *Ripping Yarns* and in such films as *The Missionary*.

Since so many television comedy series were filmed, it is surprising to notice the ones which were not. As far back as 1958 Granada and Hammer had taken a shot at filming *The Army Game*, that long-running simple-minded farce, under the disguise *I Only Arsked* (the catchphrase of Bernard Bresslaw as the dopey Private Popplewell). It was a disaster which cried out for another try, but never got one. Nor was there any attempt to film the equally successful *Bootsie and Snudge*, which took two of the *Army Game* characters into civilian life as staff at a London club. With sympathetic script and direction, splendid films could be made of *Open All Hours* and *Last of the Summer Wine* and *Hi De Hi* and

Some Mothers Do Have 'Em and *It Ain't Half Hot Mum*. But the time seems to be past for such a concept, and future researchers into these often brilliant comedies will have to look to the television archives.

TREVOR HOWARD: In laughing gas it's the impurities that cause the laughter.

ALASTAIR SIM: Ah yes, much the same as in our music halls.

Green for Danger, 1946

10

Interlude:

DRAWINGS THAT WALK AND TALK

Television schedulers of the eighties seem to think that cartoons are only for children. If they're really dumb, they can't tell the difference in quality between Tom and Jerry and Heckle and Jeckle. To me, it has never mattered that Bugs and Sylvester and Mickey Mouse and Mr Magoo aren't characters of flesh and blood. Nor are the images we carry in our minds of the human comedians who entertain us. Max Miller off-stage was apparently a very domesticated man. Bob Hope, of the quicksilver tongue, is often tongue-tied at home. Zany Groucho Marx was a buddy of T. S. Eliot, and the apparently shy Stan Laurel was an inveterate womanizer. So what can it possibly matter if a few brilliant comedy writers at Warner and MGM and UPA preferred to channel their best gags through animated drawings? The double takes which resulted were as effective as anybody's, the fade aways more astonishingly acrobatic than a mere human could manage.

From the days of the fairground peepshow cinemas, it was obvious to all that movie magic derived from the animation of a progressive series of still pictures by flashing them on to a screen one after the other. Only the hard work involved in drawing one frame at a time, 16 or 20 frames to the second, prevented more immediate use of animated figures as an alternative to real people; and when the professional cartoons did come, it was predictably from go-getting America. *Gertie the Dinosaur*, the brainchild of comic strip artist Winsor McCay, is usually credited as the first cartoon star, and the date often given for her is 1909, but the surviving film appears not to have emerged until 1914, and was drawn not by her 'creator' but by one John Bray. Smooth, silent and ably characterized, Gertie was more sentimentally appealing than funny; but *Mutt and Jeff*, who appeared in 1916 (from a newspaper strip by Bud

Fisher), were suburban, accident-prone clerks whose antics bore a striking similarity to the later adventures of Laurel and Hardy. They survived into the twenties, but *Krazy Kat*, another newspaper hero animated in 1916 by George Herriman, had nine lives, lasting in all 23 years. The first of many cartoon cats, he was comparatively cuddly and realistic.

Koko the Clown may be the first animated figure to stray into the world of utter fantasy which is so appropriate to filmcraft. He was first seen in 1918 in Max Fleischer's *Out of the Inkwell* series, a highly stimulating concept in which characters sprang from the artist's paper after the pen had been dipped in the ink and created them. The level of humour is simple, the level of technical accomplishment extremely high. Also deliberately two-dimensional was *Felix the Cat*, whose familiarity was extended into the fifties by means of a television series in colour. Reprehensibly, Felix may be the first instance of cartoon violence. A diagrammatic kind of feline at best, he was quite capable of making jokes with his creators, who sometimes omitted essential parts; and once, after an adventure in a flour mill, he had to wait for a hand to come into the picture and blacken him up again. Mysteriously, he could come to pieces and be smartly reassembled; but though he always 'kept on walking', as the song said, the frustrations he suffered made him something of a wise guy, if only in subtitles. Pat Sullivan is usually named as his creator, but recent evidence suggests that Sullivan was an entrepreneur with very limited draughtsmanship skills, and that the real work on Felix was done by a self-effacing gentleman named Otto Messmer, who in the eighties was rediscovered and fêted on film.

It was not until the mid-twenties that a British cartoon character emerged. This was *Bonzo*, a detailed and rather lovable puppy dog: he was well known in various media, including advertisements, before George Studdy presented him in 24 short cartoons. Bonzo however could scarcely compete with the New York sophistication of *Betty Boop*, Max Fleischer's sexy flapper with a huge head and shapely figure. Based on singer Helen Kane, who styled herself the 'boop-oop-a-doop' girl, Betty remained decidedly feminine throughout her wild but often satirical adventures. Her way with a predatory male raised quite a few eyebrows even in the seventies, when her films became the first 'black and whites' to be 'colorized'.

Meanwhile a graphic artist named Walt Disney, with considerable help from the more skilful pen of his friend Ub Iwerks, was sitting in his Kansas City studio turning out animated snippets called *Laff-o-Grams*. After a skirmish with *Oswald the Rabbit*, he found his first real success with the *Alice in Cartoonland* series, in which the heroine was live and everything else drawn. But Disney realized that he needed to create something more vivid, a likeable anthropomorphic figure which, placed against a recognizable modern setting, could be fantastic and funny at the same time. The first result was a somewhat grotesque *Mortimer Mouse*, gradually smoothed down to *Mickey* and given only three fingers on each hand for purposes of economy. Mickey developed a gentle personality (far removed from the brashness and crude jokes of his first appearance in 1928's *Steamboat Willie*) and there quickly grew up around him a whole menagerie of animal foils. There was his devoted partner *Minnie Mouse*, whose white gloves covered her wedding ring (if she had one). There was the usually incoherent *Goofy* (at first called *Dippy Dawg*), the dumb but faithful *Pluto* (an apparent combination of spaniel and dachshund, with a craven nature and a black whiplash for a tail), *Clara Cluck* (with a bosom like an opera singer and a voice to match) and *Horace Horsecollar*, who never really established himself and was quickly erased.

By the time colour came to cartoonery in 1933, it seemed that Disney needed just one more character to add a little vinegar to the strawberry jam. This turned out to be the vociferous and unintelligible *Donald Duck*, an unqualified success once his beak had been trimmed down to a smooth and elegant shape. Disney himself had provided the high-pitched tones of Mickey (try saying 'Hey, Pluto'), but Donald's angry squawks gave a lifetime's work to Clarence Nash, an undoubted if unseen star even though one could never tell a word he said beyond 'I wanna fight, I wanna fight'. By the mid-thirties the presence of a Disney cartoon on the bill had become almost as important as the main feature, and Disney himself was the world's Uncle Walt. The draughtsmanship which emerged from his developing factory was so admirable, the characters so fascinating and the incidents so ingenious that the mere sound of his name, along with a few others like Shirley Temple and Laurel and Hardy, cheered up the whole depression generation. Anyone who doubts that his cartoons were the work of true genius should at least review some of the shorts in which the leading figures appeared together: *Lonesome Ghosts*, say, or *Clock Cleaners*. The craft of the cinema was never more succinctly exhibited, nor the long arm of coincidence more enjoyably dislocated, than in their almost surrealist world in which a happy ending was always reached after eight minutes of exciting and hilarious action ranging from farce to melodrama.

Disney also produced musical frolics called *Silly Symphonies*, with

CLOCK CLEANERS. The bell striker starts Goofy on the road to calamity.

subjects ranging from *Father Noah's Ark* to *Wynken, Blynken and Nod*; and from time to time he varied his main group with additional characters. Donald was given three rather stridently mischievous nephews, and there were a few adventures with *The Three Little Pigs* as well as a brace of cute chipmunks called *Chip 'n Dale*. They all inhabited a perfect, detailed, sunlit world in which accidents were magically cleaned up and nobody ever got badly hurt. Perhaps for that reason they were gratefully welcomed by millions into the family circle; when war came, they made admirable propaganda figures for recruiting or air raid precautions; and in the later forties Donald was the undisputed leader of Hollywood's good neighbour policy with South America. Disappointment was audible in cinemas the world over when the word 'cartoon' on the category board proved to herald a Disney imitator rather than the real thing: a *Columbia Phantasy*, or a Paul Terry *Terrytoon*, or something from the Hugh Harman and Rudolph Ising group at MGM (*Harman-Ising*, get it?).

By the end of the thirties, however, one indisputable source of competition was well established, though the cartoon world it invented was brasher and more violent than Disney's, as befitted the Warner studio where Cagney, Bogart and Edward G. Robinson had for years prowled the 'New York' backlot. Leon Schlesinger's *Looney Tunes* and *Merrie Melodies* first erupted on to regular bills in 1930, and specialized in

BUGS BUNNY. A wisecracker *par excellence*, and the closest a rabbit ever got to being Milton Berle.

fast, wisecracking cross-talk as well as crazy action. First star into the limelight was stuttering *Porky Pig* in 1935; two years later came the unpredictably zany *Daffy Duck*, and the first sketches of *Elmer Fudd*, the fall guy who couldn't pronounce his 'R's. But waiting in the wings until 1938 was the lanky, suave and streetwise rabbit known as *Bugs Bunny* ('What's up, doc?'), braving shot and shell every minute but continuing his charmed existence through a myriad of adventures with such punning titles as *All This and Rabbit Stew, Hare Tonic* and *Knighty Knight Bugs*. Creators of these refugees from the funny farm included Bob McKimson, Tex Avery, Chuck Jones, Bob Clampett and Friz Freleng, with most of the characters voiced by the phenomenal Mel Blanc. The Warner cartoons kept America laughing through the fractious forties: if Disney was Chaplin, they were Abbott and Costello, and just occasionally they might have stood in for the Marx Brothers. Post-war additions to the tribe included *Foghorn Leghorn* (1946), a kind of southern fried chicken; Tweetie Pie the smart-alec canary ('I tawt I taw a putty tat') and Sylvester his lisping predator ('There mutht be thome eathier way for a puthy-cat to get thome thuthtenanth!'); Road Runner ('Beep beep!') with his accident-prone pursuer Wile E. Coyote; and that Romeo of skunks Pepé Le Pew. The Warner cartoons were too numerous (more than 500 in 25 years) for all to be good; but at their best, which is to say their wackiest and most irreverent, they were not only devastatingly funny but provided a recognizable if distorting mirror of their times.

Other major studios were hot to compete on the more violent level. Over at Paramount *Popeye the Sailorman* ('I yam what I yam what I yam') had held sway, courtesy of Max Fleischer, since 1933, with his retinue of simpering *Olive Oyl*, giant bully *Bluto*, and the dopey, derby-hatted *Wimpy* (a relic of the original newspaper strip, who didn't last long in the cinema but reappeared thirty years later as a string of British hamburger joints named after his favourite food). 234 cinema Popeyes were produced, and in the fifties another 200 for television. Even the best of them (i.e. the older ones) now seem a little hard to watch, as flat as a Frank Randle comedy until the last lap, when Popeye downs his spinach just as he downs his ale to work up an irresistible head of steam. Nor can a great deal be said for Universal's *Woody Woodpecker*, devised by Walter Lantz as a flying superhero but soon developing into a strident bore with a machine-gun-like war cry. Such inventions were far outclassed by MGM's *Tom and Jerry*, whose principal if not only begetters appear to have been William Hanna and Joe Barbera, though producer Fred Quimby always made sure that his name loomed largest

POPEYE. It's being so
full of spinach that
keeps him going.

on the credits. The sleek but easily outwitted cat and the thimble-sized but unoutwittable mouse got into their best form soon after their 1939 debut, and throughout the forties their appearances were a treat fit for a king. The trick was to use a Disney-like family suburban milieu (the only regular human character, a black housekeeper, was never seen above the knees), but to introduce fantastic refinements of violence derived from everyday objects such as umbrellas, electric irons and toasters. Just occasionally there was fancy dress, as in *Johann Mouse* and *The Two Mouseketeers*: in the latter Tom was finally led off to the guillotine while Jerry shed crocodile tears: 'Pauvre, pauvre pussy cat! C'est la guerre!' But house and garden generally gave scope enough for an almost incredible range of visual invention, at the end of which Tom finished up furless, toothless or variously fragmented. Luckily for all of us, he was as resilient as his ancestor Felix, and even when he fell from a great height through an iron mesh, the resultant slivers of cat re-assembled themselves in double quick time. Tom and Jerry survived censor criticism from all quarters, but they could not survive Cinema Scope or re-creation on television, both of which considerably reduced their impact as well as blunting their characters: researchers eager for the best of them should confine their inquiries to the forties and very early fifties.

Over at Fox, Paul Terry had added to his repertoire *Mighty Mouse* (1943) (a Superman rip-off) and *Heckle and Jeckle* the talking magpies, but they were low grade vaudeville compared with Tom and Jerry, who metaphorically had always played the Palace. In any case, there were too

TOM AND JERRY. Hollywood never played a better game of cat and mouse.

many cartoons about, and signs were that with escalating costs and the increasing popularity of double features the animation factories would soon have to close down: re-runs, after all, were just as popular as new episodes. It was however during this bleak period of the late forties that Columbia firmed up releasing arrangements with UPA (United Productions of America), a forward-looking company headed by innovators John Hubley and Stephen Bosustow. Their style reflected the experiments currently being made in all media: less realistic detail, more stylization of character, a *New Yorker* level of wit, a general invitation to the audience to eke out what they saw with their own minds. UPA offered six-minute treatments, in the original styles, of Ludwig Bemelmans's *Madeleine* and James Thurber's *A Unicorn in the Garden*. They invented small-boy heroes like *Willie the Kid*, who lived in a world of western fantasy, *Christopher Crumpet*, whose imaginary playmates came to uncomfortable life, and *Gerald McBoing-Boing*, who couldn't speak words, but went 'boing boing' instead. UPA's lowest common denominator (and greatest commercial success) was the near-sighted *Mr Magoo*, an elderly daredevil blessed with the voice of Jim Backus. Some of his lines have echoed agreeably down the decades: 'Didn't we meet in Heidelberg?' (to a tailor's dummy he thinks is attacking him with a sword), and 'I don't care if he *is* a walrus. I like him. I like him.' But perhaps the real UPA classic is *Rooty Toot Toot*, a joyously witty recitative based on the familiar saga of Frankie and Johnny.

The great cartoon era was nearing its end, though in 1950 Paramount did start a new and somewhat uneasy character called Casper, a baby ghost who couldn't understand why people were scared of him, when his mission was to travel through the ages helping them. Yes, well, said the public: don't call us, we'll call you. Paramount also financed George Pal's *Puppetoons*, little masterpieces of a different kind of animation; but although they achieved such individual splendours as *The 500 Hats of Bartholomew Cubbins*, they never settled on a character able to take the public fancy. Warners did a final little flip in 1955 with *Speedy Gonzales*, the zooming Mexican mouse ('Arriba, arriba!'), but by now television was so competitive as to make full animation economic, and even Disney had long since set his sights upon live action. It was in 1964, after a long gap, that the last one-reel cartoons intended for cinema outlets emerged. From the new De Patie-Freleng outfit, they were *Inspector Clouseau* and *The Pink Panther*, both inspired by a movie in which the panther appeared only as a jewel. To addicts reared on Donald and Bugs they seemed anaemic, and were quickly bundled into TV half-hours.

Television, meanwhile, had established Saturday mornings as the

Valhalla of old cartoons and the breaking-in ground for new ones. The new ones however had to be not only plentiful (so that they could also be stripped at breakfast time throughout the week) but cheap, which meant that Disney's glorious character detail was a no-no. Henceforth, cartoon characters intended for television moved little but their jaws: the backgrounds, apart from a few sweeping introductory images which were repeated *ad nauseam*, were kept as stationary as possible. While verbal invention lasted, there were a few occasions when this restricted style worked. UPA managed a witty half-hour Magoo series in which their myopic hero played a different character each week, including Sherlock Holmes, Frankenstein, and Dr Jekyll and Mr Hyde. The Hanna–Barbera studio male merchandizing hay with the dull *Huckleberry Hound*, the amiable *Yogi Bear* ('Smarter than the average bear!') and the Bert Lahr-styled *Snagglepuss* ('Exit, stage left!'), whose adventures were bundled into half-hours with those of other, lesser luminaries. Hanna–Barbera also backdated some old Burns and Allen scripts to provide 156 excellent half-hour sitcoms set in prehistoric times: Americans were comforted to think that the same petty problems were suffered by the neighbours and themselves even in those days, and some of the detail (such as rock-hewn television sets) was inventive. *The Flintstones* kept its popularity in repeats for twenty years, which is more than can be said for *The Jetsons*, which played the trick in reverse, with Pop of the future getting stuck in a helicopter jam on his way home from the office. In *Wait Till Your Father Gets Home*, produced in Australia, Hanna–Barbera also had success in a sketchier style, but the scripts, though moderately amusing, were achetypal domestic sitcom without an original thought.

Since 1960 cartoons have bred like rabbits, with Japan a potent supplier, but hardly any have been worth watching for style or content, and the music level usually deadens as much as it deafens. Occasional specials have merit: one might single out the *Dr Seuss* stories, the *Snoopy* and *Peanuts* features, and some would add *Garfield*, all from sources a cut above the average. But they did not appeal to the old crowd, and nor did the cinema's fully animated feature cartoons by Ralph Bakshi, who encapsulated an unattractive world of sex, drugs, bad language and violence. People could get all that at home, and so stayed there.

Luckily, the classic cartoons of the thirties and forties stayed around to delight generation after generation. As for the giant Disney, his image was kept burnished long after his death in 1965. His 1940 classical concert *Fantasia* was rediscovered as a 'trip' by a new drug-influenced youth audience, and parents took their children to reissues of *Snow*

THE FLINTSTONES: recognizable enough as comic actors to play *Mister Ed* or *The Burns and Allen Show*.

White and the Seven Dwarfs and *Pinocchio*, which usually outgrossed the factory's new attempts like *The Aristocats* and *The Black Cauldron*. Animation was one more aspect of cinema for which the real glory was long gone; but television found and explored new possibilities in puppetry. Muffin the Mule was a British favourite of the early days, contemporaneous with America's Kukla, Fran and Ollie. Then for a decade Gerry and Sylvia Anderson held sway with their sophisticated adventures of *Captain Scarlet* and *Thunderbirds*: here the gloss and skilful manipulation of the hardware outweighed any character deficiencies in the wire-operated figures. But even the best of Anderson seemed stiff and creaky when compared with the superb fluency of the puppets created by Frank Oz and Jim Henson, first for the educationally oriented *Sesame Street* and later for the delightful *Muppets*, forever putting on a show under their MC Kermit the frog, who stood up manfully to the frankly sexual approaches of Miss Piggy as well as to the heckling of aged theatregoers Statler and Waldorf. Alas, the Muppets had all too short a reign, being replaced after five years at the top by the grosser skills and sustained invective of *Spitting Image*, a foam rubber version of the old political cartoons of Victorian newspapers. After that, surely the next development must be a reversion to innocence?

11

*A medium so called because it
is neither rare nor well done:*

AMERICA AFTER 1945:
TELEVISION TAKES OVER

Sketch comedy became popular in music halls as an alternative to stand-up gags at the mike, partly because it was easier to write, and also because it gave a rest to the comic, who now had helpers to ease his burden. On radio, too, ten minutes was as much as the listener could take of rapid patter, but sketches could extend the format to a required half-hour. *Itma* marked a half-way stage, having very little in the way of overall plot but being divided arbitrarily into three sections by music. In the States, Hope and Benny usually had one musical break, after which the week's guest star was wheeled on for some barbed badinage. *Take it from Here*, as noted, consisted of three separate sketches, in one of which the stars played themselves, the second might be a regular feature like *The Glums*, and the third a movie parody, but the impetus all the time was towards a solid half-hour format without music, in which the star would play some fictitious character with a personality not too far removed from his own. Once the Milton Berle era was out of the way, such 'situation comedies' reigned supreme.

If television situation comedies have proved to be mainly domestic, that is partly because domestic sets are simplest, but also because of the long tradition of movie series about the Hardys, the Joneses and the Bumsteads. A half-hour slot is the preferred length, which means twenty-five minutes of film, half as much again as any of the adventures of Edgar Kennedy or Leon Errol. An obvious bait at the beginning was to cast actors who were already well known from the movies, perhaps catching them on their way down so that they would come a bit cheaper. But as soon as television got going, it was able to make its own stars. The format, the script and the personality have proved to be what count, and all the megavoltage in the entertainment world will not make a hit

out of something with which the viewers are uncomfortable. Jimmy
Stewart didn't scintillate in sitcom, and nor did Bette Davis nor Shirley
Maclaine nor Betty Hutton nor Debbie Reynolds. And even if you
make it big once, as Danny Thomas did, it isn't always easy to get
back.

Situation comedy stars seldom begin their careers as comedians, but
comedians they have to be, dextrously delivering the best one-liners
their writers can devise, and from time to time playing eyeball to eyeball
with the audience. Since in the fifties and sixties the order was for 39
episodes a year, and twenty or more sitcoms were likely to figure
simultaneously in the American schedules, it will be seen that this was an
arduous way of life for all concerned. Furthermore, all possible plots and
permutations were used up quite quickly, and the palm went to those
who were smartest at recycling. As Bert Wheeler recalled: 'Years ago I
could buy a complete vaudeville routine for a couple of hundred bucks
and use it without changing a line for five years. Today you pay a
thousand for a sketch that lasts one single television program – if some
other comic doesn't hear it at rehearsal and beat you to the airwaves with
it!'

The first sitcoms came at the end of the forties, and all were
schmaltzy. *The Life of Riley* was contemporaneous with Britain's movie
and radio series *The Huggetts,* and comparable to it in pace and milieu. The
middle-aged *paterfamilias* behind the eight-ball was played first on TV
by James Gleason, who couldn't make it work. It lasted only one season,
but became a hit when revived in 1953 with William Bendix in his old
radio role. *Mary Kay and Johnny,* forgotten now, was about newlyweds,
and featured Mary Kay and Johnny Stearns, presumably as themselves.
He was a serious young worker with a slightly screwball wife (shades of
I Love Lucy to come); and that was also the theme of another shortlived
show, *The Growing Paynes.* (With a title like that it deserved to be
shortlived.) The Paynes were played first by Judy Parrish and Ed
Harvey, then by Elaine Stritch (hooray, a known name) and Ed
Holmes.

Still featuring a family, but this time with the emphasis on Mom, was
The Goldbergs, with Gertrude Berg, who also wrote the scripts. (One
wonders whether *Hollywood* at that time would have mounted a comedy
about a specifically Jewish family?) Mother was also spotlighted (naturally) in *I Remember Mama,* a period piece from the movie about Scan-
dinavian immigrants; Peggy Wood played the Irene Dunne role. For
mainly technical reasons these shows are close to unviewable today.
(*Mama* was actually broadcast live.)

Other family shows of the 1949 season had Sam and Virginia Wren (*Wrens' Nest*), Paul and Grace Hartman (*The Hartmans*), John and Barbara Gay (*Apartment 3c*), and Lois Wilson and House Jamieson in *The Aldrich Family*, which also had a Hollywood pedigree though it had originally stemmed from a Broadway play about the problems of adolescence. ('Coming, mother!') Nothing else in the comedy field struck a responsive chord.

There were lots of new family shows in 1950, too. *Peter and Mary* (Lind Hayes and Healy, that is); *The Trouble with Father* (Mr and Mrs Stuart Erwin); Charlie Ruggles and Erin O'Brien Moore in *The Ruggles*; and *Meet Corliss Archer*, stories of the teenager played by Shirley Temple in the movie *Kiss and Tell*. (Lugene Sanders was the madcap, Frieda Inescort and Fred Shields her parents.) *Beulah* was a sassy black maid played by Ethel Waters ('Somebody bawl for Beulah?'), then by Hattie McDaniel and Louise Beavers. The character had originated on the *Fibber McGee and Molly* radio show where, strange to say, it had been played by a white *actor*. William Post Jnr and Ginger Jones were Beulah's employers.

1950 brought another Jewish show, but *Menasha* failed despite the efforts of Menasha Skulnik as the trouble-prone hero. Another bumbler was *Hank McCune*, played by Larry Keating: that was the first show to have a laugh track. There was quite a welcome for *Amos 'n Andy*, with black actors Spencer Williams Jnr and Tim Moore, but a few years later its reruns were being denounced as racist, portraying black folk as shiftless no-goods. In fact, Amos was a sharp con man in this version; only Andy was wide-eyed and gullible. Critical consensus had it that the show was better left to radio where the heroes were unseen, so that their colour couldn't bother anybody.

The real smash hit of 1950 – it ran until 1958 – was 'Burns and Allen', or to give it its full title *The George Burns and Gracie Allen Show*. This was archetypal domestic sitcom complete with next-door neighbours, but it was given a freshness by the front and end pieces performed by George and Gracie before the curtain. He didn't do much more than smoke a cigar and nod while she prattled inanities, but that was enough to make fans tune in each week in their scores of millions, for Burns and Allen had been around a long time. The radio had made them family friends – and no one minded if they now recycled their old radio scripts – while they were known, too, from film appearances in the thirties. These hadn't seemed to work very well, even when the Burnses were co-starred with Bing Crosby or Bob Hope or Fred Astaire, and on their own they had never caused the payboxes to shake. Now, suddenly,

GRACIE ALLEN and GEORGE BURNS in the days before television: a
hard-working team which never hit the high spots.

their time had come: they were comfortable to be with, good fireside
friends, and that is what television has always wanted. Sample
dialogue:

> GEORGE: You're brilliant. I'm beginning to think you're a wizard.
> GRACIE: I'm a what?
> GEORGE: A wizard. You know what a wizard is.
> GRACIE: Sure, a snowstorm.
> GEORGE: Well, if that's a snowstorm, what's a blizzard?
> GRACIE: Oh, you can't fool me, a blizzard is the inside of a chicken.
> GEORGE: Did something happen to you when you were a baby?
> GRACIE: Yes, when I was born, I was so surprised I couldn't talk for a
>   year and a half.

Or:

> GRACIE: I'm going into the department store business. I made up my
>   mind.

GEORGE: What mind?
GRACIE: Somebody told you to say that. I'm going to open up five or
   six; of course, that's only for a start.
GEORGE: No doubt in a few months you'll have several hundred
   department stores.
GRACIE: Well, maybe, but I don't want to count my chickens before
   they're department stores.

Gracie retired in 1958 and died in 1964. To everyone's surprise,
George then made it on his own, in a couple of television series and as a
stand-up comic; he was also in great demand as a talk show guest. At
eighty he won an Oscar for *The Sunshine Boys*, his first film in thirty-odd
years, and went on to play the title role in *Oh God* and two sequels, still
making wry remarks from behind his cigar. At ninety he was still on the
night club circuit as top of the bill. There is nothing predictable about
show business.

It was in 1951 that *I Love Lucy* sneaked its way into the communal life
of America. Like George Burns, Lucille Ball had been no more than
mildly popular as a movie player: Hollywood since 1932 had found her
modest roles in modest pictures, but only occasionally had she been
allowed to be funny. Some thought that her Cuban bandleader husband
Desi Arnaz was a millstone round her neck, but she was in love, and it
was because of him, and to save their marriage, that she agreed to try a
television comedy series. The situation was little different from *The
Burns and Allen Show* except that Lucy was to be even zanier than Gracie,
in a more acrobatic way, and Desi was to get excited and have harebrained schemes. The house of Burns and Allen became an apartment,
but there were still neighbours: familiar face William Frawley and less
well known Vivian Vance, a grouch and a scatterbrain. There was no
reason whatever for the show to become a hit . . . until it became clear
that a great American clown had been hiding her light under a bushel.
Lucy was bigger than the confines of the very ordinary set: her desperate
measures included routines borrowed from every slapstick comedian in
living memory, and her Hollywood years enabled her to call upon top
guest stars, who soon learned to enter into the spirit of the thing: Harpo
Marx, for instance, came on to do his mirror routine from *Duck Soup*.
Lucy had a tremendous rapport with the live audience before whom the
show was filmed, and she insisted on 35mm film for quality, television
recording being then in its infancy. Producer Al Simon and photographer Karl Freund came up with a new multi-camera system which
meant that the show was filmed five times from different angles, then
the best bits from each angle were edited into the final print. This was

I LOVE LUCY, and its four stars who became members of the American
family: Bill Frawley, Desi Arnaz, Vivian Vance and Lucille Ball.

especially helpful for the slapstick sequences: Lucy needed to get that pie
in the eye only once.

Before the end of the first season, *I Love Lucy* was a national
institution, and no nine days' wonder because it is still being rerun

around the world 35 years later. No dialogue excerpt would tell you why: the fun is all in what you see happening to the characters you know so well, and above all in Lucy's reaction shots. The show was even written around her real life pregnancy, a notable television first, and the nation waited eagerly to discover how she would break the news to Desi:

> DESI (*complaining of his difficult business affairs*): You should be happy you're a woman.
> LUCY: Oh, I am, I am!
> DESI: You think you know how tough my job is, but I tell you, if you traded places with me, you'd be surprised.
> LUCY: Believe me, if I traded places with you, *you'd* be surprised.

Beside Lucy, the other 1951 shows pale into insignificance, though *My Little Margie* rated well enough at the time. The scene was a New York apartment, with another family in it, but the emphasis was on a girl (Gale Storm) and her widower father (Charles Farrell) each of whom thought the other out of hand. It lasted three years; *Mr Peepers* lasted four. Peepers was a mild-mannered bespectacled schoolmaster, played by Wally Cox, and his adventures were amusing rather than funny, but women across the country felt sorry for him: he was so nice, and clean, and unused. What may have killed off the show was the misguided decision that he should marry: there was nowhere for the scripts to go after that.

Mr Peepers had *not* essentially been a family show, but 1952 made up for that. *The Adventures of Ozzie and Harriet* (does anybody really file it under A?) lasted thirteen seasons, and could scarcely have been more traditional, except that the family was already known. Ozzie Nelson was a bandleader, his wife had danced with Fred Astaire as Harriet Hilliard, and there were two readymade sons who could grow up before the nation's eyes. They were all nice people; but you couldn't find anything as complimentary to say about the show. It was there, and not offensive, but not very interesting either. The Nelsons were just a little too concerned always to be doing the right thing. There was much more zest in *I Married Joan*, even though the title had the faint sound of a copy. Joan Davis had long been a successful female clown in the movies, her routines filled with grotesque faces, voices and body movements; now she was the silly wife of a tolerant judge. The show did well, but after four seasons the public was tired of it. The revised version of *The Life of Riley* was a little luckier, for crumple-faced Bendix was always a popular favourite, and a lot of midwestern family men recognized themselves in his portrayal of what Gary Cooper used to call Mr Average Joe American – pratfalls and all. Another big hit of the season was *Our Miss Brooks*, which launched second-stringer Eve Arden on a new star career as a basically warm but acid-tongued schoolteacher. Almost as funny was Gale Gordon as the bossy, self-important headmaster, and he was to fill his mature years as Lucy's foil in her later shows. Another faded female star, Ann Sothern, started a four-season comedy called *Private Secretary*, with Don Porter as her boss: it was all banter, but it caught on. Less successful shows of the season were *Heaven to Betsy*, with Jack Lemmon in a department store; *Leave it to Larry*, with Eddie Albert as a downtrodden family man; *Life with Luigi*, with J. Carrol Naish as an antique dealer; and *My Friend Irma*, with Marie Wilson in her dizzy blonde role.

All this time Jack Benny had been more or less a permanent Sunday night fixture, though his presentation varied from variety special to sitcom. Even if nothing much seemed to happen some weeks, Jack was always welcome, for he could be funny without opening his mouth. And having forsaken Hollywood in 1945, after dissatisfaction with his last vehicle *The Horn Blows at Midnight*, he was well placed to make television his own. As in radio, he remained the butt of other people's humour, but now you could see his reactions. 'Hm,' he would say (laugh), and look at the audience (laugh), and then look back at the offender, a little more sharply this time (laugh). He would remain almost immobile: the eyes might glare, but the lips would be set firm, and the arms often folded. One of the running gags was that he remained 39 until he was well over 70; but although balding, he never wore a toupee. In fact he was careful never to drive any of his comic attributes into the ground, and nor did he rely on catchphrases. He no doubt remembered advising Jack Pearl to acquire more material than 'Vass you dere, Sharlie?' and Joe Penner to lay off 'Wanna buy a duck?' Both declined his advice, and both were forgotten comics within a very few years of their eminence. The meanness however was too rich a vein to ignore. When he and Jimmy Stewart battled for a restaurant check, you just knew that somehow or other Benny would wind up not paying:

> STEWART: I'll feel much better if you let me pay it.
> BENNY: Well, all right, Jimmy, as long as your health is involved.

Most of Benny's weaknesses became famous during his famous feud with Fred Allen. 'When Benny plays the violin,' said Allen, 'it sounds as though the strings are still in the cat. I don't want to say he's cheap, but he has short arms and he carries his money low in his pockets.' Benny was stung to retaliate: 'Listening to Fred Allen is like listening to two Abbotts and no Costello.' And when the pair guested on each other's shows, the sparring continued:

ALLEN: You couldn't adlib a belch after a Hungarian dinner.
BENNY: You wouldn't say that if my writers were here.

As the years went by, Benny, surrounded as ever by his familiar foils (his wife Mary Livingstone, Mel Blanc, Dennis Day and Rochester forever cleaning up the vintage Maxwell), assumed an increasing air of petulance about these jibes, which were even given to the programme's celebrated guest stars. Ronald Colman and Benita Hume, given occasional appearances as Benny's supposedly stuffy English neighbours, got a whole series, *Halls of Ivy*, to themselves out of being rude to him. Even Martha Tilton was unable to resist:

BENNY *(applauding her aria)*: What about an encore?
TILTON: Well, I could sing –
BENNY: And this time how would it be if I accompanied you on my violin?
TILTON: Er, well, Jack, I don't know how to say this, but the arrangement is all set and the violin would interfere.
BENNY: For someone who didn't know how to say it you phrased it beautifully. Sing your lousy encore.

Benny knew too how to roast a guest:

And now, ladies and gentlemen, Errol Flynn, the only man who is mentioned in both *Who's Who* and the Kinsey report.

He could be commercially knowing, and still get the audience's blessing:

BENNY: Rochester, I'm tired. Run upstairs and plug in my General Electric blanket.
ROCH.: But Mr Benny, we don't *have* a General Electric blanket.
BENNY: We do now.

(And they did: next day both Benny and Rochester received the super version, compliments of General Electric's president, for the best free plug of all time.)
Benny happily shared his laughs with his colleagues, notably in the

JACK BENNY, still fiddling, looks as though he might have been asked to stop. This was a face that could get laughs without dialogue.

side-splitting routine developed between himself and Mel Blanc as a lisping Mexican. Blanc gets the scripted laughs; Benny makes do with nods and winks and looks of surprise to the audience, which the reader has to imagine. The pace, to say the least, is leisurely.

BENNY: Does this train go to Chicago?
BLANC: Si.
BENNY: Is it on time?
BLANC: Si.
BENNY: What's your name?
BLANC: Sy.
BENNY: Sy?
BLANC: Si.
BENNY: Are you married?
BLANC: Si.
BENNY: What's your wife's name?
BLANC: Sue.
BENNY: Sue?
BLANC: Si.
BENNY: Does she work?
BLANC: Si.
BENNY: What does she do?
BLANC: Sew.
BENNY: Sew?
BLANC: Si.

And so on.

By all accounts Benny, a workaholic, was no one to spend a quiet day at home with. Like Jolson, he ached for an audience. He was also uncomplaining: whatever he was asked to do in the cause of laughter, he did, including the drag role of all time in *Charley's Aunt*. 'The only complaint I had,' he said, 'was that with all the petticoats and underwear and girdles, I had the damnedest time going to the bathroom.' Whatever he tried, he found that the best way for him to get laughs was still through self-deprecation. Towards the end of his career he started his television show with an explanation to the studio audience:

> I do some shows on tape and some shows on film, and last month I asked people to write in and say which way they like me best. You'd be surprised how many don't like me at all.

It was during the 1953 season that Danny Thomas became a superstar in the television firmament, with a domestic comedy series originally called *Make Room for Daddy*. He soon turned it into *The Danny Thomas Show*. It ran for ten seasons, even though at around the half way mark he had to 'kill off' his first wife, Jean Hagen, who got bored with the show, and romance a young Irish widow played by Marjorie Lord. *Make Room for Daddy* was only different from the other family sitcoms in that Daddy was never quite behind the eight-ball; indeed he was smart enough to be a successful night club comic, and many episodes contained generous helpings of his act. The humour came from his attempts to combine his two lives. Danny, long-nosed and rather unsympathetic looking, generated more warmth than might have been expected from a feisty ex-vaudeville comic who had been a Hollywood flop. But when I tried to buy the show for British television, the deal stalled because he wanted twice as much as we paid for *I Love Lucy* . . .

Looked at in the eighties, *Topper* seems thinly produced to say the least, but it was a two-season hit. As replacements for Roland Young and Billie Burke, television couldn't have done much better than Leo G. Carroll and Lee Patrick, but Robert Sterling and Anne Jeffreys were just a shade dull as the jovial ghosts who haunt the home of Thorne Smith's stuffy banker, and both the gags and the technical tricks were pretty limited. Another middle-aged comedy star with a hit that season was Alan Mowbray, as a con man called *Colonel Flack*, who had a heart of gold. Then there was the old warhorse *Life with Father*, agreeably but not sensationally starring Leon Ames; and *Meet Mr McNulty*, with Ray Milland teaching English at a girls' college; and *Where's Raymond?* with Ray Bolger as – guess what? – a song and dance man. But the domestic format was not forgotten: Joan Caulfield played Barry Nelson's scatter-brained wife in *My Favorite Husband*, which Lucille Ball had previously done on radio. (Could it have given her ideas?)

1954's biggest hit was undoubtedly *Father Knows Best*, about a sickly sweet midwestern family that actually prayed together. Honest, it seemed okay when Robert Young was Pop and Jane Wyatt (remember her in *Lost Horizon*?) was Mom, but outside America the show was received with a shade of disbelief. Even inside, it was originally sup-posed to have more comedy – the writers put a question mark after the title – but somehow it started sentimental and the audience lapped it up that way, so who was arguing? Another hit that year was *Love That Bob*, with Robert Cummings as a middle-aged playboy who lives with his widowed sister. (Wouldn't that have been inconvenient?) Cummings was a bigger hit than in any of his movies, and the audience also liked Ann B. Davis as his sassy secretary. Another movie exile was 62-year-old Spring Byington, who in *December Bride* (which she had also played on radio) got to be sweet and sharp at the same time, as a bubbly senior citizen who moves in with her daughter and family, and cheers every-body up when she isn't exasperating them. And yes, as the title suggests, she still feels eligible for marriage, which provides plenty of scope for comedy. Enough for 154 episodes.

Lower-rating shows that season included quite a number of Holly-

wood residents who had found their star appeal to be on the wane.
Ronald Colman in the aforesaid *Halls of Ivy*; Donald O'Connor in
Here Comes Donald; Mickey Rooney in *Hey Mulligan*; Peter Lawford
in *Dear Phoebe*; Charlie Ruggles in *The World of Mr Sweeney*; June
Havoc in *Willy*; Thomas Mitchell in *Mayor of the Town*; David
Wayne in *Norby*; Celeste Holm in *Honestly, Celeste!* None of them made
waves.

But in 1956 *The Honeymooners* did. Jackie Gleason had also been in
Hollywood, but not so that anyone would notice. In the history books,
the career of this heavyweight will begin with his incarnation as Ralph
Kramden, a bus driver with delusions of grandeur and a friend (played
by Art Carney) who works in the New York sewer. Ralph came across
as an American Tony Hancock, forever railing against the world, and
although most of the episodes were confined to a single scruffy set,
audiences saw the world through Ralph's eyes . . . and they saw it in
terms of farce and melodrama. Take the show in which Ralph thinks he
is dying, because the doctor has somehow mixed up a dog's diagnosis
with his. (Yes, it *was* used later for the Rock Hudson movie *Send Me No
Flowers*.)

THE HONEYMOONERS. Lower right, Jackie Gleason, Audrey Meadows, Art
Carney, Hoyce Randolph. When they were around, production values were
not required.

> RALPH (*who has been trying in vain to get his long-suffering wife Alice to notice his sadness*): Dinner? I think I'll just have a glass of warm milk. And if you don't mind, I'll have it in the bedroom.
> ALICE: Ralph, I think you're blowing your top. One of these days they're going to come and take you away!
> RALPH: Yes, Alice, one of these days they *will* take me away. And that's why I'd like a little talk with you. Look, Alice, if anything ever happened to me, would you get married again?
> ALICE: Don't be silly, Ralph, I think I learned my lesson.
> RALPH: It's no time for cracks, Alice. I'm talking seriously.
> ALICE: Well, I don't think I would. But I guess if I got lonely and the right guy came along, who knows?
> RALPH: Well, I guess I can't blame you, Alice. You're young and in the prime of life. I can see it all now. For a little while after I'm gone, you'll miss me. Then you'll meet some guy and the two of you'll hit it off fine. Then you'll marry him. He'll move in here. Living in my apartment, with my furniture, and with my luck he'll be just my size. And he'll probably wear the new overcoat I bought last winter. Alice, you've gotta promise me one thing.
> ALICE: What's that?
> RALPH: If anything ever happens to me, I want you to bury me in my new overcoat.

Like Hancock, Gleason was allowed to call too many of the shots, and only 39 of the shows were recorded. (It began as a sketch in a regular variety programme.) But most of the scripts remain, and thirty years later they form a tribute to the writing skills of Marvin Marx, Leonard Stern and their team.

Almost incredibly, a second famous comedy series also bloomed in 1955. *You'll never Get Rich* was its first title, but it soon became *The Phil Silvers Show*, though the nation and the world came to know it as 'Bilko', after the character played by the star. Bilko, master sergeant and master conniver in a forgotten army camp, was Phil Silvers's finest hour. Though in the confined sets there ran amok a fine team of farceurs, from Maurice Gosfield's unlovely Private Dwayne Doberman to Paul Ford's easily conned Colonel Hall, viewers switched on to see and hear what the fast-talking and even faster thinking Ernie Bilko was up to this week. It was always something reprehensible, but the public loved him to get away with it:

> COLONEL: Bilko, you know I've tried to arrange the military schedule of this post so as not to interfere with your poker games . . .
> BILKO: Sir, I'm merely trying to create an atmosphere for my men.
> COLONEL: I know very well the atmosphere you're creating round here. They're starting to call this post Little Las Vegas.

PHIL SILVERS had a distinguished comic career before television posted him to Fort Baxter, but it is as the conniving Sergeant Bilko, who consistently avoided committing himself to his girlfriend (Elizabeth Wilson) that the world will remember him.

> BILKO: Sir, you have the knack of turning a phrase . . .
> COLONEL: Bilko, do you know why you're here?
> BILKO: Yes, sir. And I can assure you that jeep engine I had installed in
>   my own car is just temporary until –
> COLONEL: It's not that. It's another matter.

BILKO: Oh, yes, sir. I assure you I'm still looking for that scoundrel in my platoon who whistled at your wife last Wednesday.
COLONEL: Forget it.
BILKO: You will convey to her my sentiments that she was just made for those shorts. You're a lucky man.
COLONEL: Bilko! This is serious. I just received orders from the Pentagon.
BILKO: You're leaving us! Sir, this post will not be the same without you. We'll have a party. I'll get the cold cuts.
COLONEL: Bilko! Why must the simplest conversation with you become a sparring match? The order from the War Department concerns you. It concerns what happened when you were on the island of Kabuchi.
BILKO: Oh, no. Are they bringing up that old thing again? Sir, the court of enquiry definitely established that that native girl was lying.
COLONEL: Bilko!
BILKO: I did pay her for that laundry. Twelve cigar coupons . . .

Nat Hiken's scripts were simply brilliant: it is a pity that the execution was not always up to them. Although the episodes were filmed by the multi-camera system, some are marred by hesitations and bad moves, even by mistiming of lines, so that to read the scripts is now funnier than to see the films. That even goes for the most frequently quoted story, *The Case of Harry Speakup*, in which an attempt to speed up routine procedures leads to a chimpanzee being inducted into the army. And when the pace falters, Bilko becomes rather dislikeable: to win our hearts, he has to operate at high speed. He did so, more or less, for four seasons.

1955 was also the season of *The Charlie Farrell Show*, *The Great Gildersleeve* and Jackie Cooper with a basset hound in *The People's Choice*. The following season, with so many top shows still running, could produce only also-rans: *Hiram Holliday* with Wally Cox; *Blondie* with Pat Harty and Will Hutchins (also Jim Backus as Mr Dithers); *Hey Jeannie!* with Jeannie Carson and Allen Jenkins; *The Brothers* with Gale Gordon and Bob Sweeney as photographers; *Mr Adams and Eve* with Howard Duff and Ida Lupino; *Oh Susanna* with Gale Storm and ZaSu Pitts. At least they all stayed away from the cute family format. But in 1958 it was back with a vengeance. *Leave it to Beaver* was the American equivalent of Britain's naughty boy *Just William*; *The Real McCoys* a sweet slice of hillbilly Americana, with Walter Brennan as the irascible old head of the clan. Also that year, the head of the Carrington clan of the eighties, John Forsythe, got his first big break with *Bachelor Father*, as a wealthy womanizer who had to find time to bring up his orphaned niece.

We can roll right along now because television, well established, began to repeat itself. In 1959 *The Ann Sothern Show* was a variation on *Private Secretary*, and *The Donna Reed Show* was an upper-crust *Father Knows Best. How to Marry a Millionaire* borrowed from the movie. George Burns and Ed Wynn both had shows to themselves, but ran into format trouble. Nor was 1959 much fresher, though *Dennis the Menace*, as mischievous small boys go, still seems better than *Leave it to Beaver*, and Joseph Kearns as the next-door neighbour had the funniest explosive anger since Donald McBride. *The Many Loves of Dobie Gillis* was sophomoric college stuff with Dwayne Hickman as Dobie and Bob Denver (who will recur frequently) as his wiseacre friend Maynard G. Krebs, a kind of warm-up for the Fonz of *Happy Days* to come. Jackie Cooper lasted two seasons as a navy doctor in *Hennessey*, but Betty Hutton couldn't get going as *Goldie*, a manicurist who becomes the beneficiary of a millionaire, and Dennis O'Keefe only stumbled through as a widower columnist in something not very brightly called *The Dennis O'Keefe Show. Fibber McGee and Molly* lasted thirteen episodes before radio's favourite liar was banished back to the airwaves.

The Andy Griffith Show was the big hit of 1960, and of the next eight seasons. Griffith was never exactly a comedian, just a pleasant-spoken, easy-going fellow with a fund of crackerbarrel philosophy: Will Rogers reincarnate. He cast himself as sheriff of a sleepy midwestern hamlet called Mayberry, and it rapidly became America's favourite town, though the humour never seemed to travel. Though not serialized, it was closer to Britain's *Coronation Street* than anything. Another easy-going long runner was *My Three Sons*, with Fred MacMurray as yet another eligible widower, his household run by the boys' maternal grandfather played by William Frawley, ex-*I Love Lucy*. (When he retired four years later the spot was filled by William Demarest, ex a hundred movies plus *Love and Marriage*, a cute little series, which had failed in 1959, about a music publishing company.) This family too became part of America; it could hardly fail to, in the course of thirteen seasons of 39 episodes each.

Variations were now flooding in thick and fast: J. Carrol Naish as a Red Indian quietly running the affairs of a dude ranch behind the backs of the owners, in *Guestward Ho*; Jim Backus running a deadbeat press service in *Hot off the Wire*, with the toothsome Nita Talbot as chief wisecracker; Elaine Stritch performing a similar function for *My Sister Eileen*; *The Tom Ewell Show*, with the amiable crumpleface playing an estate agent afflicted by wall-to-wall women. *The Tab Hunter Show* was about a comic-strip artist; *Pete and Gladys* had Harry Morgan in an offshoot of *December Bride*; Pat O'Brien ran a law firm in *Harrigan and Son*. The success or failure of all these shows depended not on the fame of the star but on how comfortably the elements jelled: setting, style, jokes, compatibility of actors, even make-up and set design. The show had to look lived in from the word go, for with doubt came cancellation.

One of my favourite series played the 1961 and 1962 seasons, and then quit while the going was good. It was the creation of Nat Hiken, who since leaving Bilko had been searching for another format to which he could apply his ready wit. He found it in the idea of a crazy New York police precinct, and the show which resulted was only marginally more exaggerated than *Hill Street Blues*, which followed nearly twenty years later. The title was *Car 54, Where are you?* and no audience could resist it after hearing the catchy theme song under the credits:

> There's a hold-up in the Bronx,
> Brooklyn's broken out in fights,
> There's a traffic jam in Harlem
> That's backed up to Brooklyn Heights.
> There's a scout troop lost a child,
> Krushchev's due at Idlewild –
> Car 54, where are you?

CAR 54, WHERE ARE YOU? Joe E. Ross and Fred Gwynne, otherwise known as Toody and Muldoon.

Of the two cops who shared a car, the bumbling one was Toody, played by a rasp-voiced comedian from burlesque, Joe E. Ross. His long, lugubrious partner Muldoon, more imposing but just as dumb, was in the hands of a character actor named Fred Gwynne, who later rose to greater fame as Herman Munster. The show was farce with a real background, filmed on the streets of New York, and all concerned were proud of it . . . except the network. A contemporaneous series which ran longer was *The Dick Van Dyke Show*. There was nothing very original about it, except that the hero was a staff writer on a television comedy series, but it was written and acted with freshness, and the fact that the industry was spoofing itself gave it some pretensions to be satire. Van Dyke and Mary Tyler Moore were simply splendid at tossing dialogue to each other; the swollen-headed comic star of the series within the series was chief writer Carl Reiner, and also around were old vaudeville hands Rose Marie, Morey Amsterdam and Richard Deacon. None of it was really witty, but the folk were nice to be with. Personally I got more laughs out of *Mr Ed*, a Burns-and-Allen-and-the-neighbours format with one difference: the hero owned a talking horse. This was of course a direct steal from the movie series about Francis the Talking Mule, except that the television animal was a thoroughbred palomino with views about art. His voice was supplied by Allan 'Rocky' Lane, star of countless 'B' westerns, and the nervous marrieds were Alan Young and Connie Hines. After the show folded, the horse enjoyed a fifteen-year retirement.

Another pleasant show of 1961 was *Father of the Bride*, a development from the Spencer Tracy movie. It ran only one season, but Leon Ames walked straight from it into *Mr Ed* (as the neighbour, replacing Larry Keating who had died). One season was all the ABC network could manage with a show about a childless couple who adopted three chimpanzees: Jack Weston tried hard, but it was all too obvious that the writers of *The Hathaways* had seen *Mr Ed*. *Hazel* was a four-season hit about a sassy maid, but the black Beulah of yesteryear was replaced by Shirley Booth, a long way from *Come Back Little Sheba*. *Holiday Lodge* wasn't bad either, with the Canadian comics Wayne and Shuster revamping all Abbott and Costello's old routines. Lucille Ball came back again that year, as a widow in *The Lucy Show* (the credits always said 'based on a book *Life Without George*, by Irene Kampen, but I never met anyone who'd read it). She did have kids, and Vivian Vance for best friend, and a boss in the shape of the invaluable, explosive Gale Gordon. *The Joey Bishop Show* was too much like *The Danny Thomas Show* for its own good; *Margie*, based on the twenties-set Jeanne Crain movie, was simply too mild and aimless. Another movie steal was *Room for One More*, but Andrew Duggan was no Cary Grant, and there was more sentiment than comedy in the adopted kids situation. *Mrs G Goes to College* was a genuine curiosity, with Cedric Hardwicke as a stuffy dean trying to implant college attitudes into a middle-aged Jewish widow played by Gertrude Berg from *The Goldbergs*. The one that I liked, but which didn't get anywhere, was *Oh Those Bells*, with the slapstick-prone Wiere Brothers running a prop shop. Thirteen episodes was all.

1962 brought two biggies. Ernest Borgnine in *McHale's Navy* was nearly though not quite another Bilko – which was clearly the design. The first two seasons were set in the Pacific during World War II, but after that for some obscure reason everybody moved to Italy. Characterization and casting were alike predictable, but the viewers loved it. Not so much, though, as they loved *The Beverly Hillbillies*, the show by Paul Henning which started CBS off as the cornpone network. The Clampetts were a family from way back yonder who struck oil and were persuaded to move to Beverly Hills . . . but let us hear it to the twangy musical accompaniment which Henning set to his lively words:

> Come'n listen to my story 'bout a man named Jed –
> Poor mountaineer, barely kept his family fed.
> Then one day he was shootin' at some food
> When up through the ground came a-bubblin' crude.
> Oil, that is . . . black gold . . . Texas tea.
> Well, the first thing y'know, old Jed's a millionaire,
> The kinfolks said, 'Jed, move away from there.'
> They said, 'Californy is the place you oughta be',
> So they loaded up the truck and they moved to Beverly.
> Hills, that is . . . swimmin' pools . . . movie stars. ★

Jed (Buddy Ebsen) actually took some persuading to move – looking at his mountain plot, he muttered, 'Man'd be a durn fool to leave all this' – and the Clampetts never did seem to think much of their adopted milieu. Indeed, the studio set of their 'cement pond' never appeared to admit much sunshine; but they stayed around as much as anything to annoy their next-door neighbours, banker Drysdale (Raymond Bailey)

★ There was a farewell verse each week too:

> Well, now it's time to say goodbye to Jed and all his kin,
> And they would like to thank you folks for kindly dropping in.
> You're all invited back next week to this locality
> To have a heapin' helpin' of their hospitality.
> Hillbilly, that is . . . set a spell . . . take your shoes off . . .
> Y'all come back now, y'hear?

THE BEVERLY HILLBILLIES. The Clampetts on the lookout for 'them movie stars'. From top, Donna Douglas, Irene Ryan, Buddy Ebsen, Max Baer Jnr.

and his snooty wife (Harriet FitzGibbon). Jed could have made a passable gentleman if he'd ever changed his old suit, but Granny was forever stirring her mountain medicines and threatening to cook uneatable things like possum and grits. Young Jethro (Max Baer Jnr) was a giant who didn't know his own strength, and his sister Elly May (Donna

Douglas) fairly bulged out of her Li'l Abner dresses. Only their millions made them welcome, and if any of the neighbours hoped they'd mellow with time, they were doomed to disappointment. It was a show for the midwest, complete with prissy spinster Nancy Kulp, but the urban areas watched it too, or it wouldn't have got such staggering numbers as to warrant the spinoffs and imitations it did. And although you'd never call it clever stuff, the first few seasons had sufficient zip to make them welcome before invention withered.

A movie spinoff that year was *Going My Way*, with Gene Kelly and the indispensable Leo G. Carroll. And another navy comedy was *Ensign O'Toole*, with Dean Jones. More experimental were *I'm Dickens He's Fenster*, well remembered slapstick about two carpenters (John Astin, Marty Ingels), and *Fair Exchange*, about an American and a British family who agreed to exchange their teenage daughters for a year. (Judy Carne and Dennis Waterman were two of the children involved.)

1963 was not exciting. Patty Duke got her own series, playing twins in *The Patty Duke Show*; Ray Walston as *My Favourite Martian* turned up to bother Bill Bixby; and in the backwoods farce *Petticoat Junction*, Bea Benaderet of *Burns and Allen* and *Beverly Hillbillies* got her own show at last, only to die of cancer during its run. Imogene Coca was funny in *Grindl* as a temporary domestic who got herself employed in some pretty screwy households: Telly Savalas was an axe murderer in the first. (We in the trade remember best the hard sell by writer-director David Swift, walking down a dark corridor and having a hairy hand reach through a grille to grab him by the chest. 'This is where we keep the writers,' he said as he extricated himself.) Pleasant too were *Glynis*, with Glynis Johns as a crime writer who was also an amateur sleuth; *Our Man Higgins*, with Stanley Holloway as a very English butler bequeathed to an American household; and *Harry's Girls*, with Larry Blyden as the song and dance man played by Clark Gable in *Idiot's Delight*. Other movie spinoffs were *Mr Smith Goes to Washington*, with Fess Parker, and *The Farmer's Daughter*, with Inger Stevens; both had more competence than most things you could see on the box twenty years later. *The Bill Dana Show*, about a Latin American bellhop, was a spinoff from *The Danny Thomas Show*. *The New Phil Silvers Show* tried to place Bilko as foreman of a factory, and failed miserably: it was the end for the star's Gladasya Productions.

1964 was pretty good, if only for the rival horror comedies, neither of which would back down. *The Addams Family* derived from the Charles Addams cartoons with their cobwebbed Gothic mansion and residents who looked like refugees from a funeral parlour. Morticia and Gomez were clearly into death as a hobby, Lurch the butler was the Frankenstein monster, Uncle Fester was a toothless ghoul, and there was another servant called Thing, a disembodied hand which popped up all over the place. The theme song set the style:

> They're creepy and they're kooky
> Their life is kinda spooky
> They're altogether ooky –
> The Addams Family.
> The house is a museum
> It makes you want to scre-am
> You really ought to see 'em –
> The Addams Family.

Both they and *The Munsters* lasted only two seasons, for black humour is hard to sustain, but more than twenty years on their reruns keep fan clubs happy. *The Munsters* was a little more openly spoofy, but casual viewers would have judged the shows almost identical. At 1313 Mockingbird Lane the Munster family consisted of Herman, a monster

THE MUNSTERS. A chance for Universal Studios to spoof its own horror shows. Fred Gwynne, Butch Patrick, Yvonne de Carlo, Al Lewis, Beverly Owen.

lookalike who had vampires for wife and father-in-law, and a werewolf for a son. Only Marilyn the niece looked like you or me, and the rest of the family pitied her because she was so normal that she couldn't hold a boy friend.

It must have been a year for the supernatural, because *Bewitched*, an eight-season runner and frequent rerunner, also debuted in 1964. Elizabeth Montgomery was the pretty witch who helped her businessman husband by twitching her nose to induce magical mischief. In this aim she was variously helped and hindered by her mother Endora (Agnes Moorehead), her father (Maurice Evans), her Uncle Arthur (Paul Lynde) and Aunt Clara (Marion Lorne). They all had supernatural powers, so the shows got a bit cluttered with magic, but basically *Bewitched* was just Blondie with a twist, and the poor befuddled husband (Dick York) was the one who got twisted.

Other comedies of the season had a shopsoiled look. *The Bing Crosby Show* was domestic comedy pure and simple, with Bing as a *former* crooner who'd chosen to become an electrical engineer. *The Baileys of Balboa* featured war between John Dehner, the snooty president of a yachting club, and Paul Ford, skipper of a scruffy charter boat. *Broadside* was the distaff section of *McHale's Navy*; *Gomer Pyle USMC* featured the dopey hayseed from *The Andy Griffith Show*, now in the marines (but still played by Jim Nabors). *90 Bristol Court* was a rotating comedy trilogy about selected residents of a condominium: Jack Klugman, Don Galloway and Debbie Watson were among those unhappily involved. *The Cara Williams Show* featured the star with Frank Aletter, as newlyweds who because of company policy must keep their marriage a secret. *Many Happy Returns* put John McGiver in a department store; *No Time for Sergeants* put Sammy Jackson in the air force; *The Tycoon* put Walter Brennan in big business; *Valentine's Day* put Tony Franciosa in publishing. Bob Cummings in *My Living Doll* was a psychiatrist driven off the rails by a female robot of which for some quite incredible reason he was in charge; *Mickey* was Mickey Rooney, running a hotel. Finally, *Gilligan's Island* refused to pass unnoticed, and indeed ran three seasons. A simple-minded farce which shipwrecked assorted folk on a desert island and left them to fend for themselves, its mission in life was to recall every gag ever perpetrated by Harold Lloyd, Charlie Chaplin, Laurel and Hardy or the Three Stooges, and reuse each week as many as would fit into half an hour. The audience must have enjoyed it, for it made stars of Bob Denver, Jim Backus, Alan Hale Jnr, Natalie Schaefer, and even Tina Louise. And at least two generations of kids have since lapped it up in reruns.

BEWITCHED. A witch and her family. Elizabeth Montgomery, centre: then clockwise, Maurice Evans, Agnes Moorehead, Dick Sargent, Erin Murphy.

Get Smart in 1965 was a newish concept, at least for television: a bumbling spy. To be brutally frank, the title sequence was always funnier than what followed, for Don Adams's insistence on repeating the same catchphrases every week became a little hard to take. But at the time the show seemed to have smart pace and even wit, and people now attribute this to the fact that Mel Brooks was one of the writers. It could be that there wasn't much else to enthuse about that season. *The Double Life of Henry Phyfe* (Red Buttons as a Milquetoast who looks exactly like a dead spy); Sally Field as the awful teenager *Gidget*; Ken Berry in a set-bound western spoof called *F Troop*; Eddie Albert and Eva Gabor in *Green Acres*, as city slickers being taken to town by country cousins; Juliet Prowse as *Mona McCluskey*, a cabaret and movie star who tried to continue her career without letting her husband know; *The John Forsythe Show*, about the headmaster of a school for girls; and Roger Smith as *Mr Roberts*, from the naval play. *The Smothers Brothers Show* concerned an angel who came back to help his dim brother. *Tammy*, another movie steal, had Debbie Watson as a Louisiana girl in the big city. *Please Don't Eat the Daisies* (yet another) was about a suburban family (Mom is a writer) who live with their big shaggy dog in a big shaggy house. *O. K. Crackerby* was Burl Ives, as a multi-millionaire with his feet on the ground. And *Hogan's Heroes* was a comedy ripoff of *Stalag 17* (the author of which sued) and of every other prisoner-of-war drama in which the guys spent their time thinking up escapes and the Krauts all said 'Ve ask ze qvestions.' Actually, the funny Nazis, Werner Klemperer and John Banner, were much funnier than supposed star Bob Crane.

The most revived show of that season is probably *I Dream of Jeannie*, in which Larry Hagman, now the wicked J. R. Ewing, played hubby to a beautiful genie who promised to carry out his every command. Barbara Eden being a pretty shapely lady, this rehash of *Bewitched* ran five seasons.

We have left the most grotesque of 1965 till last. *My Mother the Car* delivered what the title promised: Jerry Van Dyke bought an old car which turned out to be the reincarnation of his mother. Ann Sothern played the voice of mother: she and the network must have been pretty desperate.

1966 wasn't much in television terms. In *A Family Affair* Brian Keith as a rich playboy, and Sebastian Cabot as his portly manservant, played daddy to two orphan children, who had five seasons over which to grow up. Then there were *The Monkees*, who won all hearts despite being a flagrant steal from the Beatles. Stephen Strimpell as *Mr Terrific* took pills to become Superman; so a few months later did William Daniels as *Captain Nice*. *Occasional Wife*, about a spouse for platonic hire, was clean and forgettable. *Love on a Rooftop*, despite Judy Carne and Rich Little, likewise (especially to anyone who'd seen *Barefoot in the Park*). Jean Arthur in *The Jean Arthur Show* was a talkative legal eagle: so talkative that the folks stopped listening. *The Hero* had Richard Mulligan as a western hero who's afraid of horses, *Hey Landlord* had Will Hutchins as a

TV writer who misguidedly bought a share of a Manhattan brown-stone, *That Girl* had Marlo Thomas as an actress in New York. The movie spinoff was *The Rounders*, about modern cowboys.

There were three candidates for the lemon of the season. Phyllis Diller gabbled through *The Pruitts of Southampton*, with a splendid but disarrayed cast including Reginald Gardiner, Billy de Wolfe, Paul Lynde and Gypsy Rose Lee, but this spoof of the idle rich failed to rise. *Pistols 'n Petticoats*, set a hundred years ago, was a cross between *The Beverly Hillbillies* and *The Martins and the Coys*. Glamour star Ann Sheridan, soon to die prematurely, was lost in it. The undoubted winner however was *It's About Time*, a farce about two astronauts being lost in a time warp and finding themselves back in prehistoric times, with Imogene Coca and Joe E. Ross wearing skins and perpetrating hoary jokes which would have been turned down by *Hellzapoppin*. When this format didn't work, it was reversed: the cave folk came forward to modern Manhattan, and didn't care for what they found. *It's About Time* was what the viewers said when the network cancelled the show.

1967 was pretty well all lemons. *The Mothers-in-Law*, one supposes, was okay domestic farce for fans of Eve Arden and Kaye Ballard, but against that one had to set *The Flying Nun*, which meant what it said: Sally Field literally flew around, assisted by trade winds and her religious headgear. How this helped to convert people to good works, and why the Catholic Church approved of such a whimsy, is not clear. Otherwise, Richard Benjamin and Paula Prentiss, married in real life, played professional marrieds in *He and She*; Jerry Van Dyke, in *Accidental Family*, was given custody of his eight-year-old son and took him to live on a farm. In *The Second Hundred Years*, a young prospector is frozen alive in an avalanche; thawed out 67 years later, he finds that being technically a centenarian, he has a son who looks twice his own age. It was high on ingenuity and low on watchability.

It was really too complicated a comic idea for a series, as was next season's *The Ugliest Girl in Town*, the basic premise of which had Peter Kastner posing as a 'glamorous' female model in order to be with his fiancée in London. More popular items were *Here's Lucy*, yet another variation on the Ball saga in which she worked in her brother-in-law Gale Gordon's employment agency; *The Ghost and Mrs Muir*, in which Hope Lange as a widow falls for the ghost of the former owner of her seaside cottage (the piece was played more for laughs than the movie); and *The Doris Day Show*, which went through various formats without ever finding the right one. Basically she was a widowed mother who divides her time between the health-giving country and the big city where she must work. *Mayberry RFD* was *The Andy Griffith Show* without the original star but with Ken Berry and any old crackerbarrel regulars who happened along. It lasted a good deal longer than *The Queen and I*, with Billy de Wolfe as first mate of an ocean liner which had seen better days. Most talked-about show of the season was *Julia*, a fashionable tearjerker in which widowed Diahann Carroll (widows were *in* in the late sixties) toyed with the colour problem while working for a living and living in a curiously sumptuous apartment with her roly-poly kid, who may have looked adorable but badly needed elocution lessons. The level of the social consciousness may be gauged by her telephone conversation with her prospective new employer (Lloyd Nolan as an old crusty with a predictable heart of gold):

> SHE: I'm coloured. I'm a Negro.
> HE: Have you always been a Negro or are you just trying to be fashionable?

In 1969 there was *The Bill Cosby Show*, but that version ran only a couple of seasons and never hit the top of the ratings; the star was a school gym teacher. More successful (five seasons) was a 'cute' family sitcom called *The Brady Bunch*, in which Robert Reed with three sons marries Florence Henderson with three daughters; between them they add a cat, a dog and a housekeeper. Yuk. *The Courtship of Eddie's Father*, from the movie, was of the same ilk: a seven-year-old boy looks out prospective mates for his widowed dad. (Jodie Foster made an early appearance, though not as one of the mates.) *The Debbie Reynolds Show* was an *I Love Lucy* lookalike which failed. *The Tim Conway Show* limited itself to the adventures of a decrepit aeroplane. *To Rome With Love* found John Forsythe landing a job in Europe and taking his family with him. Monte Markham, who never struck lucky in sitcoms, failed again with a good ex-movie premise, *Mr Deeds Goes to Town*. And Dan Dailey did poorly with his gambit, *The Governor and J.J.*, as a politician ruling the state with the help of his zoo-keeping daughter. The hit of the season for my money was *My World and Welcome to It*, in which William Windom more or less played James Thurber (as he subsequently did many times on the stage). The role was that of a much-married cartoonist who contrasted drab and difficult reality with little cartoon fragments of imagination about the way he would like things to be. It was too smart and too subtle for the network.

Three long-runners began in 1970. *The Mary Tyler Moore Show* was basically another sitcom about an assistant producer in a Minneapolis television newsroom, but the difference was that all the people involved were not only funny but real, and the star, playing a character with a slightly jaundiced view of life, did not hog the limelight. Indeed, Ed Asner, Valerie Harper, Cloris Leachman, Ted Knight and Gavin McLeod all used MTM as a springboard to their own TV series, and also around were such familiar faces as Betty White, Harold Gould, Nancy Walker and Nanette Fabray. The whole thing was as close to life as TV comedy is required to get, and sometimes, though momentarily, it became drama too. *Lou Grant*, *Rhoda* and *Phyllis* all sprang directly from it, and *Hill Street Blues* derived something from it too, that sense of ensemble playing by characters for whom life goes on after the end titles have faded.

All in the Family was thought of by Americans as a big new American hit, and few people acknowledged its derivation from the British series *Till Death Us Do Part*. It certainly brought a fresh aspect to sitcomland: here was an unattractive middle-aged hero, sloppy and not very successful, constantly railing at his wife, his family and his neighbours, with special reference to any blacks or Jews who might come along. Anything was grist to Archie Bunker's mill of bad temper: sex, politics, feminism, menopause. To make it clear where the show stood, the Bunkers had a very loud toilet which was often heard flushing, a real conversation-stopper after twenty years of sitcoms in which nobody ever went to the bathroom. To begin with, the network ran a disclaimer before each episode, alleging that the show 'seeks to throw a humorous spotlight on our frailties, prejudices and concerns'. This quickly proved unnecessary: the nation took Archie to its heart, for reasons right or wrong. After all, he was a close approximation to what the trade had been saying for years was the typical television viewer: 'a fat little guy in Milwaukee, slouched in an old armchair with an empty beercan in his hand'.

These two shows between them revolutionized American television comedy; a third in the same season trailed a little way behind in originality, but still had more caustic wit than televiewers had been used to hearing. This was *The Odd Couple*, from Neil Simon's one-set comedy; Paramount stretched it out into five seasons. The two male divorcés putting up with each other were Jack Klugman (the slob) and Tony Randall (the wimp), and the penalty of success was that they remained perpetually associated with the characters they played.

Just to show that the old forms still existed, 1970 also produced *The Partridge Family*, about a widow and her five kids who were all musical. Andy Griffith was *The Headmaster*. *Nancy* was about a veterinary

ALL IN THE FAMILY. A copperbottomed American hit based on Johnny
Speight's East End shouting match *Till Death Us Do Part*. Rob Reiner, Sally
Struthers, Jean Stapleton, Carroll O'Connor.

surgeon who falls for the daughter of the President. *Nanny and the
Professor* was about a Mary Poppins-type governess who appeared as
from nowhere to help a maths teacher with his tiresome kids. *In Make
Room for Grandaddy*, Danny Thomas updated his original family, but

nobody cared. *Barefoot in the Park* chose to recast Neil Simon's play with black actors: it didn't feel right. *Arnie*, with Herschel Bernardi, was a factory foreman with doubts about his sudden promotion to an executive desk. And *From a Birds Eye View* had Millicent Martin as an airline stewardess with a penchant for helping people.

1971 found some stars in trouble. Even a genial Academy Award winner whom everybody liked couldn't save an archetypal sitcom like *The Jimmy Stewart Show*, perhaps because everybody knew him as James and thought that this undue familiarity must denote a rock star. Nor could Shirley Maclaine save *Shirley's World*, nor Don Adams *The Partners*, nor Dick Van Dyke *The New Dick Van Dyke Show* (in which he played a talk show host in Phoenix, Arizona). Richard Castellano, who had played the fat slob in *The Godfather*, was given something called *The Super*, which quickly died, as did Castellano's career. *The Chicago Teddy Bears* was a gangster spoof with too big a cast (though it included some familiar faces from the past). *The Good Life* had Larry Hagman and Donna Mills as middle-class dropouts who work as servants for a wealthy family. All very old-fashioned and ho-hum, but the new traditions were maintained by *Sanford and Son*, a black Americanization of the BBC's *Steptoe and Son*. Redd Foxx and Desmond Wilson were the junk dealers who expressed themselves at the top of their voices. It ran to 136 episodes, chiefly on the same basis as *All in the Family*: insult comedy. 'I can't eat that Chink food,' said old Sanford: 'those people do their cooking and their laundry in the same pot.' And when he complained: 'I still have some wild oats to sow', his son's reply was: 'At your age, you ain't got no wild oats, all you got is shredded wheat!'

M★*A*★*S*★*H* was the undoubted innovation of 1972, and of the next ten seasons. In fact, it was a great deal more enjoyable than the movie on which it was based, a black comedy which thought it clever to interpose outlandish jokes about army doctors in Korea with operation shots of blood and tissue. (M★A★S★H stood for Mobile Army Surgical Hospital.) The show kept the operations but omitted the gore, and concentrated on the cynical humour which must prevail when intelligent men find themselves in such a situation a long way from where they want to be. Practical jokes and sexual hang-ups proliferated, and Alan Alda loped through it all, tossing away one-liners like a rather more realistic version of Groucho Marx. He could not pass a group of female recruits without remarking: 'See you later, girls: go to my tent and lie down.' He called Korea 'the latest war to end all wars'. He didn't even keep quiet during surgery: 'While I'm cutting, Frank, you give him a manicure.' When a visiting officer took umbrage and pointed to his collar, saying

'This happens to be a gold oak leaf,' 'Hawkeye' Alda replied: 'I thought it was a little large for dandruff.' And when his commanding officer, after a telephone call from home, told him 'Imagine that, I'm becoming a father for the third time,' the only answer he got was, 'They know what causes that now.' Whole books could be written about *M★A★S★H*, which although set in the fifties mirrored American mores of the seventies; its plenitude of gags was truly dazzling, and it always left you with a twinge of guilt for laughing at something which was innately serious. And looked at fifteen years later, it hadn't dated at all.

Another trailblazer that year was *Maude*, a spinoff from *All in the Family*. Maude was Edith Bunker's redoubtable cousin, a woman ready to bend the world to her will until it broke. And her show went in for even more serious issues than had its source: drugs, abortion, rape, homosexuality, death. Oddly enough, it never travelled: Beatrice Arthur was simply too abrasive, it seems, for the English to take, though some of her scripts were remodelled, without much success, for London's tame American Elaine Stritch.

The third big hit of 1972 was *The Bob Newhart Show*, in which the star played a somewhat unlikely psychologist. He was fine as always, but the show was small beer compared with the previous pair. So were *The Little People* (Brian Keith as a pediatrician in Hawaii); *The Paul Lynde Show* (generation gap comedy); *Temperatures Rising* (high jinks in a hospital); and *Bridget Loves Bernie* (*Abie's Irish Rose* come back to haunt us). Borrowed from Hollywood was *Anna and the King* (which died despite Yul Brynner). Borrowed from British television were *A Touch of Grace* (formerly *For Love of Ada*, about old folks in love); *Love Thy Neighbour*, about reluctant friendship between black and white neighbours; and *Thicker Than Water*, with Julie Harris and Richard Long competing for their aged father's pickle factory. (The last was barely recognizable as the Lancashire farce *Nearest and Dearest*, but no matter, it closed after four episodes.)

The smash hit of 1973 was *Happy Days*, an easy-going family affair looking back to the music of the fifties. Ron Howard as the teenage son was the supposed star, but the whole show was overshadowed by the freak popularity of an over-age and little known actor called Henry Winkler as his irresponsible college friend Fonzarelli, known as the Fonz. There is no explaining the way America and the world went bananas over this character, not for a single season but for twelve of them. Perhaps the characters were simply pleasant to be with, reminding many people of their own families; perhaps the slightly serialized format had the appeal of a comedy soap opera. Perhaps the Fonz safely

HAPPY DAYS. Ronnie Howard (top left) was the original star, but that overage teenager Henry Winkler (bottom right), as the Fonz, stole the show. Anson Williams (top right) and Donny Most were the also-rans.

represented that element of danger which we all need in our lives. Whatever the reason, *Happy Days* made a lot of money for a lot of people, even though Winkler was so identified with his role that he would never be accepted in any other.

   Good Times was a five-year hit, but there is little to say about this black domestic sitcom except that the central character had once been the maid in *Maude*. It wasn't exportable, but then nor was anything else that year. Here's the roll call of clinkers. *Bob and Carol and Ted and Alice*, a tame version of the movie. *Calucci's Department*, with James Coco in charge of an unemployment office. *Adam's Rib*, from the movie about married lawyers. *Ozzie's Girls*, Ozzie Nelson's last tentative fling. *Needles and Pins*, a comedy of the garment district. *Roll Out*, a World War II comedy about a black platoon, didn't displace *M★A★S★H*. *Dusty's Trail*, an inept low-budget attempt to do *Gilligan's Island* in a stagecoach. *Lotsa Luck*, with Dom DeLuise running a lost and found department. *The Girl with Something Extra*; Sally Field as a wife who bewitches her husband by reading minds. And *Diana*, with Diana Rigg imported to bring a touch of Englishness to a New York department store. Ho, hum. Goodbye, 1973.

   M★A★S★H and Mary Tyler Moore having established the ensemble comedy, there was no shortage of imitators, some of them good like *Barney Miller*, which in 1974 had Hal Linden running a New York police precinct which seemed to have more than its share of idiotic visitors. As Barney once remarked when reproved by his superior for levity, 'We manage to have a laugh or two at humanity's expense.' Barney and his friends ran six seasons. *Chico and the Man* might have done so too, had not its young star shot himself at the height of his fame. Jack Albertson played the owner of a run-down garage on Los Angeles' east side, but Freddie Prinze was the hit as the fast-talking Chicano who enlivened his days and his business. It appeared after the tragedy that Prinze had a morbid streak and fancied himself going out in a blaze of glory like James Dean; one wonders even whether he liked the idea of the show fizzling out without him, which it did.

   For white audiences, there wasn't a lot to be said about *The Jeffersons*, except that it was funnier than spin-offs usually turn out to be. (*The Jeffersons* had been neighbours of the Bunkers in *All in the Family*.) *Rhoda* worked too: Valerie Harper had played the role of the sharp-tongued ambitious Jewish girl in *The Mary Tyler Moore Show*, and now she was set loose against a New York background, marrying, and separating, and starting a new career, and so on. It was all OK, but the fact was that Rhoda was more appealing as a support character than as a lead. The

BARNEY MILLER. Ensemble comedy triumphs in the unlikeliest of settings: a police precinct house. Now everybody's a comedian: Jack Soo, Steve Landesberg, Ron Glass, Hal Linden, James Gregory, Ron Carey, Max Gail.

same might be said for *Karen* (Karen Valentine) who had been a perky schoolgirl in *Room 202* but wasn't so interesting as a slightly kookie Washington resident looking out for women's rights. Paul Sand had also been funny as an occasional visitor to *The Mary Tyler Moore Show*, but he failed as a rather unattractive bass player in *Friends and Lovers*. As for *Sunshine* . . . well, this jaded schlock about a widower bravely trying to bring up his kids was only peripherally funny. (The original TV movie had been about the wife who died.) *The Texas Wheelers* was a kind of updated *The Real McCoys*. Best of a thin bunch was the TV version of *Paper Moon*, with Christopher Connelly and Jodie Foster. Some thought it better than the movie, but its charm was too elusive for the mass audience.

1975 saw a decided trend away from novelty comedies which simply made you laugh, and away indeed from film techniques, which had been the norm since the early sixties, into the new area of taped one-set shows whose appeal depended entirely on the personality of the star involved. Thus *The Blackboard Jungle* was brought up to date and turned comic in *Welcome Back, Kotter*, but what viewers cared about was Gabriel Kaplan as the teacher and John Travolta as the most resistant pupil. *One Day at a*

Time had Bonnie Franklin realistically playing a divorced Indianapolis lady with two daughters. *Laverne and Shirley*, a spin-off from *Happy Days*, was about two sloppy female singles working in a Milwaukee brewery, not the kind of setting the networks would have chosen five years earlier. The ensemble show was a bit of low life called *Hot*l Baltimore* (the bulb was always missing from the sign). *The Dumplings* concerned a fat couple. *Doc* was Barnard Hughes dispensing grizzled wisdom, and *The Practice* was Danny Thomas doing the same. *Phyllis* had Cloris Leachman, another MTM alumnus, on her own in San Francisco, moving in with her in-laws. *On the Rocks* was a comedy of prison life, based on Britain's *Porridge*. *Joe and Sons* were low-life Italians, *The Cop and the Kid* was about an Irishman looking after a black orphan, *The Montefuscos* were more Italians living in Connecticut. Failing to satisfy more traditional requirements were *When Things were Rotten*, a truly dire Mel Brooks spoof of the Robin Hood saga, and *Good Heavens*, in which Carl Reiner as a Jewish angel came down to grant somebody one wish each week.

Low life was still the trend in 1976. Having little to do with the movie *Alice Doesn't Live Here Any More*, *Alice* was a long-runner set in a midwestern diner, where most of the denizens preferred to yell at each other than to speak in normal tones; but Linda Lavin fared well from it, and Polly Holliday as the biggest loudmouth of all was later given a show of her own, called *Flo*. *Ball Four* was set in a baseball locker room, which gives an idea of its level. *Busting Loose* was about teenage girl hunters. *Szysznyk* (no wonder it failed) had Ned Beatty as a playground supervisor. *Fish* was about the drab home life of the lugubrious detective from *Barney Miller*. Moving up the social ladder a little, *CPO Sharkey* had Don Rickles using his night club insult technique as a drill instructor in the marines. *All's Fair* was about a political columnist (Richard Crenna) who married a girl half his age. *The McLean Stevenson Show* found the supposed star, who had foolishly resigned from *M*A*S*H* (and been killed off so that he couldn't return), running a hardware store. All these had moderate success at best. Most of them failed, as did the only novelty comedy of the season, *Holmes and Yoyo*, one of several attempts to find fun in the concept of a robot cop.

Three's Company was the smash of 1977. Two seasons earlier, as *A Man About the House*, it had been the smash of the London scene, but this was a sexed-up, leering version of an originally rather charming comedy about two girls who take in a male roommate. It ran almost forever. Best of the rest, which meant that it didn't run at all, was *The Betty White Show*, about a TV star being directed by her waspish ex-husband (John

Hillerman). *Carter Country* was an amusing title only while Carter was President. *On Our Own* was about working women in New York. *San Pedro Beach Bums* was a West Coast update of the Dead End Kids. The only traditional comedies were *Operation Petticoat*, set in a submarine, and *Tabitha*, an attempt to get another generation out of *Bewitched*. But what really changed the face of television was *Soap*, a spoof of soap operas which certainly went further than television man had ever gone before. Sisters connected two families, one rich and one poor. The rich one alone was enough to give a headache to the censors. The husband was an adulterer, the wife a ditherer, her father mad as a hatter, her butler insolent. The other family had a manic husband and a gay son, and the things they all said and did would have brought a blush to the cheeks of Aunt Edna. A hundred episodes of this excess were too many, but *Soap* at its best had a welcome energy and edge.

1978's *Taxi* was the latest ensemble comedy, set plainly in a garage and too gritty for some; the acting ability of Judd Hirsch helped a lot. By now a blending of old and new styles was becoming evident. *Mork and Mindy* was basically an old-fashioned fantasy about a guy from outer space stranded on earth, but as played by Robin Williams Mork from Ork was an inexplicable zany, and we were expected to laugh at the star's personality rather than anything he did or said. (In fact, there wasn't much to look at, since the show was usually confined to two sets.) *Diff'rent Strokes* also sounded old-fashioned, being about a Park Avenue millionaire who adopts two children; but the children were black, and one of them (Gary Coleman) rapidly took centre-stage because of his extreme self-possession and curious cuddly look (actually caused by a chronic illness). His success was such that he became a millionaire well before he was twelve, and his expertise allowed the writers to introduce 'banned' subjects such as drugs and abortion into what was basically a cute comedy for the family. The other fantasy comedy of the season, *Turnabout*, didn't work at all, because it was sloppily made and badly cast. In fact, there was an immensely long list of failures, including *Angie* (Italian waitress marries baby doctor), *The Bad News Bears* (junior league baseball organized by Jack Warden), *Detective School* (self explanatory), *Grandpa Goes to Washington* (more cracker-barrel philosophy), *Just Friends* (Stockard Channing as a divorcée still chased by her husband), *Highcliffe Manor* (a spooky house spoof), *Hizzoner* (David Huddleston as a midwestern mayor), *Hello Larry* (McLean Stevenson as a talk show host with domestic trouble), and *Makin' It* (a teenage disco affair). But one other success (though a limited one) came from the Mary Tyler Moore production factory. *WKRP in*

Cincinnati, about an oldtime radio station having to update its image, was noisy and zany enough to appeal to the younger set, yet it had streaks of wit which appealed to a more mature following.

Everything in 1979 seemed to be a rehash. *Struck by Lightning* took place in Munster country: the caretaker of an old country hotel is actually the Frankenstein monster, agreeably played by Jack Elam; but there were no takers. *Working Stiffs* was supposed to bring echoes of the Three Stooges, but Michael Keaton and Jim Belushi didn't seem to have the right talent. *A New Kind of Family* seemed a very old idea: widow with three kids and a dog teams up with widower who has a thirteen-year-old daughter. *The Last Resort* was farce about an incompetently run hotel. *Benson* tamed the sarcastic butler from *Soap* and made him the governor's strong right arm: for no reason beyond the personality of Robert Guillaume, the show ran seven seasons. In *Out of the Blue* an angel came down to live with an average American family. The only slightly fresh show was *The Associates*, which applied the Mary Tyler Moore multi-character approach to a New York law office under the fallible direction of Wilfred Hyde White; but it was caviare to the general.

The eighties will deserve their own retrospective when they can be recollected in tranquillity, but the main trends are already obvious: cheaper sets, less action, more socially conscious jokes. By mid-decade there was a rush to be first past the post with taboo subjects like lesbianism. It surfaced first in *Kate and Allie*, the saga of two divorced women living together; in order to keep their rent low they pretend to be a homosexual couple, only to find that the landlady shares their penchant. In the following season *The Golden Girls* found that they had a lesbian friend, but the dim member of the trio, played by Betty White, was perplexed: wasn't Danny Thomas one of those? 'No, Blanche,' said Beatrice Arthur firmly, 'that's Lebanese.' *The Golden Girls* by its very being broke another American taboo, that of old age. Here were three ladies past sixty, and another of eighty, making jokes about their condition, and still interested in sex. The eldest one was also vulgar, boasting that she never got up in the night to go to the bathroom. 'I never pee till seven in the morning. Of course, I don't get up till eight.' The show was set in the Golden State, which is full of eligible elderly ladies looking for mates. This means that priests are kept busy. 'I'm afraid I can't wait,' said one. 'This is Miami: I have funerals backed up.'

For the rest, there were still more cute black kids outwitting their elders (*Webster*), and plenty of black adults too: Bill Cosby by just lying in bed and talking to himself could keep half of America tuned in. The ensemble comedy continued with *Cheers* and *The Duck Factory*, as did the family domestic sitcom, though in this department there were signs of desperation when the same joke cropped up one season in three different shows. 'Dad,' says the teenage son, 'can we have a serious talk?' Dad looks up from his office work/newspaper/breakfast. 'Is this about using the car?' The actors in such shows were more or less interchangeable: they had all learned, from playing Neil Simon in stock, how to handle one-liners; while when at liberty a few hours spent watching *Beulah* on daytime re-runs would put them in fine fettle for *Gimme a Break*, a downmarket version of same which enjoyed a curiously long run. What they did not need was stand-up comedy experience, for in the eighties everybody was expected to be a comedian, and the audience had to be able to keep up with the references. On *Glitter*, an inside-magazine format, someone asked: 'How long ago was this picture of Phyllis Diller taken?' The answer was: 'Last week, and it's Boy George.' People who didn't watch television were unlikely to get the point.

HAWKEYE in *M*A*S*H*: I don't understand a word you say, but I defend to the death your right to confuse me.

12

Back to the new routines:

THE TRIUMPH OF BAD TASTE

It may be thought that in delving so deeply into America's situation comedy of the last several decades, we have neglected the major output of stand-up comics in the Hollywood studios. The fact is that there have been very few. We reached in our chronological survey the early fifties, and the middle of that decade was more or less taken over, together and separately, by Martin and Lewis, a team which is now, rather happily, a faded memory. They began, did Dino Crocetti and Joseph Levitch, in night clubs, and in those surroundings one can imagine that the very difference between the over-relaxed crooner and the frantic face-pulling grown-up baby must have garnered a few laughs from those well wined and dined. But on the big screen, despite all the sumptuous mounting that Hal Wallis and Paramount could provide, it quickly became evident that there was no sympathy between the two, that they really didn't like each other at all and that sooner or later they must part. At the time it was thought that Martin was the passenger and Lewis had all the (misplaced) talent, but in the event Dino went on to a long and lucrative career as Las Vegas's most elegant singing drunk, and put in a few quite acceptable acting performances along the way. Jerry Lewis fans must have been dismayed by the first few movies he made on his own, his wild extravagances untempered by the soft style of his former partner, and even when he gained the approval of the highbrow French critics for such comedies as *The Nutty Professor* and *The Bellboy*, his was a minority following, insufficiently large to cover his costs. By the mid-seventies he was out in the wilderness, having failed to recover his foothold on Broadway or on television. Indeed he was considered by many to be unemployable, and when in 1982 he gave a surprisingly good straight (if sour) performance in *King of Comedy*, it was too late to salvage a lost career.

Sid Caesar is the American comedian who should have made it to the top. He got there once, in the early days of American television, but he lacked staying power, and personal problems intervened. He can be appreciated today only through fuzzy telerecordings of sketches from *Your Show of Shows*: the famous take-off of *This is Your Life*, in which he is the subject who refuses, and the sketch played entirely in pidgin French in which he constantly finds his baker friend's white handprints on his own wife's derrière. *'Explanation!'* he cries, and always one is forthcoming, until the time he gets in the way, and the white handprints are on his own backside. *'Explanation!'* he demands, and the baker says: *'Je vous aime!'* Caesar's co-star was Imogene Coca, and Carl Reiner was one of the gang, which often on the shows sat around like Hancock's on that fateful Sunday afternoon. Caesar did appear briefly in a few movies, but to little effect.

One of his writers was Mel Brooks, who more or less took over Hollywood comedy in the seventies, which is a pity since Brooks has plenty of ideas but no style. He also has no taste, which is why his *History of the World Part One* virtually brought his Hollywood career to an end, if one excepts his lamentable remake of *To Be or Not to Be* with himself in the Jack Benny role. Brooks has an obsession with farting, as demonstrated in the baked beans sequence in *Blazing Saddles*; his hero in *History of the World* was even to be called the Farting Man until the studio said 'No'. Still, in *Young Frankenstein* he re-created Universal's monster world with loving care, and before going too far inserted a few good jokes: 'Pardon me, boy, is this the Transvylvania station?' his hero asks through a train window. His *Silent Movie* on the whole fell flat, and would have fallen flatter had not the audience been waiting for the guest star appearances. Brooks's imperishable moment of glory remains the 'Springtime for Hitler' sequence in *The Producers*, a Busby Berkeley musical extravaganza performed by goose-stepping Nazis. Wherever Brooks went, Gene Wilder and Zero Mostel and Dom DeLuise were never far behind.

Comedians in Hollywood movies of the early fifties tended to take second place to romantic leads. Thus MGM always had some funny man on hand to support Esther Williams and Doris Day, but the studio's comedy films *per se* were always on the 'B' level and fairly dreadful. So Jimmy Durante contented himself with re-doing his famous numbers like 'Umbriago' and 'Inka a Dink a Dink' and 'I'm the Guy that Found the Lost Chord', and Red Skelton did his drunk act mercilessly, reserving his principal energies for television specials, in which he remained for years a potent if unpredictable attraction. Donald O'Connor was around too, but after his great start at Universal, and a useful assist to Gene Kelly in *Singin' in the Rain*, never got another chance to sparkle. As the seventies approached, two from England became useful stalwarts. His fans tend to forget that Michael Crawford played a leading role in *Hello Dolly*; later he veered towards Disney, as did Jim Dale, an alumnus of the 'Carry On' school. Ed Wynn, whose style had been too ethnic for Hollywood, also found an eventide home at 'the mouse factory'.

Mel Brooks was not the only talent in Hollywood sympathetic to 'the good old days'. Stanley Kramer, of all people, staged in 1963 a marathon chase farce called *It's a Mad Mad Mad Mad World*, and had every comic artist he could think of playing cameo roles, from Ethel Merman to Joe E. Brown and from Mickey Rooney to the Three Stooges. Unfortunately he cast in the lead Spencer Tracy, among whose many virtues there did not lurk the capacity to be funny, and it was a long four hours (even, after cutting, a long two-and-a-half). A little later, Blake Edwards determined to repeat the dose, and to dedicate his effort, which he called *The Great Race*, to Laurel and Hardy. What he had failed to note was that Stan and Olly had been adept at creating beautiful bricks with next to no straw beyond their own personalities. In *The Great Race*, skilful performers like Jack Lemmon and Tony Curtis and Peter Falk were forced to shriek at each other to avoid being upstaged by the multi-million-dollar gadgets: the saloon bar and the pie fight were classic demonstrations of overkill. Edwards went on to star Peter Sellers in a series of increasingly feeble pratfall farces about the accident-prone Inspector Clouseau, but not too many of the paying crowds found them so rib-tickling as the star and producer obviously did. In similar vein that ardent copyist Peter Bogdanovich in 1973 rubbed several old comedies together, to have them break into flame as *What's Up Doc*: it was thought funny at the time, but in retrospect only the final chase through San Francisco survives.

Little if anything has been said in this volume about foreign language comedians, because few are known to English-speakers. There must be a word, however, for Jacques Tati, who so brightened up the international post-war scene with his lugubrious postman in *Jour de Fête* and his even more sidesplitting inventions for the silent hero of *Mr Hulot's Holiday*, setting a whole seaside town askew without ever realizing that he is responsible. The scenes of his stepping on a tightening rope and being precipitated into the sea, or of his canoe collapsing scissors-style

JACQUES TATI in *Monsieur Hulot's Holiday* is so watchable that he causes
others to cause accidents. That's the chief joke, and it's enough.

around him, or of his offering at a funeral a wreath consisting of wet
leaves stuck to a slowly collapsing inner tube, these are moments to
cherish. Alas, Tati was a man with strange theories of comedy, also a
man who would take no advice, and the vehicles which followed,
despite increasing budgets, found decreasing audiences: people naturally resented having to search the frame so intently before discover-
ing what was supposed to be funny. Tati's student Pierre Etaix made a
promising start in a couple of exceedingly funny shorts, but the
complexities of feature film structure were clearly beyond him. France
also sent us Fernandel, whose long horsy face was usually funnier than
his vehicles, and Louis de Funes, who struck a comic note or two. Italy
was tentative about Toto; and Mexico did not press upon us the talents
of Cantinflas, who after a splendid first appearance in *Around the World in
Eighty Days* made a real dog's breakfast of his solo starrer *Pepé*.
    We come, surely, to Woody Allen, the melancholy Groucho Marx of
the sixties and seventies. Mr Allen presents the familiar image of the
nebbish, the little man who is put upon but finally breaks through, but he
does it at *Sunday Times* level. Right from his participation in a fashionable self-indulgent mishmash called *What's New, Pussycat*, he was the

WOODY ALLEN. Jokes about death made him the cult comic of the seventies.

darling of the intellectuals. He proceeded to delight them still further by making cheap films, short films, usually in black and white, in which against drab backgrounds he dealt with topics of the moment. This was university humour: when Allen went into production values, it was to mock Ingmar Bergman and Russian literature in something called *Love and Death*. In appearance Mr Allen is a weed, but he lets us know that he has a strong sex drive, and why not? In mournful New Yorkish tones he goes through his night club routine of one liners: he is everybody's token compulsive neurotic. When he says: 'Isn't the food here terrible? Yes, and such small portions', he is really saying 'Life is nothing but loneliness and depression, but I don't want to die.' He talks a lot about death. 'It's not that I'm afraid to die. I just don't want to be around when it happens.' And: 'With my luck, suicide would turn out to be only a temporary solution.' He is far from boastful: 'My one regret in life is that I'm not somebody else.' And his own depression touches everybody he knows: 'I met this girl, she was a streetwalker in Venice. She drowned.' So he turns back for consolation to sex. 'It's the most fun you can have without laughing.' Typical, somehow, that his most lauded film, *Zelig*, was about a man who really wasn't there at all.

Neurotic comedians are of course nothing new. Everything Woody Allen writes for himself, he might have written thirty years ago for Oscar Levant. Oscar, usually cast as the hero's baleful friend, could have lived well from his music alone: he was both pianist and composer. A close friend of George Gershwin, he was shaken by the man's death in 1937 and turned increasingly to Hollywood for a few reassuring creature comforts. He had always wanted to write an opera which included the word 'Silencio!', and Gershwin helped him arrange that: you can hear it still, in *Charlie Chan at the Opera*. A few years later, after he had become a radio hit in a quiz show called 'Information Please', he found himself playing second lead in *Rhapsody in Blue*, a film tribute to Gershwin; Levant was responsible for what humour could be discerned amid the encircling gloom. He was called back to provide the rather heavy light relief in *Humoresque*, of which he said: 'I played an unsympathetic part – myself.' He was good fun in *An American in Paris*, duetting with Gene Kelly in Just Listen to my Heart and playing, by couresty of trick

OSCAR LEVANT was another manic depressive who made his neuroses pay. Here in *Humoresque* he did what relaxed him most. Joan Leslie and Charles Coburn are among the onlookers.

photography, all the musicians in an orchestra (and even the man shouting 'Bravo' from the box). There was something irresistibly funny about this thick-lipped, stooping, cigarette-smoking, bleary-eyed self-styled genius giving vent to muttered wisecracks while he demonstrated his musical versatility. But most of the time Oscar was acting sour, he really was *feeling* sour. By the mid-fifties the state of his world had got to him: behind the guy playing the psychiatric patient in *The Cobweb* was a guy badly in need of psychiatric help. It was his last film role.

He will be remembered with surprising affection. Few of us really mind a devil at our ear providing we have the power to shake him off when we desire, and Levant was easily shaken. He had no beliefs. 'I'm an atheist,' he said, 'a person with no invisible means of support.' He certainly never took his career seriously, his summation of it being as follows: 'In some situations I was difficult, in odd moments impossible, on rare occasions loathsome, but at my best unapproachably great.' He knew the burden he placed on society: 'I'm a controversial figure: my friends either dislike me or hate me.' But he knew too that the fault was not always his, and he produced at least one imperishable thought about his adopted town: 'Strip the phony tinsel off Hollywood and you'll find the real tinsel underneath.'

In the late fifties, when Levant gave up, several young comedians were knocking at the foundations of society by questioning established concepts of morality, religion and good taste. Mort Sahl offended against all three in a somewhat grumpy way: his best remembered line is likely to be his impromptu one at the end of Otto Preminger's first five-hour private screening of his film about Israel, *Exodus*. When asked how he liked it, Sahl looked pained. 'Otto,' he said, 'let my people go . . .' More readily accepted were the academic jibes of Tom Lehrer, a Harvard professor and semi-professional singer at the piano of his own rapier-like ditties, waxing sentimental about *The Old Dope Peddler* or this version of a boy scout's call to arms:

> Be prepared: that's the boy scout's solemn creed.
> Be prepared: and be clean in word and deed.
> Don't solicit for your sister, that's not nice –
> Unless you get a good percentage of her price.
> Be prepared: and be careful not to do
> Your good deeds when there's no one watching you.
> If you're looking for adventure of a new and diff'rent kind,
> And you come across a Girl Scout who is similarly inclined,
> Don't be nervous, don't be flustered, don't be scared –
> Be prepared!

Canadian humour doesn't seem to exist, but Australian humour rates a quick mention. It revolves chiefly around Barry Humphries, who seldom appears as himself, though he was closely connected with the *Barry MacKenzie* movies about what would now be called a nerd in London. I walked out of the first one just as the hero was having prawn curry poured into his Y-fronts, but not before I had heard someone excuse himself on the grounds that he must 'go and point Percy at the porcelain'. Mr Humphries, to sensitive audiences, is not tolerable as Sir Les Patterson, a drunken diplomat who persistently dribbles food and spittle down his waistcoat, but in drag as Dame Edna Everage he has his adherents, especially when giving advice about sex. At least he's funnier than Joan Rivers.

There have been few female comedians, and even fewer prepared to do stand-up routines. The best of the latter bunch since the mid-fifties has been the American Phyllis Diller, who is probably not an unattractive person when one can get underneath the process of uglification on which she deliberately embarked as her key to show business success. Bob Hope put her in several of his later films, and she had a misjudged TV series called *The Pruitts of Southampton*, but to meet the true Diller you have to catch her act, which starts off from her garish and unlovely dress: 'I think I got this on upside down.' She proceeds to destroy her whole (fictitious) family, and anyone else within reach:

My sister's the original meter maid. You only have to meet her, and she's made.

She's spent more time on her back than Michelangelo.

She's been in more motel rooms than the Gideon Bible.

When she goes to confession, she has to take a packed lunch.

My mother hated me. She once took me to an orphanage and told me to mingle.

I admit I was an ugly child. When I was out once with my mother and a man said does your monkey dance?, she made me dance.

When I asked her how to turn off the electric fan, she said grab the blade.

My grandfather's a hundred-and-five years old. Mind you, he's been dead for twenty of 'em. Still sits there at the head of the table. You know, it's hard to get through a family meal when there's one person obviously not enjoying it.

My mother's senile. You look into her eyes and you just know nobody's driving.

Does the dog bite? Yeah, he's the only dog I know that bites his nails. When you tell him attack, he has one.

Dolly Parton, the original hunchfront. She has a yacht in Seattle, and it's windy there. One day she hung her bra out to dry, and woke up in Brazil.

In Britain, Diller's male counterpart is Les Dawson, a glum lump of a man who looks square all the way down, and has a nice line in misanthropy. His wife, he says, is a delicate woman: 'She pecks at food like a bird. A buzzard. She's illiterate: she tells a waiter in a restaurant that she enjoyed the roast peasant. ("I said it's not peasant, it's phar-tridge.") She's so ignorant she thinks the charge of the light brigade is the electricity bill.' Having temporarily exhausted this vein, Dawson looks round the studio set and is disdainful: 'Looks like an early Greek Macdonalds.' He goes into his Blackpool landlady routine, a pinch from Norman Evans. Then into Cosmo Smallpiece, a dangerous monster who starts to rattle at the mere thought of women, while the mention of knickers, knockers, bloomers or a juicy pair will turn him into a quivering jelly. Finally, as himself again, he discusses his recent holiday in Corfu.

> Did you have the shish kebab?
> – From the moment we got there.
> Did you see the Acropolis?
> – We were never off it.

His travel companion is the last one to get it in the neck:

> He has a Polaroid. I can tell from the way he walks. The doctor said try a suppository up the back passage. But we hadn't got a back passage, so he did it in the front street and got arrested.

From such ruderies it is a short step to the determined bad taste of Glaswegian Billy Connolly, all beard and devilry:

> This friend of mine came round and said help, you've got to help me, I've just done the old woman in. I said you haven't. He said I can prove it, come round. So we went to his back garden, and there she was dead, naked, under the soil with just her bum sticking up. I said why did you leave her bum uncovered? He said well, I had to have somewhere to park my bike . . .

And old reliable Bob Monkhouse, a quipster for thirty years, has become a bit on the saucy side in his older age:

BOB MONKHOUSE, in between patter routines, suffers the fate of most modern comedians, doing duty as a game show host.

My girl friend and I bought a sex manual, but half the pages were missing. We went straight from foreplay to post-natal depression.

I lack stamina, you know. Last year I was having an affair with a nympho. One night she sat up in bed and said quick, my husband. I said, thank God he got my message. Still, she made a happy man very old.

These jokes all got by on BBC television, but it is an American, Pete Barbutti, who lays claim to the joke in the worst taste of all:

I went to see this farmer, and he had a pig with a wooden leg. I said how on earth did that come about? He said, 'Oh, that's a remarkable pig, that is. Do you know, the barn set on fire and I was locked inside? That pig ran for help and saved me. And then a few months later, I fell off the tractor and hurt myself bad, and that pig came and gave me the kiss of life. I'd be dead as a doornail but for that pig.' I said, 'But you haven't explained the wooden leg.' He said 'Well, a great pig like that, you don't eat it all at once!'

Such jokes are now accepted without comment by the sons and daughters of those who were shocked by Max Miller and Donald McGill. But there are signs of reaction. Max Bygraves, everybody's favourite easygoing Londoner for more than thirty years, does in his gentle sixties an act including a few drops of sauce:

Two ladies of eighty one day were talking in a park neath a clear sunny
    sky.
They were feeding the ducks and the swans on the lake when one of them let
    out a cry.
For running towards them they both saw a streaker, you should have heard
    both of them screech:
One of the ladies, they say, had a stroke, but the other one couldn't quite
    reach . . .

But the centrepiece of his act is a dewy-eyed tribute in song to the film stars of yesteryear. Only Max can make it scan:

> When I was just a kid I'd go
> To see the local picture show:
> For tuppence I could get three hours of fun.
> There up on the screen I'd see
> Film stars looking down at me,
> And I would lose my heart to every one.
>
> I loved Roy Rogers and Trigger the horse,
> I loved Dick Powell, and Ruby Keeler of course.
> The great W.C. – my little chickadee –
> And Mae West would say 'Big boy, aren't you slow!'
> And that was my big treat – we did it every week –
> At the Trocadero in the Old Kent Road.

Max doesn't leave the stage without somewhat apologetically offering a story which reveals his own frustration and that of many others, at the way society has turned since he was a lad:

There was this fellow, he hated punk rockers. So he used to drive along in his car and run down as many as he could spot. This particular morning he'd already done one, and then as he drove along the main road he got another. So he was looking for another to make it three, but the next fellow he saw was a priest with a petrol can: he'd obviously run out and was walking to the next garage. So being a religious man, this fellow gave the priest a lift, but as they drove on he soon spotted a punk rocker and turned into the side of the road to get his three in a row. But just as he bore down on him he remembered he'd got a priest in the car. He thought I can't do this, not now, so he swerved away. And just as he did, there was the most almighty bang. 'What's that?' he cried; and the priest said: 'I could see you were going to miss him, so I opened the door . . .'

Perhaps the most popular comic entertainers in Britain as this book is being written are the Two Ronnies, Ronnie Corbett and Ronnie Barker, whose seasons of weekly BBC variety shows have enjoyed high rating success since the late sixties, when they emerged from David Frost's background to become fully fledged stars in their own right. Barker, bespectacled and stout, has been the more successful in finding long-running shows of other kinds, in *Porridge* as the wily old lag Fletcher, and in *Open All Hours* as the mean-minded, stuttering, north-country shopkeeper. Corbett, bespectacled and very short, struggles along as the henpecked son, a role he is too old to play, in *Sorry!*, which is not among the great comedy formats of our time. Rather strangely, they both seem to enjoy most of all getting together for their sparkling Saturday show, which is based almost entirely on the foisting of risqué material on to a basically family audience. I have not heard that the Ronnies have received any complaints, for their beaming smiles and mischievous eyes make them irresistible to all classes. Nor does anyone seem to mind the sameness of the jokes or their unvarying format, which is bounded fore and aft by the delivery of supposed news items. This is a device borrowed from David Frost, with the difference that the Ronnies' news is plainly fictitious:

Bad news of the Gay Lib expedition to the cannibal section of Borneo. They've been captured and made into fairy cakes.

His Magnificence the Potentate of Abu Ben Wadi returned home tonight after visiting eight other sheiks in a round of wife swapping parties. He now wishes to be known as the *Im*potentate of Abu Ben Wadi.

Good Housekeeping magazine today named Elizabeth Taylor Good Housekeeper of the Year. She's been divorced five times and always kept the house.

Today at Sotheby's auction rooms lot 36, a ton of cascara, was eaten by lot 37, an elephant. Lot 37a, a last minute surprise, failed to find a buyer.

A nationwide survey of British women's underwear preferences reveals that the most favoured garment is pants in Hants, stays in Hayes, knickers in Twickers, and in Rockall nothing much to speak of.

In Uganda today the President was asked what he was going to do about tightening up defence. He replied: 'Defence? De man with de nails am comin' to fix it.'

We have just heard that due to the electricians' strike, *Oh Calcutta* is to be renamed *Fanny by Gaslight*.

Here's a message for seven honeymoon couples in a hotel in Peebles. Breakfast was three days ago.

The British Medical Council has asked us to give a simple piece of advice to men who wish to avoid falling hair. Get out of the way.

And now, by way of light relief, we'll be taking a look at fur covered toilet seats and asking: 'Do they tickle your fancy?'

There then follows a conversational sketch, which may take the form of a surrealist send-up of a situation impossible to begin with, but in any event will depend largely on puns and *double entendres*:

> When did you last make love, then?
> – If you must know, about 1945.
> That's a damn long time ago.
> – Oh, it's only 2130 now.

The Ronnies next get away the guest singer's spot, and proceed with Mr Barker's speech, which is formal, straight to camera, and often something of a tongue twister:

> This is an appeal, for women only. No, don't switch off, it's you men I want to talk to, especially. I am appealing to you, for women. I need them desperately. I can't get enough – and the reason I appeal to you men, is that I don't appeal to you women. But I still need them . . . I expect many of you have a few lying about in drawers, that you haven't touched for years. Please post them off today. Help us set up our Women on Wheels service for old men who can't move about? I think we should all remember that Christmas is on its way. And when it comes, and you are sitting at home by a roaring great woman, think of all those unfortunate people who are having to go without. Why not send them an old flame or two, to warm the cockles of their hearthrug? . . .

Probably the next segment is an episode from some expensively mounted but too often disappointing parody serial, such as *The Phantom Raspberry Blower of Old London Town*. And before the musical finale there must be room for Mr Corbett's solo item, just as relaxed as Mr Barker's was punctilious. Mr Corbett sits in an old chair, complains about his producer and the BBC's cheapskate regulations, and more or less manages to finish a story of the shaggy dog variety:

> This evening I'd like to tell you a story about a chap who was cast away on a desert island. Oh, by the way, this is not the one about the two

shipwrecked Irishmen, who found a lifeboat and broke it up to make a raft
. . . No, this chap spent fifteen years without seeing a soul, nothing but
sand, and sea, and sky – sounds like a summer season at Cleethorpes,
doesn't it? Anyway, one day he's sitting there when out of the sea comes
an apparition . . . it turns out to be a beautiful girl wearing a wet suit,
snorkel and flippers. 'Hello,' she says, 'what are you doing here?' So he
tells her. And she says, 'Oh you poor man. How long is it since you had a
cigarette?' 'About fifteen years,' he says, 'and I'm thinking of giving it
up.' So she unzips a breast pocket of her wet suit – she's a very big girl –
and hands him a packet. 'I'm overwhelmed,' he says. 'Buster,' she replies,
'you ain't seen nothing yet. How long is it since you had a drink?' 'About
the same,' he says. So she unzips the other breast pocket and gets out a
flask. 'This is marvellous,' he exclaims. 'And how long is it,' she says
huskily, 'since you played around?' And she starts to unzip the front of her
wet suit. 'Good heavens,' he says, 'don't tell me you've got a set of golf
clubs in there!'

Though none of this would have pleased Lord Reith, it cannot be said,
in the 1980s, to be breaking very many barriers. Not like Richard Pryor,
who also got on to British television (though late at night) with lines
like:

My daddy died fucking. He came and he went at the same time.

The British establishment was appalled at that, but for them the Two
Ronnies can do no wrong. Of course, the British taste, as exemplified by
the television ratings, is nothing if not catholic. Though its special
commendation is reserved for comedy in the Ealing tradition, it will
tolerate the amateur hour inanities of Cannon and Ball, who in what one
hopes will be their only film, *The Boys in Blue*, ruined a perfectly good
Will Hay script. It laughs at the gibbering impersonations of Freddie
Starr, and the hesitant borrowings of Little and Large. It won't give up
the domestic tantrums of Terry Scott, at nearly sixty still the infantile fat
boy who never grew up. It adores Richard Briers, who has been
everybody's favourite middle-class twit since he gave up impersonating
the upper-class Ralph Lynn; he has remained popular through a passel of
sitcoms including *The Marriage Lines*, *The Good Life* and *Ever Decreasing
Circles*. It supports Derek Nimmo, who for twenty years and more has
been playing a stammering curate, and the knockabout Russ Abbot and
the fashionable Jasper Carrott. It goes for nostalgia in a very big way, as
Dad's Army and *Hi De Hi* and *'Allo 'Allo* have shown; and to judge from
ten years of *Are You Being Served?*, the jokes don't even have to be new.
The *Sunday Times* crowd is also catered for, in *To the Manor Born* and *Yes*

Minister and the perennially repeated *Fawlty Towers*, where the humour lay not in the script but in John Cleese's physical and vocal mannerisms as the megalomaniac hotel proprietor. It takes many kinds to make the world, and all kinds to appreciate humour. The funniest performers I have seen on television in the last twelve months are two elderly Americans called Bob and Ray, who it seems have been devising and presenting what they call interview comedy on the American airwaves for more than forty years, comedy with such irresistible highlights as the Slow Talkers of America and the man who can't remember the points he wants to make. With talent like that lurking unsuspected, by me at least, such a survey as this can never hope to be complete; and if it were, it would still have no hope of pleasing every reader. To quote Max Miller once more:

A joke is like a woman getting out of a car. Sometimes you see it, and sometimes you don't!

I say, how dare you belch in front of my wife?
– Sorry, old man, I didn't know it was her turn.

> – SIR HENRY at *Rawlinson End*

IT'S NEVER GOODNIGHT
FROM THEM

There is no formula for success in comedy. Success is short, and likely to depend on luck, and physical style, and the kind of comedy one chooses, which may be fashionable one year and not the next. Most comedians reach their peak in their thirties, and don't sustain much beyond that because their appeal is based on an element of foolishness, which becomes less attractive in a fifty-year-old than in a young man who has no real experience of the world and can thus be forgiven his ignorance. There are of course exceptions such as Will Rogers: age could not wither him, as Bernard Shaw remarked upon another occasion, because he had never bloomed. His appeal was that of a genial uncle, and the same might be said in different ways for Robert Benchley and Jack Warner and Bruce Forsyth. On the other hand the appeal of Harry Langdon was that of a helpless baby, and Harold Lloyd that of a shy teenager: their white make-up emphasized this. Even Laurel and Hardy became less funny as age lined their faces, in Stan's case prematurely; they came to seem like senile old men rather than amiable young idiots. With Abbott and Costello, curiously, age didn't seem to matter except insofar as it physically incapacitated them. In their last film they got away with hoary vaudeville routines just as well as they had in their first: only the audience had grown bored.

Nor does age matter to comedians who hide their real selves behind a heavy disguise: George Robey's painted eyebrows, Groucho Marx's painted moustache, Chaplin's tramp ensemble, the rubber faces of Sid Caesar and Peter Sellers. They are less able however to sustain a feature film because the disguise prevents the flow of sympathy which the audience should feel for its addled hero. But they are luckier than George Formby, who before he was forty had to stop making films altogether because his gumpish character was no longer attractive, and, despite his millions, than Bob Hope, who spent the last thirty years of his career, having grown out of his coward character, desperately seeking another which would give equal pleasure to the public.

There are of course a few comedians who don't start to be funny until they *look* middle-aged. Charley Chase was actually assisted by the ravages of alcohol, which also gave Robert Benchley his air of likeable befuddlement. Henpecked types like Edgar Kennedy and Leon Errol and Charlie Ruggles and Robertson Hare have to start with a little middle-aged dignity so that they can lose it: it is the very idea of their seeking the youth that is lost which makes the ladies laugh. Nor could Bob Newhart have amused us as a young man, being a character perpetually behind the eight-ball; while Fred Allen capitalized on his baggy eyes, Harry Worth on his bumbling unwisdom, Jack Benny on his undiminishing vanity, and Shelley Berman on his pessimism.

It is possible, too, for the cleverest of the all-round entertainers to sustain their personalities until a venerable age, simply by dropping the more physical aspects of their personae and concentrating on the trademarks which the audience knows and loves. Danny Kaye, Max Bygraves, Gracie Fields, Tommy Steele, Eddie Cantor, Maurice Chevalier and Al Jolson are or were of the stuff which, health permitting, would allow them to go on giving concerts into their seventies, knowing that the audience would still applaud. Perhaps indeed the applause would be louder than ever, for the onlookers would see in the performances a chance for their own continued vitality into old age.

We are however still speaking of exceptions. Many comedians come in like fireworks, only to fizzle out like them too, never to be heard from again. Thus the Smothers Brothers, and George Gobel, and Hal March, and Joe Penner; they were lucky enough to ride one wave of fashion, and unlucky enough to be swamped by the next one. It is a risk, too, to rely entirely on physical characteristics. To some extent Buster Keaton and Jimmy Durante did, but they had more to offer than a frozen face or a long nose. Joe E. Brown found his big mouth a liability in later years, as did Claude Dampier his toothy grin, Nat Jackley his rubber neck, John Bunny his fat stomach, and Wee Georgie Wood his dwarfish stature. Jacques Tati with his long clumsy body and Lupino Lane with his supple one which did exactly what he told it to, both had touches of genius, but they could not sustain their careers. Nor was it enough merely to be fat, like Roscoe Arbuckle and John Bunny and Graham Moffatt and Fred Emney.

Old men on the whole were seldom funny, unless they were Harry

Davenport or A. E. Matthews. But young men who convincingly pretended to be old, like Chic Sale and Moore Marriott and Andy Clyde, could command plenty of work. So could female impersonators: Douglas Byng ('Queen of the Obsceni') and Arthur Lucan and Norman Evans. (Almost every comedian had a couple of female impersonation scenes to his credit.) Camp comics were frequently popular, especially in Britain, where Kenneth Williams, Frankie Howerd, Larry Grayson and John Inman were promptly taken to the nation's heart: but it was Americans who made stars, perhaps unrealizing, of such gay bachelors as Clifton Webb and Monty Woolley. Effete silly asses like Claude Hulbert and Peter Haddon and Terry-Thomas had a bit of a struggle, but there was always a welcome for truly debonair chaps like Jack Buchanan and Bobby Howes and David Tomlinson.

Of the stand-up comics, Britain led the way in applauding the cheeky chappies, Max Miller and Tommy Trinder and Jimmy Tarbuck. But they liked innocent Arthur Askey just as well, and melancholics like Les Dawson and Tony Hancock, and incompetents like George Formby and Will Hay and Tommy Cooper and Michael Crawford and Norman Wisdom. In America these styles were a little more respectable, less dangerous. Comics didn't get prissier than Edward Everett Horton or Franklin Pangborn, or cheekier than Bob Hope or Milton Berle, or grouchier than Groucho himself or W. C. Fields (with the exception of Oscar Levant who was a true manic-depressive). But Jerry Lewis was as incompetent as all get out, and that was perhaps the beginning of the modern phase in film comedy: the comedy of irresponsibility and barrier-breaking.

There had always been barrier-breakers, of course: Max Miller and Frank Randle, to name but two. There had always been zanies also: Mischa Auer and Jerry Colonna and Hugh Herbert and Red Skelton and Martha Raye and Olsen and Johnson must surely count in that category. But in the fifties it was outwardly respectable people like Lucille Ball and Jack Lemmon who were going zany, and there was a new breed like Ken Dodd who were zany-looking to begin with. It seemed a small step in the sixties to combine this trend with the satirical bent shown by Monty Python, and come up with total iconoclasts: Lenny Bruce and Richard Pryor and Billy Connolly and Cheech and Chong, who dominate the kind of comedy on offer today, with no holds barred.

Certain kinds of comedy figure go marching on. Connivers like Phil Silvers as Bilko, whose British equivalent might have been Arthur English, the perennial spiv. Ethnic types like Issy Bonn and Flip Wilson and El Brendel. Dialect comics: Hylda Baker and Judy Canova and

Sandy Powell. Commentators on the world in which we live: Mort Sahl, Ted Rogers, Jasper Carrott. Insulters: Eric Blore, Phyllis Diller, Don Rickles, Shecky Greene. Drunks like Jimmy James, friends of the heroine like Eve Arden, cynics like Lynne Overman. Comic conjurors like Paul Daniels, half pints like Robert Dhery and Charlie Drake, impressionists like Rich Little and Mike Yarwood, ventriloquists like Edgar Bergen and Peter Brough, pianists like Liberace and Victor Borge, comic ladies like Carol Burnett, slouches like Tom Ewell, spivs like Arthur English, loudmouths like Ernie Kovacs, grotesques like Don Knotts, cads like Terry-Thomas, dancers like Roy Castle and Dickie Henderson, compères like Johnny Carson, knowalls like Arthur Haynes, bandleaders like Henry Hall, violinists like Vic Oliver and Ted Ray, windbreakers like Le Petomane, pop-eyes like Marty Feldman, patter acts like Clapham and Dwyer, bullies like Bill Fraser, routine funny men like Buddy Hackett and Red Buttons and Jonathan Winters and Jimmy Wheeler and Frank Carson. The comedians come and go, mingle and separate, each with his or her moment of glory. One way or another they enliven our world, and without their buffer the suicide rate would certainly increase. For as the man said: laugh and the world laughs with you; weep and you weep alone.

Did you ever get the feeling that you wanted to go, and still have the feeling that you wanted to stay?

JIMMY DURANTE in *The Man Who Came to Dinner*

INDEX OF COMEDIANS

Page numbers for illustrations appear in bold

BAKER, HYLDA – *cont.*
star with *Nearest and Dearest*.
Catchphrase: 'She knows, you
know.'
Best films: *Saturday Night and
Sunday Morning* 60. *Nearest and
Dearest* (as a record of the series)
73. 230
BALL, LUCILLE (1910–).
American female clown who
served a long film apprenticeship
in dull roles before TV's *I Love
Lucy* made her an international
comedy star.
Best films: *The Affairs of Annabel*
38. *Dubarry was a Lady* 43. *Easy to
Wed* 46. *Her Husband's Affairs* 47.
Fancy Pants 50. *The Long Long
Trailer* 54. *Yours Mine and Ours*
68.
TV series: *I Love Lucy* 51–5. *The
Lucy Show* 62–8. *Here's Lucy* 68–
73. 194, 249–51, **250**, 263
BANKS, MONTY (1897–1950)
(Mario Bianchi). Italian comedy
dancer who made a number of
silent two-reelers in Hollywood
before moving to Britain and
marrying Gracie Fields. Best
silent work needs seeking out. 87
BARKER, ERIC (1912–). Mild,
almost apologetic British
character comedian who made
his mark in radio's wartime
Merry-Go-Round.
Best films: *Brothers in Law* 57.
Carry On Constable 60.
Autobiography: *Steady, Barker* 56
(his catchphrase, along with
'Carry on smoking.') 230
BARKER, RONNIE *see* THE
TWO RONNIES
BAXTER, STANLEY (1926–).
Scottish comic actor and
impressionist.
Best films: *Very Important Person*
61. *The Fast Lady* 63. 208, **209**
BEERY, WALLACE (1880/86–
1949). American character star,
former silent comedian. 75
BENCHLEY, ROBERT (1889–
1945). American comic writer
who moved from the *New Yorker*
to Hollywood and became
popular as a hesitant lecturer in
many shorts, also as friend of the
hero in a host of films. An
unsuspected alcoholic.
Biography: *Robert Benchley*, 46,
by his son Nathaniel.
Best films: *How to Sleep* 35. *China
Seas* 35. *Foreign Correspondent* 40.
The Reluctant Dragon 41. *The
Major and the Minor* 42. *I Married a
Witch* 42. *Road to Utopia* 45. *It's In
the Bag* 45. 123, 162, 169, 300
BENNETT, BILLY (1887–1942).
British music hall monologuist.
38–40

BENNY, JACK (1894–1974)
(Benny Kubelsky). American
comedian of international
standing, usually acting mean or
put-upon. More successful in
radio and TV than in movies.
Best films: *Hollywood Revue of
1929*. *Artists and Models* 37.
Charley's Aunt 41. *To Be or Not to
Be* 42. *It's in the Bag* 45. *The Horn
Blows at Midnight* 45.
Biography: *Jack Benny* 76 by
Irving Fein. **61**, 161–5, **163**, 252–
5, **254**
BENTINE, MICHAEL (1922–).
Anglo-Peruvian comedian, a
former Goon who specializes in
crazy novelties. 209, 231
BERG, GERTRUDE (1899–1966)
(Gertrude Edelstein). Amply
proportioned American Jewish
comedienne, on TV in *The
Goldbergs* and *Mrs G Goes to
College*. 246, 264
BERGEN, EDGAR (1903–78).
Swedish-American ventriloquist
with famous dummies Charlie
McCarthy and Mortimer Snerd.
Father of Candice Bergen. 302
BERLE, MILTON (1908–)
(Mendel Berlinger). Brash
American TV and vaudeville
comedian; never quite a movie
star, but now revered for long
service.
Best films: *Margin for Error* 43.
Always Leave Them Laughing 49.
It's A Mad Mad Mad Mad World
63.
Autobiography: *Milton Berle*, 74.
8, 53–4
BERMAN, SHELLEY (1926–).
American monologuist and night
club comedian. On film in *The
Great Man* 64. 300
BEST, WILLIE (1916–62). Goggle-
eyed black American comic
actor, once known as Sleep'n Eat.
The prototype frightened
manservant of days gone by.
Best films: *The Ghost Breakers* 40.
The Body Disappears 41. *Hold
That Blonde* 45. 178
BEVAN, BILLY (1887–1957)
(William Bevan Harris).
Australian comic actor who
moved to Hollywood and
became a familiar second stringer
of the silents, going on in talkies
to many small parts, often as
frightened policeman.
Best films: (apart from silent
shorts): *Journey's End* 30.
Cavalcade 33. *Dracula's Daughter*
36. *Cluny Brown* 46. **66**, 74
BLANC, MEL (1908–). British
comic actor sometimes in his
own plump and cuddly person
but more usually as the voice of

innumerable Warner cartoon
characters. 252–4
BLORE, ERIC (1887–1959). British
comic actor who after stage
experience went to Broadway
and Hollywood and became
familiar as a butler who could be
unctuous and insulting almost in
the same breath.
Best films: *The Gay Divorce* 34.
Top Hat 35. *It's Love I'm After* 37.
The Lone Wolf Strikes 40. *The
Lady Eve* 41. *The Moon and
Sixpence* 42. *Fancy Pants* 50. 178
BOLGER, RAY (1904–87).
American rubber-legged dancer.
Best films: *The Wizard of Oz* 39.
The Harvey Girls 46. *Look for the
Silver Lining* 49. *Where's Charley?*
52. 55–6, **56**
BONN, ISSY (1903–) (Benjamin
Lewis). British music hall
comedian who told Jewish
stories. 301
BORGE, VICTOR (1909–).
Danish comic pianist who for
forty years has been
internationally popular with his
eccentric concerts. 302
BRENDEL, EL (1890–1964).
American comic actor who
always played a mild-mannered
Swede with fractured English.
Best films: *Sunny Side Up* 29. *Just
Imagine* 30. *If I Had My Way* 40.
50
BRESSLAW, BERNARD
(1933–). Giant-sized British
comic actor who majored in
dopey roles after his success in
TV's *The Army Game* as Private
Popplewell.
Catchphrase: 'I only arsked'.
Best films: *I Only Arsked* 57. *Too
Many Crooks* 58. *The Ugly
Duckling* 59. *Carry On Screaming*
66. *Up Pompeii* 70. 232
BRICE, FANNY (1891–1951)
(Fanny Borach). American
comedienne of homely looks, a
poor Jewish girl who worked her
way up to be star of the Ziegfeld
Follies with her blues singing and
impersonation of Baby Snooks,
but never successfully broke into
films.
Best films: *My Man* 28. *Everybody
Sing* 38. *Ziegfeld Follies* 44.
Biographical films of her life:
Broadway thro a Keyhole 33. *Rose
of Washington Square* 38. *Funny
Girl* 68. *Funny Lady* 75. 50
BROOKS, MEL (1926–)
(Melvin Kaminsky). Excitable
noisy American comedian who
began as a writer for Sid Caesar
and others before finding his own
niche in Hollywood as a wild-
shooting satirist.

Best films: *The Producers* 68. *The Twelve Chairs* 70. *Blazing Saddles* 74. *Young Frankenstein* 74. *Silent Movie* 76. xii, 285

BROUGH, MARY (1863–1934). British character comedienne, one of the Aldwych farce team. Best films: *Rookery Nook* 30. *A Cuckoo in the Nest* 33. 16

BROUGH, PETER (1916–). Elegant British ventriloquist, son of another (Arthur Brough). Peter's dummy Archie Andrews rather curiously became a radio star, and their long-running show *Educating Archie* which began in 1950 gave opportunities to other talents including Ted Ray, Tony Hancock, Max Bygraves and Julie Andrews. 213

BROWN, JOE E. (1892–1973). Wide-mouthed American star comedian of the thirties who emitted a foghorn-like sound when startled. His personality deserved better vehicles. Background: circus, vaudeville, baseball. Best films: *Sally* 29. *You Said a Mouthful* 32. *Six Day Bike Rider* 34. *Alibi Ike* 35. *A Midsummer Night's Dream* 35. *Bright Lights* 35. *Showboat* 51. *Some Like It Hot* 59. Autobiography: *Laughter is a Wonderful Thing* 56.

BRUCE, LENNY (1924–66) (Leonard Alfred Schneider). Influential, foul-mouthed, drug-riddled American comedian of the new school. (He claimed that the only obscenity was war.) His material restricted him to Greenwich Village clubs (and the London Establishment). Biographical film: *Lenny* 74. xi

BUCHANAN, JACK (1891–1957). Tall, elegant British song and dance man of stage and screen in the twenties and thirties, always incomparably debonair. Best films: *Monte Carlo* 30. *Brewster's Millions* 33. *That's a Good Girl* 33. *Break the News* 37. *This'll Make You Whistle* 37. *The Band Wagon* 53. Biography: *Top Hat and Tails* 78 by Michael Marshall. **63**, 80–81, **81**, 94, 97

BUNNY, JOHN (1863–1915). Cherubic American comedian, who always played the henpecked womanizer. One of the most popular stars of the pre-Chaplin age. Catchphrase (in vaudeville): 'Here's to our wives and sweethearts: may they never meet!' Best films: such one-and-two-reelers as survive. 300

BURNETT, CAROL (1933–). Plain and lanky American comedienne who rose to great popularity on TV in the seventies as queenpin of a long series of one-hour sketch shows. Her film appearances, sometimes dramatic rather than comic, were less successful. 302

BURNS AND ALLEN. George Burns (1896–) (Nathan Birnbaum) and Gracie Allen (1902–64) were longtime partners in American vaudeville before they married. They had some Hollywood popularity in the thirties, but their peaks came with radio and especially television: in the fifties their names were on everyone's lips, he with his cigar indulging her scatty remarks. Catchphrase: 'Say goodnight, Gracie.' Best films: *Six of a Kind* 34. *We're Not Dressing* 64. *A Damsel in Distress* 37. *The Sunshine Boys* (Burns) 70. *Oh God* (Burns) 77. Autobiography (Burns): *I Love Her, That's Why* 55. *Living It Up* 76. **61**, 247–9, **248**

BUSCH, MAE (1897–1946). Australian comedy actress in Hollywood, especially with Laurel and Hardy. Best films: *Come Clean* 31. *Sons of the Desert* 33. 127

BUTTERWORTH, CHARLES (1896–1946). Languid American comic actor who often played an alcoholic and was one. Very upper class persona. Best films: *Love Me Tonight* 32. *Bulldog Drummond Strikes Back* 34. *Ruggles of Red Gap* 34. *Thanks for the Memory* 38. *Road Show* 41. 178

BUTTONS, RED (1918–) (Aaron Schwatt). American vaudeville and TV comic in occasional movies. Usually played the little guy, slightly at odds with the world. Best films: *Sayonara* 57. *Five Weeks in a Balloon* 62. *Stagecoach* 66. *They Shoot Horses Don't They* 69. TV series: *The Red Buttons Show* 52. *The Double Life of Henry Phyfe* 65.

BYGRAVES, MAX (1922–). Easy-going, gentle-voiced British entertainer who sings a little and tells a few jokes. Catchphrases: 'A good idea, son'; 'I've arrived, and to prove it, I'm here'; 'I wanna tell you a story'. Best films: *Tom Brown's Schooldays* 51. *Charley Moon* 56. Autobiography: *I Wanna Tell You a Story* 76. 294–5

BYNG, DOUGLAS (1893–). British cabaret comedian and female impersonator, noted in the thirties for his naughty songs, which he wrote himself. He billed himself as 'bawdy but British'. 301

CAESAR, SID (1922–). American television comedian who after immense fifties popularity in *Your Show of Shows* saw his career fall away through personal problems. A gifted mimic. Best films (not so good in his case): *Tars and Spars* 45. *It's A Mad Mad Mad Mad World* 63. *A Guide for the Married Man* 67. 285

CANNON AND BALL Tommy Cannon (1938–) (Thomas Derbyshire) and Bobby Ball (1944–) (Thomas Harper). British television comedians who graduated from the working men's clubs and should have retired there. Their hope to emulate Abbot and Costello has not been fulfilled, and a veil should be drawn over their only film. Cathphrase: 'Rock on, Tommy'. 297

CANOVA, JUDY (1916–83) (Juliet Canova). Strident American hillbilly comedienne, a forties star of second features. From a vaudeville family. Best films: *Sis Hopkins* 41. *Joan of Ozark* 42. 149

CANTINFLAS (1911–) (Mario Moreno). Mexican clown, acrobat and bullfighter who had a very brief fling with Hollywood. Best film: *Around the World in Eighty Days* 56. 287

CANTOR, EDDIE (1892–1964) (Israel Iskowitz). American vaudevillian, a banjo-eyed singer and dancer with a high-pitched voice and sprightly manner. A big Broadway star, but not an unqualified success in the movies. Best films: *Whoopee* 30. *Roman Scandals* 33. *Thank Your Lucky Stars* 43. *Show Business* 44. *The Eddie Cantor Story* was filmed 53 with Keefe Brasselle. Autobiographical books: *Take my Life* 57. *The Way I See It* 59. *As I Remember Them* 62. **146, 147**, 146–9

CARMICHAEL, IAN (1920–). British light leading man who,

CARMICHAEL, IAN – *cont.*
after years unnoticed in revue and
West End plays, hit the highlight
as a nervous novice in Boulting
Brothers comedies of the fifties,
and later played Lord Peter
Wimsey on television.
Best films: *Simon and Laura* 55.
Private's Progress 55. *Brothers in
Law* 57. *Lucky Jim* 57. *I'm All
Right Jack* 59. *School for Scoundrels*
60.
Autobiography: *Will the Real Ian
Carmichael Please Stand Up?* 82. 198

CARNEY, GEORGE (1887–1947).
British revue comedian who
came to films in middle age and
played easy-going fathers.
Best films: *Father Steps Out* 37.
Love on the Dole 41. Not in text

CARSON, FRANK (1926–).
Irish comedian, on television in
the seventies and eighties.
Catchphrase: 'It's the way I tell
'em'. 302

CARSON, JACK (1910–63). Beefy
American comic actor who often
played the hero's dumb friend
but was not much of a success on
his own.
Best films: *The Strawberry Blonde*
41. *Make Your Own Bed* 44. *Two
Guys from Texas* 48. *It's a Great
Feeling* 49. *Red Garters* 54. 179

CARSON, JOHNNY (1925–).
American night club comedian,
gag writer and quizmaster who
became a television fixture (and
extremely rich) as host of NBC's
'Tonight' show. 302

CASTLE, ROY (1933–). British
dancer and light entertainer who
for some years was one of Jimmy
James's stooges. 302

CATLETT, WALTER (1889–
1960). American comic with
vaudeville and Ziegfeld Follies
experience.
Best films: *Bringing Up Baby* 38.
Look for the Silver Lining 39. **138**,
178

CHAMPION, HARRY (1866–
1942). British cockney music hall
comedian whose famous songs
include 'Any Old Iron', 'Boiled
Beef and Carrots', 'Ginger
You're Barmy' and 'I'm Henery
the Eighth, I Am'. 23

CHAPLIN, CHARLES (1889–
1977). Internationally famous
British comic who began his
career with Fred Karno's troupe
and scored an almost instant
personal success when they went
to America. His real genius
flowered in the early
unpretentious shorts; his later
features were too carefully
considered to have vitality.

Best films: *The Tramp* 15. *The
Pawnshop* 16. *Easy Street* 17. *The
Cure* 17. *The Immigrant* 17. *The
Adventurer* 17. *A Dog's Life* 18.
Shoulder Arms 18. *The Kid* 20.
The Idle Class 21. *The Pilgrim* 23.
The Gold Rush 24. *The Circus* 28.
City Lights 31. *Modern Times* 36.
The Great Dictator 40. *Limelight*
52.
Autobiography: *My Wonderful
Visit* 30. *My Autobiography* 64.
My Life in Pictures 74. xii, 64, 75–
78

CHASE, CHARLEY (1893–1940)
(Charles Parrott). Toothbrush-
moustached American comedian
who made many two-reel
comedies in the twenties and
thirties, often as a henpecked
husband or go-getter.
Best films: *Limousine Love* 27.
The Pip from Pittsburgh 31. *Now
We'll Tell One* 32. *Fallen Arches*
32. *Luncheon at Twelve* 33. *On the
Wrong Trek* 36. *Rattling Romeo* 39.
68, **69**, 300

CHEECH AND CHONG.
Richard Marin (1946–) and
Tommy Chong (1938–) are a
defiant example of anti-
traditional humour in the
eighties. Drug-ridden and foul-
mouthed, they represent the very
antithesis of the great comedians
of the past. Their pitiful films are
not worth recalling. 301

CHESTER, CHARLIE (1914–).
British radio comedian who
began as an army entertainer and
after the war became famous for
his crazy show *Stand Easy*. 217

CHEVALIER, ALBERT (1862–
1923). British cockney comedian,
half French by birth.
Famous songs: 'Knocked 'em in
the Old Kent Road', 'My Old
Dutch', 'Funny Without Being
Vulgar'. 22

CHEVALIER, MAURICE (1888–
1972). Incomparable French
revue star, the man with the
straw hat and the jutting lip, not
to mention a roving eye for the
ladies. While happiest on the
stage, Chevalier had periods of
film success, especially in
Hollywood.
Famous songs: 'Louise', 'Isn't it
Romantic?', 'I Remember it Well.'
Best films: *The Love Parade* 30.
One Hour With You 32. *Love Me
Tonight* 32. *The Merry Widow* 34.
Folies Bergère 35. *Le Silence est
d'Or* 47. *Gigi* 58. *Fanny* 61. *In
Search of the Castaways* 62.
Autobiographies: *The Man in the
Straw Hat* 49. *With Love* 60. *I
Remember It Well* 72. **63, 81**

CLAPHAM AND DWYER.
Charlie Clapham (1894–1959)
and Billy Dwyer (*c.* 1890–1943)
were British comedians who
mainly confined themselves to
radio; a cross-talk act with a
straight man and a fool, in this
case a drunken toff. 302

CLARK AND McCULLOUGH.
Bobby Clark (1888–1960) and
Paul McCullough (1883–1936)
were stalwarts of American
variety and burlesque.
McCullough was the straight
man; Clark had painted spectacles
and behaved like Groucho Marx.
As a team they made a few
shorts; Clark alone is best
observed in *The Goldwyn Follies*
(1938). 50

CLEESE, JOHN (1939–). Very
tall British comedy actor with a
fine line in mania.
Best films: *And Now for Something
Completely Different* 71. *Monty
Python and the Holy Grail* 74.
Clockwise 86.
TV series: *Fawlty Towers* 75, 79.
231, **232**, 298

CLITHEROE, JIMMY (1916–72).
Pint-sized Lancashire comedian
who as 'the Clitheroe Kid' kept in
work throughout his adult life,
not only in pier theatres but as
star of a long-running radio
series.
Best film: *Much Too Shy* 42. 114

CLYDE, ANDY (1892–1967).
Scottish-American comedian, a
vaudeville and silent film clown
who found a niche in Hollywood
playing twice his own age, and
made nearly a hundred farcical
two-reelers. Also in features and
TV series. 179

COBORN, CHARLES (1852–
1945) (Colin Whitton
McCallum). British light
entertainer of the music halls,
who in his nineties was still
singing 'Two Lovely Black Eyes'
and 'The Man Who Broke the
Bank at Monte Carlo'. The latter
can be seen in *Variety Jubilee*
(1943). 22

COCA, IMOGENE (1908–).
American revue and television
comedian, especially popular
with Sid Caesar in the fifties.
Solo in the 1963 series *Grindl*.
266, 271, 285

COHAN, GEORGE M. (1878–
1942). Irish-American song and
dance man of the American
theatre, a whirlwind of energy
who was also playwright and
producer. On film in *The
Phantom President* (1934); played
by James Cagney in *Yankee*

Doodle Dandy (1942). 50, **51**
COLE, GEORGE (1925–).
British comedy actor, long the
befuddled innocent.
Best films: *Cottage to Let* 41.
Quartet 48. *Top Secret* 51. *The
Green Man* 57.
TV series: *Minder* 79–84. 187, 192
COLONNA, JERRY (1903–86).
Wide-mouthed, piercing-voiced
American variety comedian who
appeared with Bob Hope's radio
gang and sang a number of songs
including 'Conchita Lopez'.
Best films: *Star Spangled Rhythm*
42. *Road to Rio* 47. 179
CONKLIN, CHESTER (1888–
1971) (Jules Cowles). American
silent slapstick comedian with
drooping moustaches, featured
briefly by Chaplin in his 1936
Modern Times. 75
CONNOLLY, BILLY (c1945–).
Foul-mouthed Scottish
comedian. xi, 292
CONNOR, KENNETH (1918–).
British general purpose comic
actor, a member of the Carry On
team. 201 et seq, **206**
COOPER, TOMMY (1921–84).
Giant-sized, fez-topped British
television comedian who got
magic tricks wrong. Died on
stage during a live show.
Catchphrase: 'Just like that!' 226
CORBETT, RONNIE *see* THE
TWO RONNIES
COSBY, BILL (1938–). Black
American comedy actor who was
popular from 1965 but made his
biggest commercial hit in TV's
The Bill Cosby Show 85. 272, 282
COSTA, SAM (1910–81). British
band singer with handlebar
moustache. Became a comedy
character ('Good morning, sir,
was there something?') in radio's
Much Binding in the Marsh. Not in
text
COURTNEIDGE, CICELY
(1893–1980). Punchy, sometimes
strident, British comedienne and
singer, often with her husband
Jack Hulbert. Films mostly in the
thirties, stage thereafter.
Best songs: 'Riding on a
Rainbow', 'Soldiers of the King',
'Vitality'.
Best films: *Jack's the Boy* 32.
Under Your Hat 40. *The L-Shaped
Room* 62.
Autobiography: *Cicely* 53. 84–85,
88
COWARD, NOEL (1899–1973).
British theatrical multi-talent.
186–7
COX, WALLY (1924–76). Mild,
bespectacled American comedy
actor, popular in the fifties as

TV's Mr Peepers and Hiram
Holliday. 251, 260
CRAWFORD, MICHAEL (1942–
). (Michael Dumble Smith).
British light actor, former
juvenile, who became noted also
for his acrobatic skills, on
television in *Some Mothers Do
'Ave 'Em* and on stage in *Barnum*.
Best films: *The Knack* 65. *The
Jokers* 66. *Hello Dolly* 69. 8, 193
THE CRAZY GANG. See separate
entries for Nervo and Knox,
Naughton and Gold, Flanagan
and Allen, Eddie Gray.
Ensemble films: *OK for Sound* 37.
Alf's Button Afloat 38. *The Frozen
Limits* 39. *Gasbags* 40. *Life is a
Circus* 54. 99–103, **100**, 106, 109,
185
DALE, JIM (1935–) (James
Smith). Amiable British light
comedy actor, former pop singer:
in several 'Carry Ons', also *The
National Health* 73. *Pete's Dragon*
77. Not in text
DALEY, CASS (1915–75).
American acrobatic comedienne.
Best films: *The Fleet's In* 41. *Star
Spangled Rhythm* 42. *Red Garters*
54. 149
DAMPIER, CLAUDE (1879–
1955) (Claude Cowan). Toothy,
beak-nosed British comedy
character actor, noted for nasal
drawl and references to 'Mrs
Gibson'. Much on radio.
Catchphrase: 'That's right . . .'
Best films: *Boys will be Boys* 35.
Don't Take it to Heart 44. 118
DANIELS, PAUL (1938–).
British north-country conjuror
who became a lively BBC TV
star despite, or because of, many
jokes about his wig.
Catchphrase: 'Say yes, Paul',
'Not a lot'. 302
DAVIS, JOAN (1907–61). Rubber-
faced, acrobatic American
comedienne who enlivened a
number of Fox musicals in the
late thirties and early forties
before becoming a star of 'B'
features and later of television.
Catchphrase: 'I love that boy.
Love him, I tell you!'
Best films: *On the Avenue* 37.
Thin Ice 37. *Hold that Coed* 38.
Hold that Ghost 41. *Show Business*
43. *George White's Scandals* 45.
TV Series: *I Married Joan* 52–6.
251
DAWSON, LES (1933–).
Lugubrious British comedian
mostly on TV, latterly as host of
Blankety Blank. 292
DE CASALIS, JEANNE (1896–
1966). British revue comedienne
and character actress, best known

on radio as the dithery 'Mrs
Feather'.
Best films: *Cottage to Let* 41.
Medal for the General 44.
Autobiography: *Things I Don't
Remember* 53. 121, **121**
DE FUNES, LOUIS (1908–1983).
Excitable, bald French comedian
with a streak of manic
malevolence.
Best films: *Femmes de Paris* 54.
Don't Look Now 67. *The Mad
Adventures of Rabbi Jacob* 73. 287
DE LUISE, DOM (1933–).
Roly-poly American comedian,
mostly in support of Mel Brooks
and Gene Wilder. 285
DENHAM, MAURICE
(1909–). British character actor
who can be beady-eyed and
mean, but has displayed fine
comic sense, notably as Dudley
Davenport in radio's *Much
Binding in the Marsh*.
Catchphrases: 'Oh, I say, I am a
fool,' '*At* your service', 'What have
I said?', 'Oh, jolly d'. Not in text
DESMOND, FLORENCE
(1905–) (Florence Dawson).
British revue star and
impressionist, mainly in the
thirties and forties.
Best films: *No Limit* 35. *Keep
Your Seats Please* 37. *Hoots Mon*
40. 110
DESMONDE, JERRY (1908–67).
Elegant British straight man,
notably for Sid Field and
Norman Wisdom. Not a success
on his own, except as TV host.
Best films: *London Town* 46.
Cardboard Cavalier 48. *Follow a
Star* 59. 199
DHERY, ROBERT (1921–)
(Robert Foullcy). Dapper French
revue comedian whose best
characterizations involve an
element of mime.
Best films: *Femmes de Paris* 54. *La
Belle Americaine* 61. 302
DILLER, PHYLLIS (1917–).
Grotesque American
comedienne, mostly on stage and
TV.
Best film: *Did You Hear the One
About the Travelling Saleslady?* 291
DIXON, REG (1915–84). Giant-
sized British radio and music hall
comedian who spoke slowly in a
north country accent.
Catchphrase: 'I'm proper
poorly'.
Film: *No Smoking* 56. Not in text
DODD, KEN (1927–). Rubber-
faced, toothy British comedian
from Knotty Ash (near
Liverpool). A touch of zaniness is
always present.
Catchphrases: 'Disumknockerated',

DODD, KEN – *cont.*
'Hello missus', 'How tickled I am', 'Tatty bye'. 227

DRAKE, CHARLIE (1925–)
(Charles Springall). Diminutive British comedian who scored a big TV hit in the fifties and then, quite unaccountably, 'went off', returning twenty years later as a character actor. 220

DRAYTON, ALFRED (1881–1949) (Alfred Varrick). Bald, bullying, British comic actor teamed with Robertson Hare in later Aldwych farces.
Best films: *Aren't Men Beasts* 37. *Women Aren't Angels* 40. *Nicholas Nickleby* 47. 16

DRESSLER, MARIE (1869–1934) (Leila Von Koerber). Canadian-American comedy character actress with a long career in vaudeville, burlesque and silent films before in the last three years of her life she became a major talkie star.
Best films: *Anna Christie* 30. *Min and Bill* 30. *Emma* 32. *Tugboat Annie* 32. *Dinner at Eight* 33. Autobiography: *My Own Story* 34. 51–52

DUMONT, MARGARET (1889–1945) (Margaret Baker). American character comedienne, the stately butt of Groucho Marx and other comics.
Best films: *Animal Crackers* 30. *Duck Soup* 33. *A Night at the Opera* 35. *A Day at the Races* 37. *At the Circus* 39. *The Big Store* 41. 137

DUNN, CLIVE (1923–). British character actor with a neat line in old men, especially on TV in *Bootsie and Snudge* and *Dad's Army*.
Catchphrases: 'Permission to speak, sir', 'They don't like it up 'em'. Not in text

DURANTE, JIMMY 'SCHNOZZLE' (1893–1980). Long-nosed, Brooklyn-Italian-accented, explosive American comedian with long experience in vaudeville and cabaret. Films occasional but fairly regular.
Catchphrases: 'Everybody wants to get into de act', 'I'm mortified', 'Goodnight, Mrs Calabash, wherever you are'. (Mrs Calabash was his affectionate name for his late wife.)
Best films: *The Phantom President* 33. *George White's Scandals* 34. *You're in the Army Now* 40. *The Man Who Came to Dinner* 41. *Music for Millions* 45. *Two Sisters from Boston* 46. *The Milkman* 50. *Jumbo* 62.

Biographies: *Schnozzola* 51 by Gene Fowler; *Goodnight Mrs Calabash* 63 by William Cahn. **51**, 52, 96

EBSEN, BUDDY (1908–). American soft shoe dancer of the thirties who later became both a comic and a straight actor.
Best films: *Broadway Melody of 1936. Captain January* 36.
TV series: *The Beverly Hillbillies* 62–70. 58, 264, **265**

EDWARDS, JIMMY (1920–). Heavily moustachioed, vibrant-voiced, overbearing British comic who was a big hit of forties radio and fifties revue, but later fell into a state of disrepair.
Catchphrases: 'Wake up at the back, there', 'Black mark, Bentley', 'a mauve one', 'clumsy clot', 'Gently, Bentley'.
Best films: *Three Men in a Boat* 55. *Bottoms Up* (from the television series *Whack-o*) 60. *Nearly a Nasty Accident* 61.
Autobiography: *Take It From Me* 53 (from his hit radio series *Take It From Here*). 216, 220

EMERY, DICK (1918–83). British TV comedian with a flair for heavy disguise and female impersonation. His effects were repetitive, but in his last decade he built up a large following for his sketch-filled half-hours.
Best films: *The Wrong Arm of the Law* 63. *Ooh You Are Awful* (his catchphrase) 72. 229

EMNEY, FRED (1900–80). Heavyweight British character comedian, usually wry-faced and cigar-chewing, presenting an eccentric member of the upper classes. Much in musical comedy.
Best films: *Yes Madam* 39. *Let the People Sing* 42. *San Ferry Ann* 65. **111**

ENGLISH, ARTHUR (1913–). British radio and music hall comedian who hit the heights as a loud-mouthed spiv but later gave excellent character performances.
Cathphrases: 'Sharpen up, the quick stuff's coming', 'Mum, they're laughing', 'Open the cage'.
TV series: *How's Your Father, Are you Being Served?* 302

ERROL, LEON (1881–1951). Rubber-legged Australian comedian, former medical student. In America, became a regular in the Ziegfeld Follies before settling in Hollywood for a long career in shorts and second features.
Best films: *We're Not Dressing* 34.

Mexican Spitfire series from 39. 177–8, **178**

ETAIX, PIERRE (1928–). French mime comedian, pupil of Jacques Tati.
Best films: *Happy Anniversary* 61. *The Suitor* 62. 287

EVANS, NORMAN (1901–62). Burly British north-country comedian who had a surprisingly effective line in female impersonation as a half-toothless, grimacing working class woman having a gossip 'over the garden wall'.
Best films: *Demobbed* 45. *Over the Garden Wall* 50. 44, 116

EWELL, TOM (1909–) (S. Yewell Tompkins). Crumple-faced American comic actor who enjoyed a brief spell at the top in the fifties.
Best films: *Adam's Rib* 49. *The Seven Year Itch* 55. *Tender is the Night* 61.
TV series: *The Tom Ewell Show* 60. 302

FAIRBANKS, DOUGLAS (1883–1939) (Douglas Ullman). Acrobatic hero of the American silent screen; his actual comedies were made before 1920: *The Lamb, The Matrimaniac*, etc. 75

FAY, FRANK (1897–1961). Sharp-tongued American vaudeville comic whose career was affected by his drinking. Never established himself in Hollywood. 55

FAZENDA, LOUISE (1895–1962). American silent slapstick comedienne, under contract to Mack Sennett; her work is best glimpsed in compilations. Married Hal Wallis and retired. 74

FELDMAN, MARTY (1933–83). Pop-eyed British comic and scriptwriter who had some success in Hollywood.
Best films: *Every Home Should Have One* 69. *Young Frankenstein* 73. *Silent Movie* 76. 302

FERNANDEL, (1903–71) (Fernand Contandin). Lugubrious French comic actor, a national favourite from the mid-thirties.
Best films: *Fric Frac* 39. *La Fille du Puisatier* 40. *The Red Inn* 51. *Don Camillo* series from 52. *The Sheep has Five Legs* 54. *Paris Holiday* 57. 287

FETCHIT, STEPIN (1892–1985) (Lincoln Perry). Drawling American comedian of the thirties, a black stereotype who was later much deplored.
Best film: *Steamboat Round the Bend* 35.

FIELD, SID (1904–50) British revue comedian who was just making his name in films when he died.
Catchphrase: 'What a performance!'
Best films: *London Town* 46 (for the sketches). *Cardboard Cavalier* 48. 188

FIELDS, GRACIE (1898–1979) (Grace Stansfield). British singer and comedienne who rode high on her Lancashire humour and spirit, though her peak was confined to the thirties.
Best films: *Sally in our Alley* 31. *Love Life and Laughter* 33. *Sing as We Go* 34. *Look Up and Laugh* 35. *Keep Smiling* 38. *Holy Matrimony* 43.
Autobiography: *Sing as We Go* 60. 86–7, **87**, 94

FIELDS, W.C. (1879–1946) (William Claude Dukinfield). Red-nosed, gravel-voiced, bottle-hitting American comedian who became well-loved despite his misogyny. Originally a stage juggler, he graduated to Hollywood via the Ziegfeld Follies.
Best films: *The Dentist* 32. *The Fatal Glass of Beer* 32. *The Pharmacist* 33. *The Barber Shop* 33. *You're Telling Me* 34. *The Old-Fashioned Way* 34. *It's a Gift* 34. *David Copperfield* 35. *My Little Chickadee* 40. *The Bank Dick* 40. *Never Give a Sucker an Even Break* 41.
Autobiography: *Fields for President*. 154–60, **156**

FINLAYSON, JAMES (1877–1953). Prune-faced Scottish character comedian who in Hollywood became an indispensable comic villain, especially in the films of Laurel and Hardy. Invented the 'double take and fade away'.
Best films: *Big Business* 30. *Fra Diavolo* 33. *Our Relations* 36. *Way Out West* 37. *Blockheads* 38. *Frontispiece*, 5, 130

FLANAGAN AND ALLEN. Bud Flanagan (1896–1968) (Robert Winthrop) was a genial British comedian of Jewish origin; Chesney Allen (1894–1982) was the perfect well-dressed straight man. Together, or as part of the Crazy Gang (*q.v.*), they sang their own songs, indulged in music hall cross-talk, and delighted more than one generation.
Best films: *Underneath the Arches* 37. *Okay for Sound* 37. *Alf's Button Afloat* 38. *The Frozen Limits* 39. *Gasbags* 40. *Dreaming* 44. 89, 101

FLETCHER CYRIL (1913–). Adenoid-voiced radio and music hall comedian, a splendid pantomime dame who never made it in the movies.
Cathphrases: 'Dreaming of thee', 'Odd ode number one coming up, starts', 'Pin back your lugholes'. 115

FLOTSAM AND JETSAM. Flotsam (B. C. Hilliam, 1890–1961) was the tenor, Jetsam (Malcolm McEachern, c. 1885–1945) the baritone in this genial double act which delighted fans of radio and music hall in the thirties and early forties. Flotsam was British, Jetsam Australian; the latter's rich tones can be heard in the 1934 film of *Chu Chin Chow*. 119

FORDE, WALTER (1896–1984) (Thomas Seymour). British slapstick comedian of the twenties with an affinity to Harold Lloyd; now most easily seen in an excerpt in *Helter Skelter* 49. Became a skilful director. 86

FORMBY, GEORGE (1905–61) British north-country comedian with a toothy grin, gormless behaviour and a ukulele; a top box-office draw of the late thirties. Son of George Formby Senior (1877–1921), a darling of the music halls. (See page 24.)
Catchphrases: 'Mother!', 'Turned out nice again'.
Best films: *No Limit* 35. *Keep Your Seats Please* 36. *Feather Your Nest* 37. *Keep Fit* 37. *It's In the Air* 38. *Come On George* 39. *Let George Do It* 40. *Spare a Copper* 41. *Get Cracking* 43.
Biography: *George Formby* 74 by Alan Randall and Ray Seaton. 83, 89–93, **92**, 96, 103, **104**, 180, **181**

FORSYTH, BRUCE (1927–). Bouncy, beaming British comedian of the jovial uncle type: seemed unstoppable in the fifties, but too much personal publicity reduced him to the level of quiz show host on *The Generation Game* and *Play Your Cards Right*.
Catchphrases: 'Good game', 'I'm in charge', 'Didn't he do well?', 'Nice to see you, to see you, nice'. 227

EDDIE FOY Snr (1856–1928). Irish-American clown who made his children, the Seven Little Foys, part of his act. Popular on Broadway from the turn of the century, he later became a top vaudeville attraction. He made no-films which have survived, though his son Eddie Foy Jnr (1905–83) sometimes impersonated him and Bob Hope played him in *The Seven Little Foys*. Eddie Jnr was an accomplished scene stealer in his own right, notably in *The Pajama Game* 56. 55

FRANKAU, RONALD (1894–1951) Elegant, bald-domed British cabaret and radio comedian, often a touch risqué. With Tommy Handley he formed the fast-patter radio partnership of Murgatroyd and Winterbottom. 118

FRASER, BILL (1907–). Heavily-built British actor who in the late fifties was cast as Sgt Snudge in TV's *The Army Game* and played the character through several seasons of this and its sequel, *Bootsie and Snudge*.
Catchphrase: 'I'll be leaving you now, sir'. 302

FRIGANZA, TRIXIE (1870–1955) (Delia O'Callahan). American fat lady of vaudeville, 'a perfect forty-six'. Popular for the first forty years of the century. 55

FROST, DAVID (1939–). British linkman, interviewer and occasional comedian of the seventies, a 'Mr Television' who in the words of Mrs Malcolm Muggeridge 'rose without trace'. It was in fact *That Was The Week That Was* which made him a household word.
Catchphrases: 'But seriously, though', 'Hello, good evening and welcome'. 210–11, **210**

FULLER, LESLIE (1889–1948). Beefy British proletarian comedian from the concert party circuit.
Best films: *The Stoker* 35. *Captain Bill* 36. 82

FYFFE, WILL (1884–1947). Pawky, pint-sized Scottish comic actor who moved easily from music hall to serious roles and is best remembered for his song 'I Belong to Glasgow'.
Best films: *Owd Bob* 38. *The Mind of Mr Reeder* 39. *The Brothers* 47. 38, 94

GALLAGHER AND SHEAN. Edward Gallagher (c. 1873–1929) and Al Shean (1868–1949) had an occasional comedy double act in American vaudeville, and might never have been remembered were it not for a catchy song which they introduced in 1921: 'Absolutely, Mr Gallagher? Positively Mr Shean'. It became their trademark, and after

JAMES, JIMMY (1892–1965) (James Casey). British music hall comic never recorded at his best. For years in variety he used the same few routines, two stooges and himself as a top-hatted drunk. Film appearances untypical, but his son has revived the act in a fair copy. 44

JAMES, SID (1913–76.). Crumple-faced South African comic actor with the dirtiest laugh in the business; once settled in London he became a staple of the British cinema and television. Best films: *The Lavender Hill Mob* 51. *The Big Job* 65. *Bless this House* 73. Many 'Carry Ons'. 201 et seq, **206**

JESSEL, GEORGE (1898–1981). American entertainer, producer and toastmaster, more in person than on film or TV. 56

JEWEL AND WARRISS. Jimmy Jewel (1909–) and Ben Warriss (1909–) (his cousin) were both 'born in a trunk' and teamed in 1934 as a cross-talk comedy act. After many years of success in radio and on the halls, they split up in 1967, after which Jimmy Jewel became a useful solo talent in the TV series *Nearest and Dearest* and in *Funny Man*, a somewhat doleful version of his own early life on the halls. Catchphrase: 'What a carry on'. 230

JOLSON, AL (1886–1950) (Asa Yoelson). Russian-born American singing entertainer, a powerful talent by any standard, though his use of blackface now offends some. Most of the songs which he made standards actually reflect Jewish religious music with a touch of jazz. Experience mostly in burlesque, revue and musical comedy before he settled in Hollywood after starring in the first talking film. Catchphrases: 'You ain't heard nothin' yet', 'I got a thousand songs in me'. Best films: *The Jazz Singer* 27. *The Singing Fool* 28. *Mammy* 30. *Hallelujah I'm a Bum* 33. *Wonder Bar* 34. *Go Into your Dance* 35. *Rose of Washington Square* 39. *Swanee River* 39. *The Jolson Story* (voice only) 45. Biography: *Al Jolson* 72 by Michael Friedland. 56, 60, 145–6, **146**

KARNO, FRED (1886–1941) (Frederick Westcott). British acrobatic comedian of the music halls who turned impressario and ran a 'fun factory' in Camberwell

before departing for California with a troupe which included Charlie Chaplin and Stan Laurel. Bankrupt in 1926, he recovered to stage many more productions before 1935. 77

KAYE, DANNY (1913–1987) (Daniel Kaminsky). American star comedian, who after Broadway experience became Hollywood's brightest talent of the mid-forties. Best films: *Wonder Man* 45. *The Secret Life of Walter Mitty* 47. *On the Riviera* 51. *Hans Christian Andersen* 52. *Knock on Wood* 53. *The Court Jester* 55. 14, **15**, 171–5, **171, 173**, 179

KEATON, BUSTER (1895–1966). American acrobatic clown of the vaudeville stage and silent screen: the famous 'great stone face'. Best films: *One Week* 20. *The Playhouse* 22. *Cops* 22. *Balloonatic* 22. *Our Hospitality* 23. *Sherlock Junior* 24. *The Navigator* 24. *Seven Chances* 25. *The General* 27. Autobiography: *My Wonderful World of Slapstick* 60. 65, 70–72, **73**

KELLAWAY, CECIL (1891–1973). British character actor who settled in Hollywood as a portly-cherubic but often roguish comic performer. Best films: *I Married a Witch* 42. *Frenchman's Creek* 44. *Kitty* 45. *The Luck of the Irish* 48. *Harvey* 50. *Hush Hush Sweet Charlotte* 64. 178

KELLY, PATSY (1910–81). Dumpy American comedienne of the thirties, often a pert wisecracker or frightened maid. Made some two-reel shorts for Hal Roach. Best films: *The Girl from Missouri* 34. *Kelly the Second* 36. *The Gorilla* 39. *Topper Returns* 41. *Broadway Limited* 41. 68

KENNEDY, EDGAR (1890–1948). Burly, balding American comedian with a famous 'slow burn'. Best films: *Duck Soup* 33. *Unfaithfully Yours* 48. Mostly in two reelers. 177

KENNEY, HORACE (c1890–?). British music hall performer who impersonated old men. 115

THE KEYSTONE KOPS. An American troupe of silent comedians, devised by Mack Sennett and led by Ford Sterling. Now best seen in compilations. 67, **68**, 70

KNOTTS, DON (1924–). Sour-faced American 'hayseed' comedian, a local taste who after TV popularity had limited

Hollywood success. Best films: *The Ghost and Mr Chicken* 66. *The Apple Dumpling Gang* 75. 302

KING, DAVE (1929–). British comedian, popular on TV in the fifties. 220

KORRIS, HARRY (1888–1971). Rotund British north-country comedian who scored a hit in BBC's wartime radio series *Happidrome*, which was filmed. Catchphrases: 'Ee, if ever a man suffered', 'Take him away, Ramsbottom'. **184**

KOVACS, ERNIE (1919–62). Big, cigar-smoking American comedian and TV personality. Best films: *Operation Mad Ball* 57. *Our Man in Havana* 62. Biography: *Nothing in Moderation* 76 by David G. Walley. 302

LAHR, BERT (1895–1967) (Irving Lahrheim). Wry-faced American vaudeville and Broadway comedian. Best films: *The Wizard of Oz* 39. *Always Leave Them Laughing* 49. *Mr Universe* 51. *Rose Marie* 54. *The Night They Raided Minsky's* 68. Biography: *Notes on a Cowardly Lion* 69 by John Lahr. 52–53, 55, **56**

LAKE, ARTHUR (1905–) (Arthur Silverlake). American comic actor who played to perfection the harassed suburban husband Dagwood Bumstead in the *Blondie* series (1938–48). 160

LANE, LUPINO (1892–1959) (Henry George Lupino). Dapper British stage comedian and tumbler, one of a family of such. Film success mainly in silent shorts. Best film: *The Lambeth Walk* 39 (apparently lost). Biography: *Born to Star* 57 by George Dillon White. 82, 107

LANGDON, HARRY (1884–1944). Baby-faced, melancholy American clown who enjoyed brief success in the last years of silent films. Best films: *Tramp Tramp Tramp* 26. *The Strong Man* 26. *Long Pants* 26. *Zenobia* 39. 73

LA RUE, DANNY (1927–) (Daniel Patrick Carroll). British female impersonator who had great success in all media in the seventies. Only film: *Our Miss Fred* 72. 227

LAUDER, HARRY (1870–1950). Scottish music hall entertainer, an international favourite. Made three films, all lost. Autobiography: *Roamin' in the Gloamin'* 28. 49

LYNN, RALPH – *cont.*
the Nest 33. *Pot Luck* 36. 15, **16**,
17, 94, 99
MARRIOTT, MOORE (1885–
1949) (George Thomas Moore-
Marriott). British character actor,
in many twenties films, who at
the age of fifty found a splendid
line in comic senility, as
Harbottle in the Will Hay
sketches.
Best films: *Windbag the Sailor* 36.
Oh Mr Porter 38. *Ask a Policeman*
39. *The Frozen Limits* 39. *Gasbags*
40. *Hi Gang* 41. *Time Flies* 44. 9,
44–8, **47**, 97, 108–9, **108**
THE MARX BROTHERS.
Groucho (1890–1977) was really
Julius; Chico (1886–1961) was
really Leonard; Harpo (1888–
1964) was really Adolph; and
Zeppo (who left them in 1933)
(1901–79) was really Herbert.
Their zany act was a riot in
burlesque, and their subsequent
films, though variable, are a
legacy of craziness much
appreciated by posterity.
Best films: *Animal Crackers* 30.
Monkey Business 31. *Horse
Feathers* 32. *Duck Soup* 33. *A
Night at the Opera* 35. *A Day at the
Races* 37. *A Night in Casablanca*
45.
Best biographies: *The Marx
Brothers at the Movies* 69 by Paul
D. Zimmerman and Burt
Goldblatt; *The Marx Brothers
Scrapbook* 74 by Richard Anobile
and Groucho Marx. 133–7, **134,
136**
MILLER, MAX (1895–1963).
(Harold Sargent). Star British
music hall comedian, 'the cheeky
chappie'. Basically a Londoner,
he seldom ventured north of
Watford, and his films do not
give a fair impression of the
vitality of his stage presence.
Catchphrase: 'There'll never be
another, will there, lady?' ix, 17,
31–5, **34**, 80, 93, 110, **110**, 216,
307
MILLIGAN, SPIKE (1918–).
Zany British comic, creator of
radio's Goons.
Best films: *Postman's Knock* 62.
231
MILLS, NAT (1900–) and
BOBBIE (his wife, 1905–55).
British variety act in which both
performers spoke as though half-
witted. 117
MITCHELL, WARREN (1926–).
British comic character actor who
made an instant success of the
loud-mouthed bigot Alf Garnett
in TV's *Till Death Us Do Part* and
has been doing it on and off ever

since. It was filmed in 1968.
Catchphrase: 'Silly old moo'. 229
MODLEY, ALBERT (1901–).
Yorkshire variety comedian,
especially in pier theatres but
sometimes on radio.
Catchphrase: 'Ain't it grand to be
daft?' Not in text
MOFFATT, GRAHAM (1919–65).
British comic actor, the fat boy of
the Will Hay films. 44–8, **47**, 97,
108–9, **108**
MONKHOUSE, BOB (1928–).
British rapid patter comic, also
scriptwriter and quiz show host.
Catchphrase: 'Bernie, the bolt'
(in *The Golden Shot*).
Best films: *Carry on Sergeant* 58.
Weekend with Lulu 61. 199, 226,
292, **293**
MONTY PYTHON. The
elements of this modern British
version of the Marx Brothers are:
John Cleese (1939–), Michael
Palin (1943–), Terry Gilliam
(1942–), Eric Idle (1941–),
Graham Chapman (1941–).
The original BBC TV shows ran
from 1969 until 1974, but the
team's influence has been felt in
their separate activities as well as
several films.
Catchphrases: 'Nudge nudge',
'And now for something
completely different', 'Naughty
bits'.
Films: *And Now for Something
Completely Different* 71. *Monty
Python and the Holy Grail* 75. *The
Life of Brian* 79. *Monty Python's
Meaning of Life* 83. 231
MOORE, VICTOR (1876–1962).
Hesitant, bumbling comic actor
who after a long career in
burlesque and on Broadway
settled in Hollywood and was
occasionally memorable.
Best films: *Swing Time* 36.
Louisiana Purchase 42. *Star
Spangled Rhythm* 42. *It's in the Bag*
45. *We're Not Married* 52. **161**
MORECAMBE AND WISE. Eric
Morecambe (1926–84) (Eric
Bartholomew) and Ernie Wise
(1925–) (Ernest Wiseman) were
both starstruck British kids from
the north who wove a great
variety act from copying the
masters and adding their own
characteristics. In their prime
they were a pleasure to see on the
stage, but their television
appearances are the ones which
have been recorded.
Catchphrases: 'Get out of that',
'Good evening, young sir', 'I'll
smash your face in', 'The one
with the short fat hairy legs',
'You can't see the join'.

Best films: *The Intelligence Men* 64.
That Riviera Touch 66. *The
Magnificent Two* 67. *Night Train
to Murder* (TV) 84.
Autobiography: *Bring Me
Sunshine* 75. 220–23, **221**
MORRIS, DAVE (1897–1960).
British north-country comic
famous as host of 'Club Night'.
Seldom recorded.
Catchphrase: 'As 'e been in,
whack?' 115
MORRIS, LILY (1884–1952).
Exuberant British music hall
singer. Several recordings
survive. 24
MOSTEL, ZERO (1915–77).
Heavyweight American comic
actor, usually found at the end of
his tether.
Best films: *The Enforcer* 51. *A
Funny Thing Happened on the way
to the Forum* 66. *The Producers* 68.
The Front 76. 8
MOUNT, PEGGY (1916–).
British comedy actress of
overbearing roles.
Best films: *Sailor Beware* 56. *Inn
For Trouble* 59.
TV series: *You're Only Young
Twice*. 198
MURDOCH, RICHARD (1907–)
Elegant light entertainer of the
thirties who during the war
became popular with Kenneth
Horne as commanders of the
mythical RAF station *Much
Binding in the Marsh*. Most
popular subsequent radio show:
The Men from the Ministry.
Best films: *Band Waggon* 39. *The
Ghost Train* 41. 120, 217, **217**
MURRAY, KEN (1903–).
American comedy actor and
collector of home movies of the
stars. 57
MURRAY AND MOONEY
(nda). British crosstalk
comedians of the thirties and
forties, mostly on radio.
Theme tune: 'Side by Side'. 116
NAUGHTON AND GOLD.
Resident members of the Crazy
Gang (*q.v.*), Charlie Naughton
(1887–1976) and Jimmy Gold
(1886–1967) would without the
group have been a pretty
ordinary music hall cross-talk
act. 100, 104
NERVO AND KNOX. More
resident members of the Crazy
Gang (*q.v.*), Jimmy Nervo
(1890–1975) (James Holloway)
and Teddy Knox (1896–1974)
might not have amounted to
much without the group, though
they brought a certain unusual
style to their antics. 96, 97
NEWHART, BOB (1929–).

41. *I Dood It* 43. *Dubarry was a Lady* 43. *Ziegfeld Follies* (the 'Guzzler's Gin' sketch) 46. *Merton of the Movies* 47. 184, 285

SMITH AND DALE. Joe Sultzer (1884–?) and Charles Marks (1881–1971) were allegedly the originals of Neil Simon's *The Sunshine Boys*. American Jewish cross-talkers, they played vaudeville and burlesque with just a few film ventures. 57–8

THE SMOTHERS BROTHERS. American comedians with a disarmingly casual approach, Tom (1937–) and Dick (1939–) had great television popularity in the sixties, but it somehow faded away. 270

STAINLESS STEPHEN (1892–1971) (Arthur Clifford Baynes). The British radio comedian with the punctuated patter exhausted his appeal between the mid-thirties and the mid-forties. 122

STEELE, TOMMY (1936–) (Tommy Hicks). Energetic British cockney performer, former pop singer, now everybody's favourite. Best films: *It's All Happening* 62. *The Happiest Millionaire* 67. *Half a Sixpence* 67. 199

SWAIN, MACK (1876–1935). American silent comic actor, one of Mack Sennett's heavies. Best films: *The Gold Rush* 24. 74

SYKES, ERIC (1923–). Mournful-faced north-country comedy writer and actor, popular through the sixties in his own domestic TV series, with Hattie Jacques as his sister. 192

TARRI, SUZETTE (1881–1975). British radio and music hall comedienne who impersonated a lady reluctantly left on the shelf. Signature tune: 'Red Sails in the Sunset'. 121

TATI, JACQUES (1908–82) (Jacques Tatischeff). French comic mime, restricted by his own theories of screencraft, which didn't work. Best films: *Jour de Fête* 49. *Monsieur Hulot's Holiday* 52. *Mon Oncle* 58. 286, **287**

TERRY-THOMAS (1911–) (Thomas Terry Hoar-Stevens). British comedian with high-class gap-toothed manner, a vein which was rather quickly mined and exhausted. Catchphrase: 'How do you *do*?' Best films: *Private's Progress* 56. *Carlton Browne of the F.O.* 58. *I'm All Right Jack* 59. *School for Scoundrels* 60. *Those Magnificent Men in their Flying Machines* 65.

How to Murder Your Wife 65. 302

THE THREE STOOGES. Originally assistants to the burlesque comic Ted Healy (1886–1937) who discarded them when he tried to find solo favour in Hollywood, this apparently moronic and certainly violent trio went on to fame and fortune in nearly 200 two-reelers for Columbia. In from the mid-thirties to the mid-sixties were Moe Howard (1895–1975) and Larry Fine (1911–75); Moe's brother Curly (1906–52) was replaced in turn by his brother Shemp Howard (1891–1955), then by Joe Besser (1916–) and Joe de Rita (c. 1908–). 131–3, **132**

TRINDER, TOMMY (1909–). British cockney music hall comedian who alternated cheek with pathos. Catchphrase: 'You lucky people!' Best films: *Sailors Three* 41. *The Foreman Went to France* 42. *Champagne Charlie* 44. *Fiddlers Three* 44. 20, **21**, **111**, 188

TUCKER, SOPHIE (1884–1966) (Sophia Abuza). Russian-born, American-oriented popular singer, the heavyweight 'red hot momma' of vaudeville. Best films: *Broadway Melody of 1937*. *Sensations of 1945*. 50

TURPIN, BEN (1874–1940). Cross-eyed American silent comic who in the twenties specialized in spoofs of romantic heroes. 74, **75**

THE TWO RONNIES. Ronnie Barker (1929–) and Ronnie Corbett (1930–), bespectacled TV sketch artists whose smiles rise above their blue material. Best films: *Futtock's End* 60. 295

VAN DYKE, DICK (1925–). Lanky American comic actor who was a hit in his own TV series (1961–6) but never quite made it in movies despite a big launch in *Mary Poppins* 64. 263

VARNEY, REG (1922–). British cockney character comic who hit the high with his TV series *On the Buses* in the sixties, but found himself typecast. 227

VAUGHAN, NORMAN (1927–). British television comic and compère of the sixties; never made it in other media. Catchphrases: 'Dodgy!'; 'A touch of the how's your fathers'. Not in text

VINCENT, ROBBIE (1896–1978). Plaintive supporting comic famous as Enoch in radio's wartime *Happidrome*.

Catchphrase: 'Let me tell you . . .' 184

WALL, MAX (1908–) (Maxwell Lorrimer). British music hall and radio comedian specializing in funny voices and walks. In his older age, feted by the intellectuals. No films of consequence. 217

WALLACE, NELLIE (1870–1948). British low comedienne of the music halls, more vulgar and grotesque than most of the men. No films of note.

WALLS, TOM (1883–1949). British farce actor, a kingpin of the Aldwych team. Best films: *Rookery Nook* 30. *Thark* 32. *Stormy Weather* 35. *Strange Boarders* 38. 15, **16**, 17, 80, 88, 99

WARNER, JACK (1894–1981) (Jack Waters). Genial British light character actor, famous for twenty years on TV as Dixon of Dock Green. No record of his variety act. Catchphrases: 'Mind my bike!'; 'Blue pencil'; 'He didn't orter et it'; 'It's a rill mill; 'Mind how you go'; Evening, all,'; 'Allo, allo, allo'. Best films: *It Always Rains on Sunday* 47. *Holiday Camp* 47. *The Blue Lamp* 50. *Jigsaw* 62. **119**, 120

WATERS, ELSIE (c 1891–) and DORIS (1892–1978). British comediennes long familiar on music hall and radio as Gert and Daisy, two garrulous housewives. Occasional films poor. 119, **119**

WEBER AND FIELDS. Morris Weber (1867–1942) and Moses Schanfield (1867–1941) were early American vaudeville comedians; in fact, they began in minstrel shows. They had a Dutch act as well as their Jewish one, and later were known for a time as Mike and Myer. No films survive. 57

WEST, MAE (1892–1980). American comedienne, an archetypal mocking sex symbol who shocked America for a year or two before being put in her place by the censors. Best films: *She Done Him Wrong* 33. *I'm No Angel* 33. *My Little Chickadee* 39. Autobiography: *Goodness Had Nothing to Do With It* 59. 150–54, **151**, 159–160

WESTERN, KENNETH AND GEORGE. These 'brothers', actually cousins (1900–63) and (1895–1969), were radio's upper-class 'cads' throughout the

LIST OF PRINCIPAL SOURCE
MATERIAL FROM FILMS AND PLAYS

As I hope I have indicated throughout, this book is intended to give well deserved credit to the writers who provide the material which the comedian performs. Apologies are due if the following list lacks details of any writer for film or theatre who is quoted in the text.

ROMANS, FRENCH AND COUNTRYMEN
A Funny Thing Happened on the Way to the Forum: lyrics by Steven Spielberg. Play 1958; film (United Artists) 1966
The Court Jester: lyrics by Sylvia Fine. Film (Paramount) 1955

MASTERS OF THE MUSIC HALL
Hoots Mon: script by Roy William Neill, Jack Henley, John Dighton (and, presumably, Max Miller). Film (Warner British) 1939
Oh Mr Porter: script by Marriott Edgar, J. O. C. Orton, Val Guest. Film (Rank/Gainsborough) 1937

AMERICAN VAUDEVILLE AND
  BURLESQUE BEFORE 1930
The Wizard of Oz: lyrics by E. Y. Harburg. Film (MGM) 1939

THE GLORY DAYS OF SILENCE
James Agee quotations from 'Comedy's Greatest Era', *Life* magazine 1949

THE THIRTIES HEYDAY OF BRITISH
  COMEDY
Jack's the Boy: lyrics ('The Flies Crawled Up the Window') by Douglas Furber. Film (Rank/Gainsborough) 1932
Gay's the Word: lyrics ('Vitality') by Ivor Novello. Play 1953
Sing As We Go: lyrics by Harry Parr-Davies. Film (ATP) 1934
Over She Goes: lyrics by Billy Mayerl, Desmond Carter, Frank Eyton. Film (ATP) 1937
Keep Your Seats Please: lyrics by Harry Parr-

Davies, Clifford and Cliff. Film (ATP) 1936
Feather Your Nest: lyrics by George Formby, Harry Parr-Davies. Film (ATP) 1937

AMERICAN FILM COMEDY 1930–45
Their First Mistake: script by H. M. Walker. Film (Hal Roach) 1932.
Horse Feathers: script by Bert Kalmar, Harry Ruby, S. J. Perelman, Will B. Johnstone. Film (Paramount) 1932.
Animal Crackers: lyrics Bert Kalmar, Harry Ruby. Film (Paramount) 1932
At the Circus: lyrics by E. Y. Harburg. Film (MGM) 1939
Monkey Business: script by S. J. Perelman, Will B. Johnstone, Arthur Sheekman. Film (Paramount) 1931
Abbott and Costello in Society: script by John Grant, Hal Finberg, Edmund L. Hartmann. Film (Universal) 1944
Whoopee: lyrics and music Walter Donaldson, Gus Khan
Thank Your Lucky Stars: songs by Frank Loesser, Arthur Schwartz.
The Bank Dick: script by W. C. Fields (Mahatma Kane Jeeves). Film (Universal) 1940
My Little Chickadee: script by W. C. Fields and Mae West. Film (Universal) 1940
Always Leave Them Laughing: script by Jack Rose, Mel Shavelson. Film (Warner) 1949
The Cat and the Canary: script by Walter De Leon, Lynn Starling (and Hope's writers). Film (Paramount) 1939
Caught in the Draft: script by Harry Tugend. Film (Paramount) 1941

Road to Morocco: lyrics by Johnny Burke and Jimmy Van Heusen. Script by Frank Butler and Dan Hartman. Film (Paramount) 1942

The Secret Life of Walter Mitty: lyrics by Sylvia Fine. Film (Goldwyn) 1947

The Court Jester: script by Norman Panama and Melvin Frank. Film (Paramount) 1955

Dr Rhythm: Double Damask sketch by Dion Titherage. Film (Paramount) 1938

POST-WAR BRITISH COMEDIANS AND THE GRIP OF TELEVISON

Sigh No More ('I Wonder What Happened to Him?'): lyrics by Noël Coward. Play 1945

The Globe Revue ('There are Bad Times Just Around the Corner'): lyrics by Noël Coward. Play 1952

Carry On Sergeant and other *Carry On* films: scripts by Norman Hudis, Talbot Rothwell. Films (Rank/EMI) 1958 on

TONY HANCOCK scripts by Ray Galton and Alan Simpson. Television series (BBC) early sixties

MORECAMBE AND WISE: script by Eddie Braben. Television series (BBC) seventies

AMERICA AFTER 1945: TELEVISION TAKES OVER

The Honeymooners: script by Marvin Marx and Walter Stone. Television series (CBS/Viacom) 1955

You'll Never Get Rich/The Phil Silvers Show/ Bilko: chief scriptwriter Nat Hiken. Television series (CBS/Viacom) 1955–58

The Beverly Hillbillies: lyrics by Paul Henning. Television series (CBS/Viacom) 1962–70

THE TRIUMPH OF BAD TASTE

The Old Dope Peddler: lyrics by Tom Lehrer. Published in *The Tom Lehrer Song Book* (Granada 1984).

If we may believe our logicians, man is distinguished from all other creatures by the faculty of laughter.

– Joseph Addison, 1672–1719

There was this man with two eligible sons and a daughter. And the eldest son came to him and said Dad, I'm sorry to say I've got a girl into trouble. The old man sighed and reached for his cheque book. Then one night a year later, the second son came in and said Dad, there's a girl, I've got her into trouble. So the old man sighed again and wrote out another cheque. And finally, some time after that, his daughter came in and said Dad, I'm afraid my boyfriend's got me into trouble. And the old man said: 'Good, this is where *we* cash in.'

– Max Miller, 1895–1963